Higher Education:
A Critical Business

17

SRHE and Open University Press Imprint

General Editor: Heather Eggins

Higher Education: A Critical Business

Ronald Barnett

The Society for Research into Higher Education
& Open University Press

Published by SRHE and
Open University Press
Celtic Court
22 Ballmoor
Buckingham
MK18 1XW

and 1900 Frost Road, Suite 101
Bristol, PA 19007, USA

First published 1997

A catalogue record of this book is available from the British Library

ISBN 0 335 19703 5 (pbk)   0 335 19704 3 (hbk)

Library of Congress Cataloging-in-Publication Data
Barnett, Ronald, 1947–
      Higher education : a critical business / Ronald Barnett.
         p.   cm.
      Includes bibliographical references (p.   ) and index.
      ISBN 0–335–19704–3. — ISBN 0–335–19703–5 (pbk.)
      1. Critical thinking—Study and teaching (Higher)—Great Britain.
      2. Critical thinking—Study and teaching (Higher)—United States.
      3. Critical theory.   4. Education, Higher—Philosophy.   I. Title.
      LB2395.35.B37   1997
      370.15′2—dc21   96–51029
                                                                          CIP

Typeset by Graphicraft Typesetters Limited, Hong Kong
Printed in Great Britain by St Edmundsbury Press Ltd, Bury St Edmunds, Suffolk

For Isabella (b.1993) and all her contemporaries

Contents

Tiananmen Square, 1989

Photograph by courtesy of Associated Press Ltd

And it struck me that it was precisely men like these students who embodied beauty and power of thought, and in whom was concentrated a burning, noble, philanthropic will to spend their lives reconstructing life, unhampered, along some new, humanitarian lines.

(Maxim Gorky, *My Universities*, Penguin edition 1979, p. 42)

Acknowledgements

I would like to take this opportunity to thank a number of friends and colleagues. Bob Cowan, Peter Jarvis, Malcolm Tight, Susan Weil and Geoff Whitty have all read the entire manuscript and offered me many helpful comments on it. My regret is that I have not been able to do full justice to their many shrewd insights. To do so would have required another book. Upma Barnett also read the manuscript with her customary eye for its editorial circumspection.

Gareth Williams has given my writing efforts over the years much warm support: it is a great pleasure to work closely with such a professional colleague who, even from within a slightly different field of intellectual endeavour, gives one such continuous and generous endorsement. Gunther Kress is an intellectual friend and mentor who gives me quiet support for the combined intellectual and practical project into which I seem to have fallen. Gareth Parry takes on a level of responsibility in the projects on which we are engaged which enables me to continue with my writing knowing that things are in safe hands. Nicole Levingston's cheerfulness and coolness under pressure in the office help me to retain a sense of proportion and enable me to focus on my writing with something approaching a clear mind.

I have also gained much from working with all my research students especially, so far as this volume is concerned, John Tribe and Bruce Macfarlane through their work on tourism studies and business studies respectively.

John Skelton, at Open University Press, continues to give me unhurried space to continue with my writing, while all the staff at Open University Press offer a quite excellent level of service.

Introduction

Bearings

A student stands in front of a line of tanks, halting its advance. The student knows that, in taking that stance, his life is imperilled. This is not just any line of tanks: this is a line of tanks in support of a policy on the part of the state, and the action by the student is a form of resistance – some might call it heroic resistance – against all that the tanks represent. How might we understand this action? What bearing might this action have on our thinking about higher education in Western democracies as we move into a new millennium?

The photograph depicts a form of *critical action* on the part of the student. In taking the action, the student is being critical, is entering into a state of *critical being*. The action is not blind behaviour, but is informed by a knowledge of the political structure of contemporary China and is imbued with a deep understanding of concepts such as democracy and freedom. The critical action is underpinned by *critical thought*. But, in addition to critical action and critical thought coming into play, the student is purposively taking up a stance against the world. The student is saying, literally: 'Here, I stand. This is the authentic me. This is what *I* believe.' The student has reached this position of brave authenticity through an internal process of ever-increasing self-reflection, such that he has reached a position of utter assuredness of his own values. The student would have undergone a process of *critical self-reflection* and has now become fully a *critical person.*

Understood in this way, this photograph captures the argument of this book and serves as a leitmotif for our explorations. Critical persons are more than just critical thinkers. They are able critically to engage with the world and with themselves as well as with knowledge. It follows that we have to displace critical thinking as a core concept of higher education with a more comprehensive concept. The concept that I am proposing is that of critical being, which embraces critical thinking, critical action and critical self-reflection.

The problem

Critical thinking is a defining concept of the Western university. Almost everyone is in favour of critical thinking, but we have no proper account of it. Higher education, which prides itself on its critical thought, has done no adequate thinking about critical thinking.

The result of this inattention to critical thought is three-fold. First, higher education doesn't live up to its own rhetoric: higher education is often not critical. Secondly, even where it is on offer, critical thought is construed narrowly: the freeing of the mind that it promises is not forthcoming. Thirdly, and most seriously of all, the whole idea of a higher education founded on a view of critical thought is now inadequate for the modern age, if higher education is to play its part in enabling graduates effectively to be able to take on the world.

In short, in suggesting that we need a new concept of critical thinking, I am also suggesting that we need a new conception of higher education itself.

Let it be

Some will say, why worry? First, we might feel that things can't be in too much of a mess. In the UK, higher education has moved quickly from being an elite institution to being a mass system, with around 1.75 million students. It is generally accepted that the quality of what is on offer is more than passable, even if the academic community has difficulty in articulating its sense of standards. Why then bother to spend time in trying to get to grips with a tricky notion such as critical thinking? Perhaps it just means different things to different people.

This is a 'let sleeping dogs lie' philosophy. Such a stance may be acceptable anywhere else, but it cannot be a tolerable stance for the university. According to the university's self-understanding, everything is potentially available for critical examination. No topic can be off limits.

A second response begins from the consideration that, in the postmodern world, big ideas such as critical thinking are best avoided. Critical thinking sounds suspiciously like a large idea with general application; in other words, 'a grand narrative'. We are told by Lyotard (1984), at least, that we should exhibit 'incredulity towards grand narratives'. Large ideas may seem as if they carry us forward, giving order and coherence to a world of chaos, but the sense of security is ill-founded. In truth, so the story goes, they cabin and confine us and even, *sotto voce*, represent a form of terror, constraining thought and ultimately human action and arrangements. But this is a 'let a thousand flowers bloom' philosophy and is an abandonment of any serious critical thinking. It is a form of uncritical thinking.

A third stance asserts that different epistemic communities, different disciplines, different professions and different sectors in society all have their own forms of critical thinking. The critical thinking of the historian is quite different from that of the physicist and both, in turn, are quite different from the viewpoint of the chief executive of an international corporation in proclaiming that graduate employees should be adept at critical thinking. This is a 'forms of life' philosophy. Things, on this view, are simply different and there's an end on 't. Again, therefore, we have here a view against which critical thinking will find it hard going to make any headway.

False prophets

Not all current views have this laid-back character. Indeed, part of the story to be told is that there are more optimistic voices. But, again, we run into a problem. For these more optimistic voices tend not to be disinterested. They are often representative of the critical thinking industry. Here, the danger is that folk come to believe their own rhetoric. So swept along are they by the belief that there is a single set of actions, skills, propensities or dispositions that can be labelled 'critical thinking' that they lose sight of the end of the critical thinking. Instead of being a means to a greater end – better life, emancipation, greater understanding – critical thinking here becomes a driving force in its own right deserving of curriculum space and resources. For these adherents, critical thinking deserves a significant slice of the action. This is an internal agenda of the academic community.

More recently still, however, other voices have begun to be heard in favour of critical thinking but representative of an external agenda. Two linked but distinguishable sub-plots can be identified. First, critical thinking is heralded as a key component of the competences needed for economic regeneration. The corporate world has to move on and we need critical minds to help it to do so. Secondly, in professional life, critical thinking is coming to be prized as a form of self-development: through continuing self-reflection, individuals can work out their own game plan and so go on reconstituting themselves through their lifetime. This is a human capital that replenishes itself and adds value to itself continually.

These external voices appear to be rescuing higher education from its self-doubts about critical thinking. A new role for higher education built around its own project of critical thinking seems to be opening. But the rescue is an illusion, and needs to be combated. The definitions of critical thinking may be broadening but they are also surrendering, in the different domains, to an instrumental agenda: these forms of critical thinking are intent on delivering given ends with ever greater effectiveness. Rather than being a vehicle for combating ideology, critical thinking now takes on an ideological character of its own.

In all of these redefinitions of critical thinking, the wider purposes of higher education are forgotten. This is ironic. For one point of critical thinking is to engage students in a critique of the wider context of their education; and yet here there is a critical thinking movement that declines that wider view. No wonder it has backers: there will be no boats rocked in this movement. It is a very benign form of critical thought.

What's the big idea?

Even if we cannot bring it off, let us at least be clear about the world that we might be missing. First, critical thought is potentially emancipatory for individuals. Through critical thought, students can not just come to free themselves from dependency on their former taken-for-granted worlds, but can also be free from dependency on any world, at least in theory. It is sometimes said that, through a genuine higher education, students come to live in a different world. So they may; but such an observation misses the main point, which is that through a higher education that takes critical thinking seriously – rather than as a set of intellectual games – students can come to a realization that they need not be dependent on *any* world with which they are presented. Doubtless, this is difficult for many. But it is also liberating in a radical way. Students realize that they are free to build their own cognitive universe.

Secondly, critical thought is educationally radical. No teacher who places critical thinking at the centre of her approach to teaching and learning can teach didactically as a general strategy. On the one hand, such a teacher would have an eye to the ultimate provisionality of everything she says and its potential critique by her own students. On the other hand, that same teacher would understand that the students are not going to be able to emerge from their course with the disposition to engage in critical thinking unless they are given every opportunity to develop those dispositions. In turn, the pedagogical relationship is implicated. Where everything is potentially criticizable, the teacher and the students stand on an epistemological level (Jaspers, 1960). The teacher retains her professional control but becomes, to a considerable degree, a participant in a *joint* inquiry after truth with her students.

Thirdly, critical thought is radical in social and cultural terms. The arguments of the 1960s about higher education being a base for social revolution cannot be sustained. It would simply politicize higher education in a most problematic way. However, what is conceivable is that a higher education – especially a mass higher education system – which takes critical thinking seriously can act indirectly as a formative agency in society simply through the power of critical dispositions as they are released into society. Widened to embrace not just the capacities to think critically but to understand oneself critically and to act critically, higher education becomes the formation of critical persons who are not subject to the world but able to act autonomously and purposively within it. A higher education for the modern world becomes a process in which critical being is realized.

Social and personal

This book is based on the view that a critical form of life, adequate to the problematic it faces in higher education, has to be construed and practised as a form of *social and personal epistemology*. The dual phrase is intended to do a number of things.

To begin with, the idea of social epistemology puts the category of the social on the map. Critical thinking cannot adequately be construed just as a form of individual action or mental state. We live in a knowledge society (Stehr, 1994). That *is* the case, but more to the point are the changing forms that knowledge takes according to the evaluations that society places on those different forms of knowledge. Humanities give way to science; small-scale forms of knowledge production give way to large-scale forms; knowledge for its own sake gives way to applied knowledge; pure inquiry gives way to problem-solving *in situ* (Gibbons *et al.*, 1994); propositional knowledge gives way to or at least is supplemented by experiential knowing; and ways of knowing give way to sheer information (Midgley, 1989).

Our epistemologies are, therefore, irredeemably social. Society places different kinds of value on different kinds of knowledge. The computer age, the age of action and of getting things done, extracts payment in terms of the value placed on appropriate new knowledges (information, reflective experience, problem-solving). What counts as knowledge is not just social but societal.

Accordingly, knowledge is not given: it is socially sustained and invested with interests and backed by power. On this, there is agreement both between contrasting conservatives (such as Gellner and Searle) and contrasting radicals (such as Foucault and Habermas). A critical higher education has, therefore, to take on knowledge itself. We cannot leave our students sensing that there is a givenness to the knowledge structures that they are encountering or that those structures are socially neutral.

However, a social epistemology of this kind has a deeply personal character to it. If the full promise of critical thinking is to be achieved, then it will have to be achieved not only through students but also by them. Students, individually and collectively, will have to realize that transformatory potential themselves. *This* social epistemology has a necessarily personal component. Again, the interpretation of critical thought at a personal level can be – and often is – constraining, or it can be emancipatory.

Partly, the story is that told by critical theory. That is, our cognitive efforts have the power not just to cloak us with illusions or ideologies, but also to critique the world – and, in that critique, to have a self-referential capacity. Higher education sometimes likes to overlook this capacity, but it is happy enough when students say that they have been transformed by their experience. Through higher education, students can come not just to inhabit a different universe, but also to be changed as *persons*. Critical theory posits a situation in which, through their cognitive achievements, individuals see through the misapprehensions to which they have been in thrall and, thereby, can undergo a process of personal emancipation.

Another story that directly implicates the personal component of critique is that of epistemology itself. Truth-telling is not the antiseptic process that academics like to portray it as, but calls for commitment and existential involvement. These are not adjuncts to, but are necessary ingredients of, the critical life.

Critique in context

Modern society is characteristically a changing society, but it is not yet a learning society (Ranson, 1994). The distinction here ultimately turns on a quality that we might term 'social wisdom'. Is society in command of itself as it responds to and produces change? Change might be grounded on knowledge, but to what extent is that knowledge itself under critical control? Is the use of that knowledge enlightened (Maxwell, 1987)? Has knowledge become simply the supplier of means to non-debated ends or are the ends up for debate too? We do not have to invoke an image of a worn-out and unworkable central control to ask whether society can be said to be, in any real sense, steering its changes with the maximum insight that might be available.

Change will only become enlightened if three conditions are satisfied. First, society has to form within itself a significant reflexive capacity (cf. Beck *et al.*, 1994). This would be a critique, a critical function, bent on understanding, on enlightening and on improving in every sense society and its changes. Higher education thus has to be seen as central but in a new way. No longer a vehicle for the reproduction of knowledge elites or the production of labour market competences, higher education has the crucial task of supplying in large measure this reflexive capacity.

It is often remarked that the critical spirit is unduly negative in character but the idea of reflexivity puts paid to all that. Modern society requires a reflexive capacity – at both the personal and the societal levels – which has a formative element. Modern society will move forward only through its powers of symbolic *creation* (not, as Reich suggests, just through its powers of symbolic analysis). Reflection and critical evaluation, therefore, have to contain moments of the creation of imaginary alternatives. Reflexivity has to offer resources for continuing development.

Secondly, if modern society is to be in a significant sense in control of itself, this reflexive capacity has to be significant itself. Seen in this way, higher education *has* to be a mass enterprise. (Whether, in Trow's terminology, it *has* to be universal is a further matter.) The point is that a higher education system, seen as a major generator of reflexive and steering capacities in society, has itself to be substantial. The idea, *à la* Leavis, that a critical function is synonymous with an elite system has to be repudiated as totally inadequate to the problematic we are facing.

Thirdly, reflexivity, critique and imagination have to be accompanied by personal capacities for change and for critical but constructive action. The balance between critical action and constructive action will not always be easily achieved, especially amid the conflicting values and discourses of modern society. Again, though, the furnishing of those qualities of human being has to be one of the tasks of higher education in the foreseeable future.

Critical thought is important but that importance has been underestimated. Nothing less than the future of society is at stake. Without a proper conception of criticality for higher education, there have to be question marks put against the sustainability of modern society. Yes, it will go on, but at what cost, and with what little degree of careful and informed direction? Unless higher education begins to take criticality seriously, there is little hope of critical being of the kind intended here ever taking off, for there will be few other advocates. And if higher education does not have and does not practise a proper conception of critical being, it will have little or no prospect of playing its full part in the continuing reshaping of modern society. Society will then be diminished as a rational society and as a self-transforming society. Critical being has to be *the* business of higher education.

The argument

My thesis is that we should dispense with critical thinking as a core concept of higher education and replace it with the wider concept of critical being. There are five steps in the argument:

1. Criticality takes place along two axes. First, we can distinguish a number of *levels*, from critical thinking skills through critical thought to critique. Each succeeding level offers ever higher forms of alternative possibilities of understanding. Critical thinking skills confine the thinker to given standards of reasoning within specific disciplines, whereas critique opens the possibility of entirely different and even contrasting modes of understanding.
2. Criticality can also be understood as taking place in three *domains*: knowledge, the self and the world. Respectively, three forms of critical being are possible: critical reason, critical self-reflection and critical action.
3. Critical thinking is a defining concept of the Western university but it has been interpreted narrowly, being confined largely to its place in relation to formal knowledge. The critical life in the domains of the self and the world has been given short shrift. Critical self-reflection and critical action have hardly appeared as components of higher education.
4. Now, higher education is being enjoined to widen its conception of criticality to include the two domains of the self and of the world. However, that broadening is being accompanied by a limited interpretation such that, in all three domains (of knowledge, self and world), criticality

is being confined to instrumental levels of operation. The emancipatory potential of critical being – in thought, in self-understanding and in action – is being vitiated.

5. The full potential of critical being will only be achieved, therefore, through the integration of its expression in the three domains of knowledge, self and world, and in being lived out at the highest levels of critique in each domain. Through such an integration of the critical spirit, critical but creative persons will result, capable of living effectively in the world.

It will be observed that this is a general argument. The reference to the Western university alone indicates that I intend my argument to have wide applicability. Within the text, references will be made to the UK situation, especially to the English traditions, and to a lesser extent to the USA; but those references fill out the general argument. The main issue is that of how we might construe and practise higher education in the modern age – an age, for instance, of globalization and increasing interconnectiveness in economic and intellectual transactions. The argument, therefore, *has* to be a general argument, an argument that has wide applicability.

The plan

The first Part of the book is a series of skirmishes, coming at our topic from a number of directions. On the basis of those preliminary inquiries, Part 2 starts (Chapter 5) with a summary statement of the book's analysis of critical reason and, in subsequent chapters, develops the argument, especially in relation to the underplayed forms of criticality, those of critical self-reflection and of critical action. Part 3 widens the argument and looks at the connections between critical being and the wider society. It shows ways in which higher education can be a critical business in and for society.

The reader may like some sense of the topography ahead. Part 1 can be likened to negotiating the foothills of a mountain and establishes the basecamp from which the assault on the summit is attempted. It catches glimpses of the summit from a number of angles. Part 2 attempts its assault on the summit, and secures the ground in doing so. Part 3 surveys the terrain from the summit. These three stages of the expedition have, it might be conjectured, distinct levels of difficulty. However, in this age of hang-gliders, it is always possible to start with the panoramic view (of Part 3) and descend from there.

Part 1

Rethinking Critical Thinking

1

Conditions of Critical Thought

Beginnings

In the Western university, critical thought has many factions. We can, as an opening sally, identify some contemporary fault lines:

Critical thinking as disciplinary competence

In this tradition, students at the end of their courses will be expected to have mastered the tacit norms and conventions of the mode of inquiry associated with their discipline. The norms and conventions encourage certain forms of disciplinary inquiry and communication and rule others offside. While these tacit rules have policing and socializing functions, they crucially make possible critical moves.

In the Western university, it is not enough to be a faithful rule-follower, reiterating views already enunciated. Disciplines are critical conversations (Oakeshott, 1989): one is expected to do some work on the evidence, namely to make truth claims. In so far as undergraduate work is concerned, making truth claims does not typically involve taking on established positions and authorities in the field. Rather, it points to coming to an independent judgement about the evidence. Terms like 'analysis' and 'synthesis' are code words for the kinds of metacognitive moves that undergraduates are expected to be able to make.

This is, as we might term it, epistemic critical thinking. It springs from a high value accorded to the cognitive ordering of the universe through supposedly enduring disciplinary traditions. Its pedagogical strategy is to develop a mastery of the tacit epistemological rules within a cognitive field, the students ultimately having to demonstrate that they have the competence to participate in the conversation of the discipline. Its critical standards are internal, tacit, cognitive and under academic control.

Critical thinking as practical knowledge

Another tradition of critical thought in the Western university is that of reflexive practice. Donald Schön (1987) has made much of his notion of 'the reflective practitioner'. But his elucidation of it as a form of real-time reflection and critique in action has to be seen as a variant on an enduring theme. The mediaeval universities, after all, were high-level professional schools with some – such as Salerno with its focus on medicine – specializing in particular professional fields. The disputations were a form of training in the use of rhetoric, the rhetorical skills that – in an age long before mass communication – were going to be needed in court, in administration or in Godly affairs. This critical thinking fostered thinking on one's feet. Critical frames here are looser, less under the tight control of any constituency and more responsive to the pragmatic demands of 'the real world'.

Philosophical warrant for critique in action can be found both in Greek thought and in Marxism. Aristotle's 'practical knowledge' (which he divided into *techne* and *phronesis*, or making and action) and the Marxist notion of 'praxis' both assert the legitimacy of knowledge gained through practice. The Aristotelian idea is weighted on the problem of action in a largely pre-given world; the Marxist notion is weighted on the problem of the kind of world to be constructed *through* action. But both have an inner sense of the world of action supplying the possibility of learning. And, in both cases, learning comes through a critical interrogation of practice.

One reading of professional education – and of its often begrudging assimilation into the university – is that of bringing professional action under 'critical control' (Eraut, 1994). In this, there are large questions about the relationship between thought and action and of the relationship of critique to both. But the essential idea in this tradition in the Western university is that it is possible to critique action so as to produce more enlightened or more effective forms of action. The critical thinking in this tradition is a practice in the world, a *praxis*. Knowledge situated in practice is not, as is sometimes implied (Gibbons *et al.*, 1994), a newish form of knowing alongside propositional knowledge, but is a tradition of enduring character.

Critical thinking as political engagement

The term 'political' is very much a small 'p' sense of political, and it is susceptible of soft and strident variants. The softer version is reflected in the goal of many universities in the USA to provide a civic dimension to learning. But it is also to be found in more local and small-scale activities, such as study service (Goodlad, 1995) and, arguably, even through activities of the kind prompted by the UK Government's Enterprise in Higher Education Initiative. In this softer form of critical thinking as political, there is a sense that the university owes much to its host community. The sense of political cuts two ways. On the one hand, students become sensitized to their wider society and gain direct insight into the challenges that its citizens face. On the other hand, there is an indirect impact on society itself. Through the implicit constructive critique with which students work in the community, the civic character of society is extended and deepened.

A more strident variant of the political interpretation of critical thought is also visible in the university. The image of the lone student in front of a line of tanks in Tiananmen Square in Beijing in 1989 graphically captures the point, but examples can be culled from across the world over the past thirty years. The university has been seen as a potential base of social and political revolution. The sociological explanation and legitimation was supplied by Marcuse (1968): even though society was on the verge of generating *One-Dimensional Man*, the university was not entirely incorporated into the state's apparatus and was able to operate as a semi-independent societal base for critical thought.

That account is given contemporaneous backing through the current student activism across the world, especially in newly emerging countries (where the student cadre acts as a means of injecting global criteria of democracy and social reform). However, the student body is volatile and overt political action by students may be reactionary. It was the upper-middle-class students of Oxbridge that helped to break the General Strike in 1926 by driving the buses and so keeping public transport going. Currently, too, student political opinion has taken a more conservative stance across the Western world.

Whatever its orientation, the issue is whether a political critique can justifiably be inserted into higher education. At best, is it to be tolerated as a form of personal development, on the fringe of university life, where even community service, for example, is unassessed; or is some form of political consciousness-raising to be built into the curriculum? *If* it is the case that all knowledge is political in some senses, embodying interests and ideologies of social and economic change, then, the argument might run, a proper higher education should incorporate a political dimension, at least sufficient to enable students to grasp the social and political character of the education that they are receiving.

Critical thought as corporate reform

Now being proposed by the corporate world as a university responsibility is that of providing students with the wherewithal to be critical of work and business practices. If we have entered an 'age of unreason' (Handy, 1995) and have – each of us – to bring about continuing change, and if we are to have the future built into our sense of work, then we all have to become friendly critics of work practices. And so the voice of industry is being heard encouraging universities to develop critical thinking among their students.

What kind of critical thinking is being sought here? The answer is that this critical thinking is essentially strategic in character and in two senses. On the one hand, it is a critique of operations, goals, human resources and organizational culture that is called for. This is strategic critical thinking, intent on delivering instrumental ends; this is not critical thinking that is oriented to truth or to understanding or to genuine mutual communication. So this plea for critical thought to find its way into the university curriculum *is* partial. On the other hand, this critical thinking also encourages strategic behaviours by the employee. Organizations might evince a rhetoric of change, of openness and of 'empowerment', but contain, in their culture and practices, a deep resistance to change. The graduate will have to box cleverly. Being armed with insight into ways of improving organizational culture and practices is one thing; bringing it off effectively is another. The employees can be too clever for their own good.

Uncritical thought

Critical thought is not all of a piece. Of the four forms of critical thinking in the university that we have just identified, none is reducible to any of the others. Epistemic critical thought looks to reproduce academic identities; professional critical thought looks to produce professional identities in the wider world; civic critical thought looks to have an impact on the polity (whether of a humanistic or a revolutionary kind); and corporate critical thought looks to produce an instrumental reflexivity likely to sustain economic change.

More than that, the four perspectives cut across each other in subtle ways. Internal and external to the academic world; conservative and radical; reproducing and transformatory; personal and social: all of these polarities can be found across the four forms of critical thought just identified. These polarities can also be seen *within* them. As we saw, the civic or political form of critical thought is susceptible of conservative or of radical interpretations. But so, too, critical thought aimed at professional life can take a reproducing form, in which undergraduates are socialized into a pre-given professional culture *or* – as perhaps with nursing degrees today or even teacher education in the 1970s – are given the intellectual resources to critique that professional culture.

However, although critical thought is susceptible of both radical and conservative interpretations, in higher education the weight has been on conservative formulations. Professional education has been largely an initiation into professional culture. But, equally, epistemic critical thought has tended to perform the same function for academe: it has been a socialization into the norms and styles of thinking associated with the different academic disciplines. In this sense, epistemic critical thought is a means of reproducing the academic professions (Squires, 1990).

This may seem heretical. Surely, critical thought is unbounded. The university prides itself on the openness of its thinking. Potentially, all truth offerings are open to challenge from any quarter. It may be that every truth offering is set within a framework, but that does not mean that we are condemned to live only within that framework. Such, at least, was Popper's point and to think otherwise is to bind ourselves to 'the myth of the framework' (Popper, 1977). We do not have to be the slaves of the particular framework within which we are operating.

The philosophy of this view has merit but the sociology is weak. While there are elements of openness built into the cognitive life of academics, the overwhelming message of the sociology of knowledge is that the academic identity is maintained within definite cognitive frameworks with their own norms, values and territorial defences (Kuhn, 1970; Bloor, 1976; Bourdieu, 1988; Becher, 1989). *Homo Academicus* lives in particular *Academic Tribes and Territories*, in which the cognitive life is characterized by a 'habitus' with its routines and cognitive perspectives. Even though critical thought has limited scope, even though deviance is hardly tolerated, it is still necessary in order to keep alive each academic sub-culture. In a universe of endemic cognitive and social change, no academic sub-culture can stand still. Critique, therefore, plays more than an identity-sustaining function. The economic and social capital of each discipline is maintained through critique. But it must never try to live up to the rhetoric of academe about the central value of critical thought.

I am not suggesting that critique is barely to be seen. On the contrary, in every discipline, dispute is evident and over substantial theoretical matters. But, by and large, the disputants talk easily enough to each other. They understand each other to be living in the same portion of the cognitive universe. The disputes are normally low-key and internal to the discipline, about this theory or the substance of that finding. Occasionally, they are about the character and constitution of the discipline as such. Then, complete breakdown in communication between the contending parties can result, leading perhaps to a breaking away and the formation of a rival approach. Eventually, a new 'discipline' may result. Still less do critical debates take the form of transdisciplinary debates about, say, the critical functions of the university itself. For the most part, the cognitive universe of academics is characterized by a taken-for-grantedness about its orderliness and its enduring nature within local frameworks of thought.

Analogously, those forms of critical thinking oriented towards the wider society – whether the corporate world, professional life or the wider polity – tend to operate within horizons of givenness. Revolution in the business world, in the student's intended profession or in the wider society is not typically envisaged. There may be the odd 'case study' where every assumption is up for grabs, but this is normally an indulgence within safe parameters of understanding.

So each of our four forms of critical thought exhibits radical moments, but those moments tend to be diversions from the main enterprise or tolerated minority pursuits at the margins of the kirk. In each, reproduction plays a stronger role than revolution or transformation. In each, too, elements of power are not far away: critical thought turns out to be a means by which agendas can be furthered. We arrive, therefore, at a paradox: critical thought proclaims itself as fearless, prepared to scythe away pretence, bluster and falsehood. But it all too easily harbours just such elements. There are always limits to critical thought.

What's so critical about critical thought?

I now want to unpack three terms: critical thinking, critical thought, and critique.

Critical thinking

Critical thinking I take to be cognitive acts undertaken by individuals. Students engaged in critical thinking may do so in the company of other students and their critical thinking may be enhanced by that interchange; but the emphasis in the term 'critical thinking' is on the character of the individual's cognitive acts. Critical thinking, considered as the cognitive accomplishments of individuals, has – especially in the USA – become big business. Much effort has gone into working out both the logic and the psychology of critical thinking. Since, on this view, critical thinking is what students do, the task of educators is, first, to work out the components of critical thinking: what are the logical moves that amount to critical thinking? Secondly, it is to work out pedagogical strategies for assisting students to develop the identified critical thinking skills.

Two features of this way of looking at critical thinking are apparent. First, it is assumed that there are cognitive processes that can justifiably be labelled 'critical thinking', largely independent of intellectual or practical contexts. It may be accepted that contexts are necessary for the deployment of critical thinking, but it is still considered that the strategies that take the title of 'critical thinking' can be identified *sui generis*. Secondly, critical thinking here becomes an assembly of skills. Attributes of skills are that they can be turned on a situation at will and that they are value-neutral. What matters is the application of particular techniques by individuals to given situations. The skills of critical thinking are turned on the problem situation and, providing the permitted procedures are followed, legitimate outcomes will flow.

The assumption that critical thinking is what critical thinkers inevitably do is fast yielding an unquestioned programme of activity and is even generating an intellectual sub-culture in its own right (with its journals, books and conferences). The overt signs of legitimacy cannot be persuasive. Even if context-neutral skills could be isolated, they could not provide a sufficient approach to critical thinking. The transformation of the critical thinker, as well as possible wider forms of social change, has to come into view. To see critical thinking as the deployment of cognitive skills by individuals is to adopt a blinkered approach to the matter. The upshot is that things will be left largely as they are: this is a critical thinking without a critical edge.

Critical thought

The idea of critical thought begins to supply such a critical edge. Here, the focus widens. The sense of a thinker is retained, since thought necessarily implies a thinker. But thought is also collective. As well as their formal properties and components, disciplines are forms of social interaction within epistemic communities. Knowledge *is* socially constructed and sustained. We do not have to believe in the strong programme of the sociology of science – with its central view that, sociologically, there is nothing special about science – to acknowledge the category of the social in the constitution of knowledge.

Critical thought is collaborative in character. Individuals might be doing some hard critical thinking, but critical thought develops and takes off through sustained interchange around collective standards. An intellectual field is a set of critical traditions. We do not have to follow Habermas in believing that the critical dialogue is oriented towards a consensus. On the contrary, conversation can become heated argument. But there has to be some meeting of minds for even heated argument to take place, for even polarized positions to assert themselves. Indeed, the presence of a significant level of disagreement is an indication that social space is available for dissent to express itself. Whatever the level and extent of agreement, critical thought necessarily contains a social component. We have, therefore, to ask whether our educational practices in higher education fully reflect this point. Critical thought can only be developed collaboratively.

Bodies of knowledge are also sites of organized power (Foucault, 1980). Their definitions of the world impose themselves on those who fall under their sway. Those who inhabit them rarely experience their oppressive character; but even those distinguished in their fields can feel that burdensome weight if they dare to step outside the presuppositions of understanding and the sanctioned forms of inference and presentation of 'evidence'. Both the social sciences and the natural sciences brook no dissent from the uninitiated: the non-expert are expected to accept the definitions of the world that are imposed on them. Certainly, there are now the beginnings of public resistance to this disciplinary imposition. Clients of professionals will shop around, not being ready to take the 'expert' advice on offer. Science-based definitions of the world are also being resisted. In the educated society, in theory at least, we can be our own experts. But the disciplines retain this in-built will to power.

In this context, critical thought cuts two ways. On the one hand, disciplines contain their own critical standards through which they interrogate the world. On the other hand, the critical standards generate a relatively closed world. Foucault may have overdrawn his analysis: disciplines contain their own reflexivity through which they move on. They are not unchanging monoliths. Even so, their representations of the world are a form of power, their adherents being the wielders of that power. The exercise of critical thought turns out to be the exercise of a form of power.

Higher education has understood these points and, indeed, has embraced them, seeking in the past to turn its students into faithful and expert followers of the faith. Nor, in the expert society, is that strategy without point for it produces 'experts'; but it prompts further thought. What do they know of a discipline when all they know of the world is through the perspective of that discipline? How critical is the critical thinking of those 'initiated' into such a world? How trustworthy are such experts? Critical thought is a powerful form of criticality but it, too, has its limits.

Critique

If critical thought is criticism within the discipline, conducted according to its values and procedures, critique is a form of criticism about the discipline itself. It might be conducted by the practitioners of the discipline, or by those outside it, but its logic is that it is an extramural form of criticism.

Critique is a way of placing the discipline. It may chide the discipline for becoming like this or for failing to do that, or may simply offer a commentary on it, but essentially critique seeks to set the discipline in a wider perspective than that in which the internal debates are usually conducted. The intellectual field can be the subject of critical evaluation. Critique is metacriticism.

Critique works outside the conventions of the discipline itself. Other standards can come into play, for instance the extent to which ethical considerations play a part, the degree to which the discipline represents sectional interests, or the influence exerted by particular epistemologies. Such self-analysis at the level of the discipline may typically occur, as Kuhn (1970) implied, at moments of crisis. But this need not be the case. What is in question here is the extent to which a discipline contains within itself the capacity for accepting critique.

Such a reflexive capacity can be exploited by the practitioners of the discipline: Are the inmates prepared to chance their arm and mount a serious evaluation of the discipline? What fate awaits those who dare? Is there a spirit of generosity abroad or will the discipline close ranks against such an inner scrutiny? However, a generosity that amounts to a toleration only of those on the inside is a limited form of generosity. Charity may begin at home but it doesn't have to stop there.

Real generosity reveals itself when comment from outwith the kirk is not only heard but also seriously considered. Since critique does not have to obey the rules of the internal game – being a commentary *on* the game

– others can legitimately comment. This, of course, will be denied. How can non-medics comment, for example, on medical science? The response is understandable: it is a defence mechanism to maintain control over the definition of a discipline by its practitioners. But, in logic, critique can be *legitimately* mounted by external commentators, and may be all the more insightful for that. In time, as with complementary medicine, a contending perspective may begin to be accepted within the dominant field itself.

The educational implications of these observations on critique are two-fold. First, interdisciplinarity is of critical importance. Interdisciplinarity is necessarily *critical interdisciplinarity*. It encourages the possibility of different cognitive perspectives being turned on a subject and so illuminating it in different ways. This can be said simply enough but it is fraught with problems, both of an epistemological and of an operational kind. Precisely how, in any one course, are such multiple perspectives to be opened to students in a serious way? A superficial encounter with a rival disciplinary perspective could be counterproductive: it could present unwelcome cognitive challenge and fail to bring even the cognitive transformation that a deep familiarity with a single intellectual field would bring.

More problematically still, issues arise as to how different forms of thought are to be brought into a relationship with each other such that the student really gains from her experience. The student does not have to feel that it is a 'coherent' experience: intellectual progression can arise out of a sense of disjunction (Jarvis, 1992). The comfort factor is not necessarily an educational guide. But there are limits to incoherence: the student is not usually required to stand entirely outside herself. Yet this is what critique as external reflection ultimately requires – the capacity to become an *other*, to inhabit, if only briefly, a cognitive perspective that is unfamiliar.

From critical thinking (with its connotations of critical thinking skills) to critical thought to critique, the sequence posits an ever-broadening horizon in which critical reason can operate. Through such a sequence, thought becomes increasingly critical. In critique, quite different views of an object or a topic might be proffered as alternative perspectives are taken on board. This is real cognitive and personal challenge, and it may open up the way to a transformation of the individual student.

Positive or negative?

Is criticism necessarily negative in character? Clearly not. The critical mind is, in essence, an evaluative mind. Critical thought is the application of critical standards or values – sustained by a peer community – to an object or theory or practice. There are evident and explicit examples of this understanding of critical thought *institutionalized* in higher education. In art education or in literary criticism, for example, criticism is a process of evaluation. There, the critical process as evaluation is a central part of the curriculum. Here, positive features are to be celebrated.

And yet the idea of criticism as a negative form of thinking dies hard. First, since evaluation takes place against standards, critical judgements quite properly can show how the object under discussion falls short of those standards. The judgement will also often imply that things could have and should have attained more closely the critical standards in question. And perhaps the review or the paper or even the remarks on the student's essay carry something of that judgemental tone. Secondly, where the judgement attempts to be formative, indicating how things might be taken forward, its recipients are often left in the dark. This is because, in academic life, the critical standards are seldom made explicit. Being tacit within the discipline, they are not known in any articulable form even to the initiated.

Unfortunately, judgement can end up purely as summative. In that case, we have a doubly skewed example of negative criticism. It neither identifies areas in which the critical standards are – more or less – reached, nor indicates how things might be taken forward.

The negative tone of academic criticism is a reflection of the structural features of academic life. In the Western world, academic life has become – indeed, has been made – competitive. Collaborative features are downplayed, despite their increasing significance. Career development, rewards, prizes, status and power attach almost entirely to individuals. Universities have become part of larger societal processes linked both to a capitalist economy and to a post-Enlightenment culture in which high marks go to individuals. 'Fast capitalism' (Agger, 1991) has no time for solidarity and the resulting individualism produces a destructive competitiveness.

Certainly, science and technological research, and indeed social scientific research, are built largely around the efforts of teams. Those teams collaborate, often on a worldwide basis, sharing research paths. Priority disputes are balanced by genuine mutuality of endeavour. But the unduly negative tone of criticism is still noticeable. It may be that *that* form of criticism is to be found even more in the humanities; or that it is topic-sensitive. That would be a matter for empirical investigation. But the negativity of academic criticism is endemic.

Springing from a competitive environment, criticism may have the social function of producing rival formulations of an issue or approaches to a practice. Its virtue remains that it reminds us that things could be otherwise. However, it can be corrosive. Criticism can easily turn its attention from the theory or idea or practice under consideration to a commentary on the individual. Such criticism can induce natural feelings of anxiety and even fear. Individuals can feel damaged; students' confidence can be easily dented. The upshot on the part of the student is caution, a playing safe and a keeping within agreed norms. Risk-taking and creativity are marginalized. Far from opening our cognitive universe, criticism ends up by keeping things safe but unchallenging.

If, therefore, higher education is to engender critical dispositions of a robust kind, able to withstand the world and assist in moving it forward, our pedagogical practices certainly have to engender a critical spirit that is evaluative against the severest standards; but those critical practices have to be conducted in a way that is also positive, affirming, supportive, collective, constructive and even utopian in character (Kress, 1995).

Angles on critical thinking

We can reclassify the views we have explored in the following way.

1. *Critical thinking as control*, through the tight imposition of largely taken-for-granted rules and standards: the invocation of terms such as validity and reliability are symptomatic of this view of critical thinking. Talk of critical thinking here is a rhetoric for a pedagogy that acts tightly to control the formation of 'students'.
2. *Critical thinking as reconstitution*. This notion has three sub-plots:
   (a) reconstitution of knowledge;
   (b) reconstitution of the self;
   (c) reconstitution of the world, especially the world of work.
   There are subtle relationships and even tensions between these sub-plots. In particular, (b) can look towards either (a) or (c). Coupled with (a), it can promise the possibility of the formation of 'the passionate sceptic', in which the student does not passively consume but critically engages with the intellectual frames that she experiences, becoming an active participant in the critical dialogues around her. Coupled with (c), however, the student can easily become simply an extension of the manufactured world, certainly helping to reshape it but in its own instrumental terms.
3. *Critical thinking as the development of wisdom*. Key ideas here are understanding, autonomy and contemplation: through grappling with multiple intellectual frames, the student's understanding of any one frame develops and her possibilities for autonomous thinking grow. A critical space emerges between the individual and her hold on the world. Intellectual frames are understood to offer resources that can be imaginatively deployed to illuminate the world. In itself, this is a contemplative view of critical thinking.
4. *Critical thinking as praxis*. Here, the alternative frames of understanding are put to work in action towards a better life. Emancipation is part of this view of critical thinking, but only a part. Critical thinking or, rather, critical reason understood as praxis is both fundamentally collaborative in character and rooted in interventions in the world of action.

Conclusions: Conditions of the critical life

From our discussion, three conditions can be identified which are necessary for the critical life:

1. *Critical reason calls for a framework* – of rules or values or theories – from which the critical commentary is mounted and which supplies the standards embedded in the critical commentary. The framework may be internal to the object of the evaluation or may be external to it; but a framework has to come into play in some way. A complex text, such as a book, may draw on many frameworks. But, in turn, the critical frameworks can themselves be critiqued. A review of a book on music education may query the value attached in the book to the work of Adorno: essentially, critical reason is a contest over critical frameworks. A challenge for our pedagogies in higher education, accordingly, is that of imparting frameworks to students that enable them to view their studies in a genuinely critical way. In turn, this condition calls upon their lecturers themselves to show that their favoured intellectual frames can be critiqued by other frames. A genuinely higher education has to be an education of multiple frames.

2. *Critical reason calls for a critical space*, a space in which a critical commentary can be mounted. The corporate world is recognizing just this in its flatter structures and its talk of empowerment, allowing employees the space in which to critique their immediate environment. Critical spaces have to be sustained collaboratively, and cannot be secured in the presence of power. Our pedagogies in higher education, accordingly, have to accord real critical space to students, and to encourage them to take advantage of it rather than to fear it.

3. *Critical reason calls for a disposition on the part of the individual to be critical.* Through critical reason, individuals assert themselves and constitute themselves. The exercise of critical reason calls for brave acts, even if it is exercised in what appears to be the most theoretical of domains. Higher education, accordingly, cannot be seen as purely cognitive, but has to be seen as experiential: the development of critical reason calls for the development of whole persons. This observation alone runs against the grain of most of our practices in higher education.

   Multiple frames, social space and the development of persons: these are just three conditions of a higher education understood as the development of the life of critical reason. These conditions alone present major challenges to academics and others responsible for the student experience. But the life of critical reason is a contentious idea, especially in a postmodern world. It is to postmodernism and its challengers, therefore, that we turn next.

2

Uncritical Theory

On critical standards

Critical thought has to start somewhere. It takes place against a background of values, standards or truth criteria. Two sets of questions arise immediately. First, is that background necessarily domain-specific? Can we identify only the presuppositions of, say, this historian or that physicist or that doctor or this corporate manager? Or are there any universal standards of, for example, the rational life against which criticism can gain a purchase?

Secondly, how secure is any framework of knowledge or values, whether context-specific or not? Frameworks are always susceptible to criticism: that was a point made by Popper. But the critical enterprise, as Popper construed it, was worthwhile because it contained valid standards. That he spent much of his intellectual life attempting to identify and to shore up those critical standards is a matter germane to our discussion. Piecemeal criticism was both possible and legitimate. Through critical and rigorous examination of each theory and even of its accompanying framework, through a process of conjecture and refutation, we can approach nearer the truth – so gaining for our theories greater verisimilitude – even if we cannot ever entirely reach it.

The Popperian strategy, however, has come under two massive and entirely opposed challenges. The first was that of critical theory, especially in the hands of Habermas. The essence of that challenge is that piecemeal criticism is an unduly limited form of criticism, despite the rigour that Popper (and others such as Lakatos) attempted to insert into the process. The problem is that, because it is piecemeal, it fails to take on the form of knowledge as such. Any ideological presuppositions – for example, about the epistemological or even the technological superiority of a form of knowledge – will go unchallenged. Any distortions or imbalances in the process by which the form of knowledge is constructed and maintained will go undetected. The edifice of this knowledge will remain intact, safe from criticism.

The second challenge to Popper's critical rationalism is more recent and is that presented by postmodernism. Postmodernism denies that there are secure critical standards of any kind. Whereas Habermas's critical theory impugns Popperianism for having far too limited a conception of criticism, wanting criticism instead to have a much broader sweep and, potentially, a transformatory effect, postmodernism implicitly repudiates the notion of criticism. For postmodernism, both Popper and Habermas are in the dock together. They both believe that valid critical standards can be identified, albeit of a quite different order. Postmodernism, on the other hand, refuses to accept that there are *any* secure frameworks or critical standards on which we can agree and from which criticism can get going.

This, then, is the territory of our discussion in this chapter. Are there any critical standards that we can hold on to? If so, are they simply expressive of different forms of life, embedded in contrasting language games (the postmodern position)? Or are there any universal critical standards which might also inform our practices in, and our understanding of, higher education (as implied by critical theory)? Is there a critical life as such? This seemingly arcane discussion is of some importance. It bears upon what we take higher education to be and what we take society to be.

Anything goes?

Actually, it is not true to say that postmodernism eschews criticism. For postmodernism, criticism is fine. What is in doubt for postmodernism is that there can ever be any substance to any evaluation. To assume that evaluation can ever amount to anything much is to believe that it rests on some firm ground of knowledge, of principle or of value. Any such firm ground would require assent from others. It would call forth a belief in some large story about truth or value or an ideological project. And just this kind of belief is explicitly ruled out of court by the postmodernists.

There are no large stories or general descriptions of the world that are available to us any longer. All we have are our local stories, activities and projects. There cannot be any real communication between them either, for they are characterized by incommensurable language games. Transferable communication skills, on this view, are not just a nonsensical construction. Since there are no universal forms of communication, the attempt to identify any such 'transferability' is an imposition of a particularly favoured set of performativities backed by powerful alliances.

Why is the postmodern view so determined to drive out all belief in anything that smacks of the universal? At bottom, there is a fear of terror. The view is that any attempt to identify elements of human action or thinking – whether in the form of knowledge, bodies of thought, ethical principles, modes of language and communication, or forms of life – amounts, ultimately, to totalitarianism. My suggesting that you should assent to this view of the world or to these moral principles because they have some kind of objectivity or general applicability to them amounts to a form of dictatorship. It is tantamount to my saying: really, you have no choice in the matter. This is the way the world is. You can't even take it or leave it: you *have* to take it. You might not see the world the way I do or readily assent to these moral principles. Nevertheless, because I am more insightful than you, or because I have considered these matters more carefully, it so happens that the picture of the world I am putting before you is not just my view – it has universal validity.

This, then, is the terror that lies behind postmodernism: the fear that particular pictures of the world will be paraded as if they are universal. It is not, therefore, just a fear of 'grand narratives' as such that characterizes the postmodern viewpoint. It is the underlying fear that grand narratives – claims to universality – turn out to be particular perspectives, particular ideologies or particular positions in disguise. The postmodern outlook is the fear of the universal and the totalitarianism that it appears to presage.

One extraordinary thing about this postmodern reaction to potential totalitarianism is that the major rival position, as enunciated by Jurgen Habermas, is also driven by a fear of totalitarianism. The readings of the world are the same: the world is largely oppressive and liable, unless we can develop counter-forms of life, to become totalitarian. The proffered solutions, however, are diametrically opposed. The postmodernists, such as Lyotard (1984), would have us turn to our particular forms of life, with all the admitted complexities to which they give rise. Let us work things out in all our separate localities, discourses and ideologies. Let us eschew large plans, thoughts and ideas. Habermas, on the other hand, resolutely would have us hang on to the universal, even in the face of totalitarianism.

How does his argument work? And why is he so opposed to postmodernism? The two questions and the answers dovetail. The first is the key question but we can come at it through the second. Habermas is opposed to postmodernism because he sees in it, through its celebration of the particular, two worrying possibilities. The first is that the constitution of the self, through the particular, renders the self liable to ideological takeover. The world is *not* composed of competing but equal forces; rather, it is composed of competing but unequal forces. The celebration of immediate projects, self-made identities and modes of communication renders the self vulnerable to an unnoticed domination by the dominant powers.

The second point is that different forms of life, on the postmodern story, have no means of communicating with each other. Since universal forms of communication have been repudiated, different forms of life have only their own inner resources with which to face the world. One reading of such a position is that postmodernism ushers in contrasting forms of reason, with each form of life secreting its own way of engaging, if only within itself. But an alternative reading is that this is no way towards the rational life at all. Non-communicating forms of life, each with its own conception of what is to count as rational, as worthwhile and as intelligible, hardly end up as a babel of voices. A voice, after all, is a relatively coherent contribution to a larger conversation, which is just what is in question here. What we are left with, on the postmodern view, must be just a number of tongues talking different and mutually incomprehensible languages.

A third point can and should be made about postmodernism from the standpoint of Critical Theory, which builds on both the previous two points. It is that postmodernism leaves things entirely as they are. It is an utterly conservative philosophy. The postmodernists would deny this. In celebrating difference, in encouraging playfulness and in trying to undermine the universal, they would claim that they are opening the way for new possibilities of taste, of experiment and of communication. Perhaps; but at bottom, nothing *much* will be disturbed. If critical standards are denied – as they must be, on the postmodern story – the world, with its configurations of power, manipulation and ideological manoeuvrings, will be left largely as it is. Postmodernism may offer us some new forms of decoration around the edges or some new insights into our surroundings, but we will not be offered a comprehensive new way of looking at the world, since just that has been repudiated. This is a philosophy that suits the contented and the powerful.

The phrase used by Paul Feyerabend (1978) – 'anything goes' – is often taken to encapsulate postmodernism (although Feyerabend was no postmodernist). Prima facie, this may be understandable: postmodernism, in wanting to get outside any binding rules of rational discourse or of the framing of knowledge or of the construction of moral rules, seems to usher in lawlessness. 'Anything goes' seems to be an apt summary of postmodernism. But on the analysis just given, it should be clear that anything does not go in postmodernism. It may seem to be supremely non-judgemental, allowing all comers; but, in fact, it has its own limits. The 'ism' in postmodernism is indicative: there is a definite viewpoint at work. It may be largely negative; postmodernism may constitute itself largely through what it is not. It is not the modern, whatever that may mean. It is not in the business of endorsing general principles or knowledge-constituting rules. It is not prepared to underpin large ideologies. But in declaring what it is not in business for, it also puts boundaries around itself. Those things – rules, ideologies, universal projects – that it does not endorse are beyond the pale. So postmodernism is not as charitable as it makes out. Anything goes only within its own rules.

Strange bedfellows

What does all this have to do with higher education in general and critical thinking in particular? The connections may seem elusive but, as I hope to show, they are of some importance.

We touched on one of the connecting issues in this chapter's opening section, that of critical frameworks. In developing a sense of the place and character of critical thought in higher education, how are we to understand it? Is it a limited affair, restricted to working within the rules of only the local discourse, or are there larger contexts and frameworks that can be drawn on? Are our critical standards set by the immediate form of thought or can we introduce others, from quite different perspectives? Answers to these questions will determine nothing less than the scope of and character of higher education itself. Is there a set of processes that can justify a universal appellation such as 'higher education', or is it merely a matter of separate processes, markedly different according to the rules of the local epistemic community? Can we talk meaningfully of higher education in an unqualified way, or is it really a cover for unbridgeable forms of experience to which we blithely, but unwisely, affix the same label?

Earlier, we noted that, for the postmodernists, Popper and Habermas were in the same camp, despite their profound differences. Both believe that the notion of critical standards makes sense. Popper wanted to wield critical standards by attacking particular theories or ideas in a piecemeal way, whereas Habermas wanted criticism to extend to take on a form of thought itself. Popper wanted to restrict criticism to internal standards, whereas Habermas wanted to allow for the possibility of external critique or, to use his term, 'metacritique'. Nevertheless, despite their differences, from a postmodern point of view there is much to unite Popper and Habermas in their sense that criticism is both possible and desirable.

But, in applying these views to higher education, another reading offers itself to us. It is that Popper and the postmodernists should be put together in opposition to Habermas. Such a suggestion will seem heretical, to both postmodernists and Popperians. The postmodernists seem to rail against the very notion of reason, whereas the Popperian framework is built on it. The postmodernists cut away the ground from under their own feet so far as the idea of critical standards is concerned, whereas it is central to the Popperian perspective. And the postmodernists would deny the universality of objectivity, whereas Popper asserts it boldly. Nevertheless, the two camps have much in common. Both look to local languages or forms of life as setting the context for conversations, both deny the possibility of panoramic critique, and both recognize the essential differences in forms of life.

This juxtaposition, in which Popper ends up with the postmodernists, is crucial for our understanding of critical thought. Is it just a local affair, respecting only the traditions of the immediate form of thought and the knowledge community that sustains it? Or can we justifiably bring other frames of thought to bear on a topic? Do we *necessarily* live in separate worlds, critically speaking, or might we live in a unified world? Are we destined to be critical citizens of multiple universes, or might the day come when we are critical citizens of one universe?

Locals *and* cosmopolitans

In fact, it is both – at least, that is my argument (and it is a crucial part of the argument). We can both inhabit and gain our critical standards from particular communities – say, those who teach business studies or those who teach philosophy – *and* we can deploy critical standards from wider fields. But to say this, that we can be both locals and cosmopolitans, critically speaking, is to say a great deal; and it opens up many questions for our subsequent inquiries.

It is to say a great deal because the view that we can be attached to a larger community in addition to our immediate circle or reference group is tantamount to saying that there are ties or rules or principles or approaches that could potentially, at any rate, unify in some sense all the epistemological villages in the world. The local communities might be able to identify larger interconnections between themselves, even though those communities might be unaware of what those linkages might be. Both the tribes and the territories might be linked in some way. We just may be able to talk with a straight face of critical reason as such.

But these are large claims and they open up a number of large problems. To say that, if only potentially, critical standards from a wider frame of reference than the immediate form of thinking can be drawn on is ambiguous. It could mean that the critical standards of other disciplines or modes of thinking could be brought into play; or it could mean that there are cross-disciplinary critical standards to which we could resort. The first possibility is that of linking territories together, if only in a piecemeal way. This is the Bailey bridge route to critical reconstruction: creating new linkages but probably of a limited and temporary character. The second possibility is the cartographer's route in which we detect new connections in the map of knowledge, local territories being seen to be part of a new and larger map of the whole territory.

Postmodern cul-de-sac

Postmodernism would repudiate both possibilities. Since forms of life have incommensurable language games and since academic knowledges and their associated sub-cultures can be – if only just at times – forms of life, there can be no real communication between them. There will be no firm anchorage for the Bailey bridge on both territories: there is no connectivity. If the first possibility of mutual critique is problematic for postmodernism, the second possibility will seem completely nonsensical quite apart from its undesirability. There are no universal critical standards: end of story. *Vive la différence!*

Postmodernism may seem to be an arcane academic or cultural phenomenon, but it should be clear that our response to it should affect the way in which we conceive of and practise higher education. Is critical thought at most to be understood as relative to particular frameworks or might there be some sense in which we could talk meaningfully of critical thought as such, transcending particular frameworks? Is higher education, especially mass higher education, to be seen as a postmodern phenomenon, mainly a matter of personal consumption (Scott, 1995), devoid of any substantial critical elements? Or might it be understood as a – if not *the* – social institution with a particular role to play in sustaining a critical capacity in modern society? Is higher education simply a collection of discrete academic sub-cultures with their own languages, values and relationships to the wider world of work, or can higher education be understood to have a potential for forms of critical reason which cross the disciplines and the curricular fields?

In each of these pairs of questions, it is the first that might be prompted by the postmodern outlook. And those questions, both separately and – with even greater force – taken together, provide a severely restricted conception of the way in which critical thought can get a hearing in higher education. Indeed, as I have already intimated, thoroughgoing postmodernism in the end does not merely curtail but actually forbids even the motivation towards critical thought. Postmodernism abhors judgement since judgement calls on independent criteria. (Postmodernism has got itself into an unnecessary hole here: in repudiating grand narratives such as cross-disciplinary criteria of assessment, it has ended up ruling out of court even internal truth criteria.) Playfulness, not judgement, is the watchword of postmodernism.

If this is postmodernism, it may be felt that it has nothing to offer higher education, and that no one in higher education would seriously entertain such nostrums. They run counter to the Western conception of the university, they would reduce its social and educational value, and they can hardly do justice to the way in which Western academics conceive of their own role (since, in surveys, they always give high priority to the value of higher education in promoting critical thinking). But times are a-changing. Virtual universities, mass higher education, and the reduced economic value of higher education, accompanied by a renewed interest in higher education as a form of personal consumption: all these arguably lead higher education away from a sensitization to the critical standards enshrined in disciplines standing externally to students and more towards a higher education as personal, experiential and process-based. In the age of the consumer, it becomes a case of goodbye, higher education as discipline; hello, higher education as play, as enjoyable discrete experiences and as an extension of popular culture. Higher education becomes a form of 'infotainment' (Ritzer, 1996).

So the postmodern world beckons both in theory and in fact. And with it, therefore, comes the ultimate abandonment of critical standards and an abandonment of a larger view of life. Bloom (1987) was wrong on this point: we are not there yet. But that is the direction in which we are going. The remedy does not lie, as Bloom argued, in identifying and asserting the dominant Western canon. A 'great books' approach will serve only to ossify a tradition, not to sustain it. The remedy lies, instead, in the first place, in becoming clearer about what it is about critical thought that is ultimately of most worth and, therefore, about our efforts to develop.

The lure of transcendentalism

As I indicated earlier, Jurgen Habermas has entered the lists against the post-moderns by opposing them directly. Where they seek particularity, Habermas seeks universality; where they emasculate the idea of reason, Habermas vigorously defends the idea (albeit distinguishing substantively different forms but still with a universal character); and where they deny the possibility of communication across forms of life, Habermas insists on it as a necessary condition of human life. Is there, then, in the Habermassian framework, a set of ideas that can help us to understand the character of critical thought as it might apply to higher education in the modern world?

There are, in fact, two Habermassian frameworks. In Habermas's first Critical Theory, knowledge is seen as being imbued with deep-seated human interests. Habermas (1978) distinguished between an interest in prediction and control, an interest in communication and an interest in emancipation. He believed that, respectively, these three interests were latent in the sciences, the humanities and critical studies. With modifications – principally, that all three sets of interests could characterize any field of knowledge – this schema has obvious attractions in working out a critical theory of higher education (cf. Grundy, 1987; Young, 1989).

At the heart of Habermas's contemporary framework lies the idea of universal validity claims. Habermas (1989, 1991) contends that any rational speech act has to take an attitude with respect to four in-built critical standards. The critical standards are those of veracity, comprehensibility, sincerity and appropriateness. Any speech act, in other words, can be interrogated in any one of four ways. Is it true? Does the account hang together? Do you really believe that? And is its form appropriate to the context? When I say that these are 'in-built critical standards', I mean that, for Habermas, they have come to be constitutive of what we take a rational discourse to be. They are not in-built in the Chomskian sense of innate structures of the mind; nor are they in-built in the sense of having some kind of anthropological necessity. They have come, over time, to form part of what, in Western life, we take a rational discourse to be.

To say this is not to say that a discourse will become interrogative in all of the four ways suggested. It is to say that a serious participant in a discourse opens herself up to a challenge in any of the four dimensions – of truth, comprehensibility, sincerity and appropriateness – and understands this, if only tacitly. There is, therefore, on Habermas's view, a kind of discourse behind the discourse. There is an invitation to engage in inquiries along any of the four dimensions; that that invitation is not fully taken up is only an indication that, say, one or more of the validity conditions are not giving immediate cause for concern at this juncture. The text will have been examined against all four criteria: that hidden dialogue will have taken place. It just so happens that the text at the moment is to be tested, say, in terms of its coherence with the speaker's other utterances (and, thereby, against the comprehensibility criterion), rather than in terms of any of the other three validity conditions.

This framework casts light on the critical enterprise as such. It implies that, in the university, the historian and the physicist, the architect and the nursing studies lecturer, whether they realize it or not, all subscribe to the same set of rules of rational life. More, they all agree on certain critical standards as fundamental to serious inquiry. They have much more in common than they realize. They really are engaged in the same form of life, much as their own territories, languages and practices within it may mislead us to the contrary. Their overt discourse and their elaborated code vary; but these are just surface phenomena.

There are three questions worth posing of the contemporary Habermassian framework: Is it true? Even if it is true, so what? It may be true, but is it – in important ways – only partially true?

In answer to the first question, it may be tempting to say that the jury is still out. Habermas has his critics on several flanks. But that would be a trivial response. Naturally, Habermas has his critics. He is taking them on; and it would be astonishing if they were all to cave in and accept the Habermassian edifice as entirely sound. A much more telling response to the question (Is it true?) is that one's response will depend on one's prior disposition as to the value of the Habermassian approach. If one seeks security, and if one hankers after a sense of humankind (as distinct from lots of kinds of human being), then one will give the Habermassian approach a fair wind. If, instead, one recoils at any suggestion of universal rules and wishes to work things out in more local domains, then one will resist the Habermassian framework.

Too much or too little?

But if we are of a disposition to see value in the Habermassian framework, so what? What are its implications for higher education? There are dangers in reading both too much and too little into the framework. First, it may be tempting to believe that Habermas is opening out to us a means by which all the sub-cultures within the academic world can unite around a critico-rational calling. The rational life is universal and has critical standards written into it. Critico-rationalists of the world unite! You may have the particular truth criteria and procedures of your immediate calling, but you all share fundamental assumptions of what counts as a serious investigation into truth. There are transcendental critical standards which unite you all.

But if there is any real substance to these universal critical standards, and if they are so important, why do academics not recognize them? Why do they not understand that they have at least as much in common as segregates them? These validity claims, or critical standards (as I am calling them), surely operate at such a deep level that they are buried. We can get along without bringing them to the surface. Either they do not exist or, if they do, they lie dormant. Either way, they seem to be impotent.

More than that, Habermas undermines his own argument. His project of Critical Theory is structured around a search for universal standards of the rational life which do not smuggle in disputable values or presuppositions or normative hopes. Habermas is attempting to run philosophy and sociology together. He is offering an account of human life – albeit modern life – that is both descriptive and critical, the critical element being universal and, therefore, outside criticism itself. But, if true, his account is just, or so it might appear, a high-level description of the way things are. If it is true, it simply tells us how the rational life is constituted. If academics, for example, are conducting a rational form of life, albeit different varieties of it, they will have *ipso facto* adopted these critical standards. If Habermas is right, his critical framework seems to lack a critical edge. We might come to understand the rational life a little more clearly than we did, but we are not taken forward substantively. We simply understand better the world (the university, at least) that we live in. Transcendentalism has no practical lessons for us.

There are, therefore, dangers in reading too much into Habermas. But we can also read too little. In part, the fault lies with Habermas who, over time, has equivocated over the status of his validity claims. More recently, he has come to slough off the transcendental overtones of his framework to suggest that the validity claims can act as a critical standard after all. A key concept in this latter turn has been that of the ideal speech situation, in which he posited a discourse in which the participants have equal dialogical chances. Where such a discourse does not obtain, the discourse is liable to become distorted. The upshot will be that the critical standards will be themselves distorted, if not made inoperative. The inquiry may look serious, but real interrogation – along the dimensions of the four validity claims – will be thwarted.

The ideal speech situation is an ideal. It offers a critical standard against which we can test discourses in higher education. To what extent are there interests or power structures at work which prevent a fully open inquiry? Do the participants really feel that they are equal? Do they fear the worst if they ask their critical questions or speak their mind? Given the way money, power and external interests play an ever-increasing part in higher education, these are real issues.

So it is possible to read too little into the Habermassian framework. It *can* offer us critical standards against which we can interrogate the character of the discourse present in higher education.

Putting thought in the dock

The key question in this chapter has been: are our critical standards local or universal in character? The contemporary Habermas implies that they are universal, that there is an implicit set of validity claims in any rational discourse and that they derive their force from being situated in a communication structure in which all the parties have equal dialogical chances. The postmoderns deny that there can be universal standards of right reason. Each discourse has its own way of going on. It is tempting to say that both perspectives have merit: that we should embrace the tolerance of differences that postmodernism opens out but hang on to more general criteria of what it is to be rational (of the kind Habermas offers us). But that marriage is not one made in heaven.

The problem lies not with the postmoderns. Their position is incoherent, as we have seen, but we could overcome that. Observing local differences in critical standards requires a position outside the immediate language games. Postmodernism isn't as parochial as it would have us believe.

The problem comes with the later Habermas, whose transcendental approach to critical reason operates at such a stratospheric level that it hardly obtains a purchase. If everyone is signing up to the validity claims *tout court*, then that's it; end of story. These critical standards can hardly serve as discriminators. Even in the Habermassian unpacking of the communicative structure of open discourse we run into problems, since the notion of participants being equally competent is bound to be problematic in an educational situation, especially in higher education where lecturers are expected to be authorities in their own right. Certainly, the working out of the idea of an open dialogue within the confines of an educational process is far from straightforward.

More fruitful, for our situation, is the earlier set of differences between Habermas and Popper. Popper seemed to offer the best of all possible worlds: a receptivity to the differences of forms of human reason together with critical standards that traversed their specific forms. But Habermas, both in his dispute with Popper and in his early magnum opus, *Knowledge and Human Interests* (1978), pointed up the limitations in the Popperian strategy. First, he called attention to the interests embedded in human thought as such, which Popperian critical strategies were never going to uncover. But, secondly, and much more important (and unnoticed), is that, implicitly, Habermas called up the idea that critical thought could operate at different *levels*. It was possible for thought to critique thought. It was possible for thought to put thought in the dock. Through metacritique, we could step right outside our frameworks of thought and bring to bear the firepower of alternative critical frameworks.

It is, therefore, possible to be both locals and cosmopolitans with respect to critical thought. We can both operate with the critical standards of our own local framework of thinking and come at the framework itself from an external vantage point. This prospect opens up the possibility of emancipation, at least in our thinking and in our understanding of the world we are in. We do not have to succumb to the postmodern image of being entrapped by our local frameworks.

Conclusion: the critical spirit

Critical Theory supplies the crucial idea of metacritique, of critiquing whole forms of thought, and with that notion comes the idea of levels of thinking. More can mean not just different but higher. A higher education, therefore, will have to embrace such higher forms of critical thought.

But this is all very cerebral. At least, coming through Foucault's poststructuralism, we have a sense of disciplines possessing, literally, a physical presence in their framing of human being. Postmodernism, too, offers us a sense of the plasticity of the self in the modern world. The self constitutes itself through the discourses it encounters. Such a line of thinking raises sharply for higher education the issue of the self that it would wish to construct. If the self is to be more than simply a collection of dominant discourses, if the self is to be a person, it has to be itself. The self has to be alive as a self, authentically and even passionately. Students have to come into themselves, the selves that they construct for themselves. Notions of being, of a self, and of commitment, authenticity and emotion have, therefore, to come into our account. The critical self is an involved self. We look to our students to be fully themselves.

The Habermassian perspective offers us the prospect of leaping out of our immediate critical frameworks, but it is unduly abstract, is overly rule-based and sees individuals only from the neck up. There is pain (amidst distorted dialogue) but not much passion in the Habermassian notions of critique. The critical spirit is spirited. Students are human beings and higher education has the responsibility of developing their humanness still further, and their criticality at the same time (witness the Tiananmen Square student). What it means to live the critical life in higher education, and engender a critical spirit, must be a key topic in our inquiries from here on.

3

Discourse and Critical Potential

A critical voice

The image of the lone student facing a line of tanks in Tiananmen Square is a telling motif for this chapter. The scene was part of an effort, albeit abortive, by Chinese students to bring about a political revolution in China. That the effort failed is largely immaterial to our purposes here. The events of that time provide a particularly vivid example of a collective effort on the part of students to engage directly with the state, even with all its military forces.

Since the contemporary examples of student radicalism are mostly to be seen in developing countries, it is tempting to develop an account of such events in terms of the stage of political systems. Student activism, it might be said, is likely to be seen where democratic processes are weak: student activism fills the vacuum, providing perhaps the only serious opposition to the otherwise unchallenged might of the state (Marcuse, 1968). Such a reading is clearly too simple. Only a generation ago, governments in the Western world were almost brought down by a wave of student activism where, again, the students acted collectively and in direct confrontation with the forces of the state.

It is a matter still on the table as to whether there might or could be a new wave of student activism in the West. The growth of higher education markets, with more consumer power being given to students; the development of a more uncertain relationship between higher education and the labour market; and the growth of mass higher education itself, in which the student experience is more uncertain (although we can hardly say more prone to stress), present a new situation. We are not in the late 1960s. But the new situation of higher education and of the students within it could conceivably give rise to a deep dissatisfaction, a sense of unmet expectations. On the other hand, the uncertainties of the world, of the student career, have brought a narrowing of the student horizons. Now, less collective and more solitary; with less intimate and more instrumental pedagogical relationships; and less internally driven and more susceptible to the external educational messages (of competence, enterprise and transferable skills): the idea, and the social identity, of the student is being remade.

Against this background, the key question before us in the chapter is this: in what way, if at all, can we identify a wider critical function for higher education in the modern world? If we can envisage such a function, is it to be confined to the extramural activities of students, or can we develop a legitimate set of educational practices in which a wider critical function has a place? And if the latter, is the idea of student as critic to be confined to some disciplines rather than others? Might we identify a universal responsibility, which we take the role of student to include? The argument here is precisely that: that the idea of student has been emasculated and that it needs to be reconceived so as to embrace a wider conception of the student's critical tasks. Our educational practices, accordingly, should also be refashioned to that larger end.

I want to pursue that argument through the notion of discourse. As the university opens itself to, and becomes the repository of, many discourses urged on it by the wider society, a discourse of critique has to fight its corner. It is liable to be expunged as the more instrumental and operational discourses colonize the discursive territory of 'the university'. If the university is to have any role as a social critic it, in turn, has to maintain vigorously and vigilantly a discourse of critique, of commentary and of fearless evaluation. The maintenance of such a discourse will be no easy matter. It will require a discursive competence from the university that, as yet, it barely possesses. After all, the challenges now opening up to the university – of fulfilling external agendas while retaining a discursive space to itself – are new, so the discursive competence needed to sustain a discourse of critique has yet to be forged.

The centre cannot hold

To develop a properly founded conception of the student as social critic requires a preliminary sense of the place of the university in modern society. The character of modern society is itself disputed and so no straightforward account can be given of the university, of society or of their relationships. It may be helpful to remind ourselves of some of the contemporary insights, even if many are in tension with one another.

One large idea in understanding modern society is that of fragmentation (Touraine, 1995). Whether in the cultural sphere, the economic sphere, the corporate sphere or the intellectual sphere, the dominant message seems to be that 'the centre cannot hold'. More parochially, we have similar messages coming at us from higher education.

In the cultural sphere, anything goes. That, at least, is the message of postmodernism in its cultural aspect. Playfulness, kitsch culture and no limits to experimentation: there are no limits to what is to count as art and culture. In the economic sphere, the development of financial practices in which – with the arrival of computers – business is enacted around the clock has produced volatile markets. Globalization, in which not just products but labour markets are internationalized, act as a force for detraditionalization. More broadly, governments have attempted in the economic sphere 'to roll back the state', even if with limited success, and to encourage the growth of consumer markets. In the corporate sphere, two developments are notable: first, customer-sensitiveness accompanied by computer-controlled processes of production have led to an abandonment of traditional practices of mass production, replacing them with a 'post-Fordism' in which a 'just-in-time' set of business practices is accompanied by a customer-driven corporate culture. Secondly, and as a complementary development, corporations have become flatter organizations, with employees being supposedly 'empowered' to make and be accountable for their own decisions.

The intellectual sphere, too, is witnessing signs of fragmentation, not only or not so much through a splitting off of the conventional modes of academic inquiry from each other. On the contrary, in some senses, they are coming together, or at least are seeing increasing intellectual trade across their boundaries. The greater sign of fragmentation is that of the augmentation of what counts as knowledge and knowing. The range of permissible knowledge acts is widening. This is not a matter of postmodern experimentation or playfulness affecting the academy. In this sense, postmodernism is a little local affair noticed largely in certain disciplines and even sub-disciplines within them (aesthetics rather than logic; social theory rather than empirical sociology; some schools of architecture; and psychology hardly at all).

The wider source of fragmentation is that what counts as knowledge and knowing in society is witnessing a fundamental moment of change. Recently, it has been described as a shift from mode 1 of theoretical knowledge to a mode 2 of applied and problem-based knowledge (Gibbons *et al.*, 1994). An alternative description of the change is that from knowing as contemplation to knowing as action. As society grapples with increasing and complex change, as its economy struggles to maintain its competitiveness, knowing about the world gives way to knowing as practised in the world. This is none other than a fundamental shift in our social epistemology.

We can argue whether this change is a shift or whether it is additive; and, in the end, the matter would have to be investigated empirically. The point is that the academy is not immune from all this but, as a key knowledge institution in modern society, is bound to reflect these changes. The arrival of action research, problem-based learning and experiential learning, and of a discourse of competence, outcomes and skills, are indications that, gradually, knowing-how is coming to find a legitimate place in the university at least alongside knowing-that, even if the former has not yet supplanted the latter.

These signs of fragmentation – cultural, economic, corporate and epistemological – are not isolated phenenoma but are interlinked (Scott, 1995).

Certainly, too, the university in a mass higher education system is bound to respond to some degree – even if, depending on its position in a differentiated system, each university will have its own set of responses.

Options for critical thought are, on this view, limitless and yet lacking in critical purchase. In a totally fragmented world, our critical standards evaporate. Critique lacks bite. Ultimately, deep critique is epistemologically off-limits. Curricula in business studies, say, will vary: they may be a study *of* business or confine themselves to being a study *for* business, serving up to business the competences and problem-solving capacities it thinks it needs. But we have no way of comparing these different approaches: we are doomed just to observe that they are different. So critique dies on two levels: it dies pragmatically, as a response to our situation. And it dies dispositionally. We are no longer constituted as critical persons. The fragmented world is post-critique and, therefore, lacking in any direction that critique might impart.

But against this idea of fragmentation, and a sense of anomic absence of any direction, we have to put the idea of systematicity. The state is caught in a double-bind. It wants to release the energies that it believes a free market – of production and consumption – will generate, but it believes that it is best placed to identify the main challenges of a world of change and the social and ideological tensions that that changing world presents. And so, especially in its human services, it seeks to retain both control and direction (Jenkins, 1995). The result is not necessarily greater planning as such, but it is steerage, guidance and certain kinds of reward structures backed up by evaluation, monitoring and surveillance. In this context, self-assessment in universities becomes the internalization of state-set agendas, human 'outcomes' and even processes of interaction. We can now talk of a higher education system with a straight face. This is the formation of a body politic writ large.

Responding to change in higher learning

Society, then, is doubly uncertain, theoretically and practically. We are uncertain of the character of the change we see, both in describing and accounting for it, and in experiencing it and determining the options in front of us. We live in a world of change but we are unclear as to the nature of that change: Is it a set of random changes? Is it rather an example of genuine chaos, in which order can be detected within? Is the order being built in, so far as it can be, overtly by state action? Fortunately, we do not have to answer these questions here. The question that does have to be answered is this: what are the implications of this double uncertainty for higher education, particularly a higher education in which critical thought is central?

The first response is sociological. Uncertainty is written into modern society not only in the modes we have been discussing – culturally, intellectually, economically – but also ontologically. An important manifestation of this ontological uncertainty is that of reflexivity which, as Giddens (1990) has observed, is a defining characteristic of late modernity. 'The reflective practitioner' may have the ring of a worthwhile set of educational and professional aims about it: this is how things *ought* to be. But on Giddens' analysis, this is a brute description of late modern society. It is how we are – how educated professional people are, at any rate. And this is to be understood not as a particularly praiseworthy feature of professionalism as such, but as a natural response to the predicaments that modern society faces us with. Schön (1983) thinks that he is describing how the skilled professional functions; in fact, he is telling us about the character of modern society as such. We are all reflective practitioners now. Critical thought, as reflective practice, is a constitutive element of the working life of the highly educated. In taking on, therefore, the idea of 'the reflective practitioner', all higher education is doing is reflecting back to society both its embedded and its contemporary idea of what it is to be a fully participant member of this society, at least so far as working life is concerned. In that sense, the idea of the reflective practitioner may be 'reflective', but it is thoroughly uncritical.

The second response of higher education to a world of uncertainty is a search for stability of some kind. One form of stability that attracts is that of 'transferable skills'. The world might change; even persons might, indeed must, change and, with them, their skills must change. But the idea of transferable skills offers the hope that, in this world of instability, persons can be the carriers of enduring capacities. The whole idea is, of course, curious in its own terms. Why should any form of durability be sought in a world of uncertainty? It is asserted continually that we require adaptability and flexibility among employees. Why, then, should *any* form of continuity be required? Again, there is a double-think at work: we want change but we want stability. We want responsiveness but within limits: 'transferable skills' supply those limits.

We shall eschew debate over the existence of transferable skills or their appropriateness in higher education or even for the world of work. The question here is: how are we to construe the relationship between transferable skills and critical thought? Are they likely to further critical thought or to hinder it? One response is that, in themselves, transferable skills are neutral in regard to critical thought. There need be no surreptitious influence at work in the importation of transferable skills. Critical thought, after all, could be critical of transferable skills. But that view begs questions. 'Transferable skills', as currently advocated, are a state project, underwritten by a number of state agencies. They are largely a given, both as a policy and in terms of their ontological import. As policy, they are not proffered in a spirit of debate: they are produced and developed as part of the systematicity we noted earlier in this section. As skills, they are lacking in reflexivity. They do not allow for their own development and modification. An individual might be – we can be charitable – skilled in her transferable skills, but will not be furnished thereby with the capacity to critique her surroundings. The skill lies in the competence to perform instrumentally and not in the capacity to form a deep understanding of her environment and to critique it. As policy and as educational project, critique is doubly written out of transferable skills.

A third response of higher education to its sense of social change is that of problem-solving. There are, admittedly, in this idea a cluster of related ideas: if problem-solving is largely the use of given techniques to reach a given solution to a given problem, variations on the theme can be derived by injecting some measure of openness at each of the three key elements (definition of problem, problem methodology and problem solution). With increasing openness in the elements, the process of problem-solving becomes the focus as distinct from the solution itself. Ultimately, we might be in the presence of problem-based learning in which it is understood that there is no one legitimate 'solution'; that learning is derived from the refinement of the problem and even its redefinition; and that 'solutions' are pragmatic in character and, therefore, may require negotiation and astuteness in their achievement.

In this family of curricular strategies, three underlying ideas are present. First, for personal survival in this world of change, pure knowledge is no longer sufficient. Individuals have to be able to apply it in action in presenting situations. The carry-over from knowledge as reflection to knowledge as deployable has to be made effective. Secondly, situations and problems are readily identifiable. The problems are clear for all to see: the problems are unproblematic. Thirdly, life presents with problems which are soluble and which must be solved. We make progress in the world by solving our problems. All three assumptions are problematic.

The epistemology of knowledge in pragmatic situations is quite different from that of knowledge in contemplation: compare the surgeon presented with a problem in the operating theatre with that of the medical scientist in the hospital's laboratory, where the exigencies of time and immediacy of impact are evidently in contrast. Situations and problems, in any case, are not given *in any sense*. A higher learning should be focused on developing the capacity to redefine and reconceptualize what counts as 'the situation'. In reconceptualizing a 'problem', quite new conceptual frameworks might be brought into play, which might be threatening but which nevertheless could be educationally worthwhile. Lastly, the ideas that problems are soluble and, in principle, should be solved are both symptoms of technological reason, of an unbridled will to power and mastery over the world which, again, a higher learning should be in business to expose and put in its place.

These three contemporary responses to a sense of societal and even world change – 'the reflective practitioner', transferable skills and problem-solving – turn out to be resistant to critique. Their increasing presence in higher education – and we might have looked at others, such as experiential learning or action learning – is an indication that, at a time when critical thought is especially needed, its possible presence in higher learning is being curtailed. It is not that critical thought is disappearing, for such a judgement would imply that critical thought has characterized higher education in the past. Rather, the position is that the possibilities for critical thought – its conception, its practice, its forms – are being limited. Whether we are seeing a shift from academic competence to operational competence, or whether operational competence is additive to academic competence, the effect is the same: limited opportunities for critical thought when it is needed more than ever, when we should be giving it a greater significance than ever, and when we should be practising a wider range of forms of critical thought than ever.

Discourse and critical potential

In so far as critical thought *is* taken on board in our curricular practices and in our thinking about higher education, that presence is wholly inadequate. The challenge before us is that of coming to an adequate account of critical thought as part of a higher learning within a changing world. We saw earlier that there are few, if any, non-contestable readings of even the major characteristics of late modern society. Yet perhaps *this* can be said relatively uncontroversially: that the contemporary world and, therefore, society holds within it multiple discourses. Indeed, that was always the case. And it may be said that globalization, marketization and the onward sweep of technological reason are reducing the range of discourses in society: some discourses are more dominant than others. These qualifications are valid. But, as we saw, other forces are at work – cultural, economic, intellectual – which are not only expanding the range of permitted discourses, but also expanding the range of what are seen as *legitimate* discourses.

Higher learning, as represented by the mass university, cannot be immune from this situation. Whether simply assimilating the external discourses, or resisting them; whether seeking an accommodation between those external discourses and its more internal discourses; or whether being willing to supplant its internal discourses with the external discourses: the university in late modernity becomes a site of multiple discourses. Liberal, technological, pragmatic, critical, experiential, professional, humanistic, operational, technical, reflexive: all these and more are among the discourses of a single university within what passes for its higher learning.

The critical discourse, it will be noted, becomes simply one among many. At best, it fights for its place. No longer, if ever, can it be assumed that it has a special place. Since the critical voice is just one voice among many in the wider society, so it has – apparently – to accept a corresponding fate in higher learning. 'Where is the critical element?' becomes a telling commentary on a course proposal today. The critical element falls off the edge, not necessarily through a conspiracy; in a situation of multiple discourses, some discourses just won't get a hearing. They are not the dominant discourses; they become marginalized. And this we saw in the last section: the new forms of pedagogic developments are not characteristically critical in character. They are representative of other voices.

As a site, then, of multiple discourses, what is to be the proper stance of the university to critical thought? Does the mass university just allow it to fight its corner, to be just one voice and possibly a marginal voice at that amid the many on campus? It might be felt that in the modern world, faced with demonstrable challenges, the critical voice does not warrant a special place. Alternatively, in a differentiated mass higher education system, some universities might be expected to give particular consideration to critical thought, even if it is barely to be found in others: some universities will be more critical than others (Brosnan, 1971). Both stances should be repudiated and through the same reasoning.

In an elite system of higher education, critical thought will have two orientations. First, it will reflect the capture of higher education by epistemic elites: the scope and range of critical thought will, in the first place, be framed by each academic tribe acting in and for itself, and for whom critical thought will be confined to its own territory. Critical thought here is as much a matter of learning the rules by which the territory may be maintained and interlopers resisted as it is of genuine critical thought (Chapter 1). Secondly, in an elite system, critical thought at the margins will be allowed – through extramural activities – to take on a wider social and political ambit. The so-called critical thinking becomes a training for the administrative and leadership roles that are to be followed.

In a mass higher education system, by contrast, critical thought takes on – or should take on – a central place. Higher education expands and takes on 'mass' characteristics, not fortuitously but because higher education is seen as meeting societal and economic needs. In this context, higher learning has to become higher critique. We noted that reflexivity is becoming a defining characteristic of our age. This is not just a matter of a personal attribute or disposition. Rather, this is a matter of our social epistemology and ontology. Self-monitoring becomes an embedded assumption in relation to our conception of what it is to be a fully participating member of society. Self-monitoring can be read essentially in two ways. It can indicate an internalization of others' agendas. Here, self-monitoring is self-censorship. Or it can stand for powers of self-control *and* self-agency. Here, self-monitoring can have emancipatory overtones: through self-reflection, we put new possibilities to ourselves and so extend ourselves and our potential range of actions.

Reflexivity arises as a constituent of our age through two features. First, in a world of change, uncertainty is generated. Reflexivity becomes a strategy by which individuals might cope with uncertainty. That is a psychological response. But a second, more sociological explanation can be suggested. Reflexivity supplies a general resource for responding effectively to change. Consequently, reflexivity is seen as a means of generating knowledge. Nor is this just self-knowledge. Reflexivity provides new cognitive resources for the community, especially when generated and exploited collaboratively.

Reflexivity, then, is both an epistemological concept (containing a theory of knowing) and an ontological concept (to be a person in modernity is to take on powers of self-reflection).

If this analysis is right, we can now see why the two ideas encountered earlier which would marginalize critical thought have to be repudiated. Neither the claim that critical thought is a characteristic more of some disciplines than others, nor the claim that critical thought would be more appropriate to some universities than to others in a mass system, can be allowed to stand. Critical thought, at least in so far as it implies critical self-reflection, has to be considered to be a desirable property of a higher learning.

Questions are being begged here that deserve answer. Are critical thought, critical self-reflection and reflexivity synonymous? In any event, why does critical thought have to be considered to be a universal desideratum of higher education? We shall come to these issues in just a moment. What I wish to urge here is the much more general point that a full account of critical thought in a mass higher education system has to be placed in the context of late modernity itself. Critical thought has to be central to higher education because critical thought, in certain senses, has to be central to the kind of society we have to live in. Modern society is a complex of multiple and, indeed, contending discourses. But the critical discourse as a synonym for reflexivity is, in a certain sense, characteristic of late modernity. It is not just one voice among many. It has to be the defining voice.

All this has yet to be justified. But if it can be justified, then critical thought has to take on a central place in higher learning. Another way of putting the point is that, in modern society, higher education has available to it new forms of critical potential.

Discourse and the university

We can develop the argument by turning to the university itself. We noted earlier that the modern university, placed as it is, is the home of an array of discourses, including those that are emancipatory, instrumental, hermeneutic, action-oriented and contemplative in nature. The mass university is a mansion of many rooms; and they seem to be unconnected, non-communicating. Notwithstanding postmodernism, the discourses are contending grand narratives. They are educational projects which are opposed to each other. This is not just a matter of the different disciplines being unable to communicate. A single discipline can be subject to contrasting interpretations such that, even in the same department, so-called colleagues find it difficult to communicate with each other.

We saw earlier that business studies might be understood as the study of business or a study for business. What counts as business studies is contestable. Its framing is the result of the outcome of a negotiation between the relevant discourses and their relative influence in a particular situation.

The discourses of economic competitiveness, of business change, of the analytical understanding of business, of research into business, of action to 'improve' business and of radical reconceptualization of business: all these will be jostling in the framing of any business studies curriculum. It is hardly surprising if there are party lines within the same department. In that case, too, what counts as critical thought will itself be subject to alternative interpretations.

The discourses of mass higher education, then, are inevitably multiple and provide the resources for the way in which academics come to constitute themselves as much as they provide the resources from which curricular and other academic practices are framed and, indeed, fought over. Discursively, the university is situated in society more than ever. It takes on an increasing spread of the discourses of the wider society. In so doing, it plays its part in shaping those discourses through all the main activities of the university (Fairclough, 1993). The university cannot help but be discursively implicated in society.

This discursive implicatedness, this entanglement in society's discourses, at once reduces the critical scope available to the university and expands it. The assimilation by the university of the newer discourses widens the potential scope for criticality because the domains of critical being now embraced by the university are themselves wider. Students are expected to show that they can perform in various ways and to be self-reflective and in control of themselves. But the instrumental, the technological and the performative are liable to squeeze out the hermeneutic, the liberal and the contemplative. The possibilities for critical thought are not being extinguished but they are reducing. Critical thought becomes defined by interests in promoting effectiveness, economy and control. Reflection that modifies practices and thinking towards those ends is acceptable, indeed welcome. The centre of gravity around which critical thought turns shifts.

But the university neither needs to nor should allow the newer definitions of critical thought to be construed and practised in this way. It does not need to do so precisely because there are new demands for self-monitoring, self-critique and self-agency. This spirit of reflexivity could be interpreted through the perspective of instrumental reason, such that self-critique is a means for promoting technological change (understood broadly), or it could be interpreted as a vehicle for emancipatory ends. Higher education, therefore, has a choice: does it sponsor reflexivity for instrumental or for emancipatory ends?

Three elements, then, provide the context for understanding the mass university as a site of critical potential: that modern society is characterized by multiple and conflicting discourses (a matter celebrated by postmodernism); that the university is embroiled in many of those discourses and is a part-shaper of those discourses; and that the way in which critical thought can be brought to bear on those discourses is largely open. The university has both discursive and critical opportunities, and it has a responsibility to deploy those opportunities fully and wisely. Of course, terms such as 'responsibility' and 'wisdom' will make many feel uncomfortable; but we have to recapture such terms and use them without embarrassment if we are to work out a theory of the modern university, and if our universities are to be more than merely responsive institutions.

A culture of critical discourse?

The 'culture of critical discourse' is a phrase of Alvin Gouldner's (1979), which he developed in working out a theory of intellectual life. With it went a debatable theory about the existence of an intellectual class. Still, the idea has attractions for us here. Against the context of rapid change, of multiple discourses which are themselves far from equal and of the difficulty of holding on to grand narratives of truth and knowledge, critical thought is not to be construed as particular sets of techniques. That strategy will surrender critical thought to the narrow definitions that press onto higher education. Nor can critical thought be seriously confined to particular disciplines. A theory of critical thought has to be found that transcends all disciplines and which will be adequate to the discursive insertion of the university into modern society. It also has to be such as to take advantage of the critical potential now available to the university, precisely because of the discursive insertion of the university into society and because of society's demand for reflexivity.

Against this background, the idea of a culture of critical discourse is beguiling. If this can become the dominant culture of the mass university, much of value would appear to flow. All the discourses present in the university and, indeed, outwith the university would be susceptible to critical interrogation. All frameworks for knowing and becoming that are deployed in the university would also be candidates for critical examination. At the same time, the idea of a *culture* of critical discourse turns us helpfully away from techniques of critical thought and from criticism oriented towards a particular purpose towards an interest in critical thought itself. A culture of critical discourse understands that, while critique cannot supply the only educational value for the modern university, critique is a worthwhile form of life as such. It is so for the reasons that we have identified. Reflexivity is necessary if we are to gain critical control over our world and critical thought is a necessary element of reflexivity. Through such critical self-reflection, we become more fully human: we realize the personal potential for reflexivity that lies in language. And through critical self-reflection, we come to a fuller insight into our knowledge frameworks and their ideological underpinnings, which we might otherwise take for granted.

So a culture of critical discourse seems to be what is required, but it has to be interpreted with care. There are three challenges in its interpretation in the contemporary era.

First, the slide in the argument just made will have been apparent in the move from talk of a culture of critical discourse to critical self-reflection.

These are related ideas but they are not synonymous. Both ideas are concerned with the ways in which those in universities are fundamentally to be constituted. The first idea focuses on the collective culture, the ways in which persons in that setting understand their interrelationships and their mutual responsibilities. The second idea focuses on the implications for individuals. Individuals who internalize a culture of critical discourse will engage in critical self-reflection. But both are separable: either could be found without the other.

An adequate account of critical thought in the modern university has, therefore, to work at the two levels of culture and personal dispositions: the intersubjective and the personal. We have to give an account of both. What, for example, does it mean concretely to expect that a student will take on the dispositions of critical thinking? The idea of a *culture* of critical discourse, therefore, is inadequate by itself. We have to supplement it with the personal dimension of criticality.

Secondly, we saw earlier that the character of modern society is contestable: it is constituted by multiple discourses, but those discourses are being skewed through colonization by dominant interests in technological reason. In this context, a culture of critical discourse cannot be construed – as Gouldner (1979) was able to do – purely cerebrally. Since the new discourses in higher education seek to widen what it is to be a student to include aspects of the student's reflective self and of the student as actor in the world, a culture of critical discourse must also widen beyond knowledge to take in those domains of the self *and* of the world. The reflection must be critical self-reflection and the action must be critical action. Enabling students to inhabit fully a culture of critical discourse requires that it permeates not just their cognitive world but their entire critical being.

Thirdly, in a world saturated by discourses impregnated with power, the university acquires new responsibilities for symbolic creativity. In late modernity, there are any number of sites of symbolic creativity, so this role is not distinctive. The particular responsibilities here are two-fold: to provide society with a site of alternative views of the world, and to proffer those alternative views in such a way that they are likely to gain a hearing. The university is a critical voice through its supply of new meanings: it has available to it not just a commentating and certainly not just a voyeuristic stance, but a constructive, albeit critical, stance. This critical discourse is an engaged discourse.

Conclusion

To return to the starting point of this chapter, the university gains new responsibilities and a new potential as a critical voice in society through its capacity to offer society alternative conceptual resources; society is then better placed to understand itself and to move forward productively in the challenging world it faces. The university assists society in its 'reflexive modernization' not simply by holding up a mirror to society but by enabling society to see itself anew. The university fulfils its critical function by injecting new forms of knowing and action into society.

Knowing, reflection and action on the one hand; imagination and creativity on the other hand; and all taking account of both the personal and the interpersonal dimensions of criticality: these, then, are the challenges in working out a proper conception of the critical function of higher education. We take up this challenge in the next chapter by addressing the issue of the extent to which our universities are organized to sustain this critical function.

4

The Closing of the
Critical University?

Introduction

At this juncture, two points should be captured from our unfolding story. First, there are tendencies that would see critical thinking as an attribute of individuals or would see it as a characteristic of a social structuring of the world. On the one hand, the criticality resides in individuals: it is what they can do. On the other hand, the criticality lies in forms of thought: it is an indication of their power to enlighten and to go on refining themselves. Individuals or forms of thought – this polarity is a way of distinguishing current approaches to criticality. The theoreticians tend to focus on forms of thought, on socially structured ways of thinking, and the problem becomes one of: how do we ensure that thought is critical? The practitioners and the policy-makers tend to focus on individuals, and the problem becomes one of: how can we enable students to become more critical? But, clearly, a full account of criticality has to take on both dimensions. A critical higher education has to be sensitive both to the social character of thought and to its acquisition by individuals. Criticality is both social and personal.

Secondly, pretty well all the contemporary formulations of criticality are deficient in that they focus on thinking. Critical thinking is more than thinking. It involves action, if only in the sense that the expression of a critical thought is a definite intervention in the world. And it involves the self. The development of critical thought brings the development of the self. The self is not outside the critical thinking but is intimately implicated in it; and nor is this only the cerebral self. The expression of critical thought calls for emotion (if only emotional control), commitment and courage. Criticality, therefore, embraces action and the self just as much as it embraces thinking. Accordingly, we should abandon the notion of critical thinking as central to higher education and replace it with a more encompassing idea of critical being, which embraces action and the self together with thought.

We now pursue these reflections by coming nearer home, through focusing on the contemporary university. Universities all over the Western world, and especially in the UK, are changing as they are called to account by the wider society. Is the contemporary university, as a result, more or less conducive to the critical life? Does it nourish the development of the critical self? Are there tendencies in the modern university that will thwart the development of criticality, even if universities would generally claim that they were still committed to that purpose? Are there perhaps features of the modern university that render such a mission impossible? The argument of this chapter is that such a mission is by no means impossible, but that the realization of such a mission demands strategies and actions that are little in evidence. The university as a centre of and for a critical life is an endangered species.

On university differences

Before embarking on the argument, an immediate criticism should be deflected. It will be said that, especially in a mass higher education system, universities differ considerably. Some may choose to give space to critical thought, however defined. Others may choose to put their energies into action, whether in the curriculum or in applied research or in consultancies. In any event, it has already been part of the argument here (Chapter 1) that critical thought can come in all manner of guises. No general comments can usefully be made, therefore, about universities and critical thought. Each university will develop its own position on the matter for itself.

That is true, but it is only partly true. Certainly, a mass higher education system is a differentiated system, whether the lines of demarcation are clear or ambiguous, whether they are institutionalized or informal, and whether they are horizontal (built upon hierarchical forms of knowledge or activity) or vertical (built upon disciplines nominally equal in status). Generalizations, therefore, need to be qualified and to be subject to empirical investigation. But the modern university is implicated in the projects of late capitalism and late modernity. Both the modern economy and the character of modern society require higher-order cognitive and interpersonal capabilities which, it is to be hoped, the university can supply. Universities will relate to these external influences in different ways: they will find their own niche. But an accommodation of some kind by each university there has to be.

Further, in the UK at least, there is the formal shaping of a single system by the state over the past forty years. There are significant informal forms of stratification, but they are by-plays within a unified state policy for higher education. All universities are, therefore, subject both to informal messages and networking negotiations with the wider society and, through state steering, to a common set of bureaucratized mechanisms.

We can, therefore, without diffidence, embark on an exploration of the general character of the modern university: each one has to live in something of the same world.

Mission impossible?

Most universities have a stated mission, usually indeed in the form of a 'mission statement'. But we should distinguish between a mission as stated and a mission as practised. It is the latter that concerns us here. The question before us is not whether universities refer to the idea of critical thought in their manifestos, but rather whether universities are in practice conducive to the development of the forms of critical thought that we have begun to sketch out. The university may now be a repository for several forms of critical thought in the different disciplines, some of which are directly connected to wider societal and economic activities. Critical thought as a commentary within a disciplinary mode of thinking; or as a form of high-order problem-solving (where the problems may well be real-world problems in the form of case studies); or as a critical examination of cultural texts (understood in the widest sense); or as strategic planning (for example, in management courses of all kinds); or as personal reflection: all these and other forms of critical thought *are* to be found within the interstices of curricular practices. If this is the case, critical thought would appear to be an indissoluble aspect of the university's mission as practised, whether or not there is mention of it in the published mission statement.

The conclusion, however, does not follow from the premises. The fact that a wide range of activities that can be termed 'critical thought' can be detected in the teaching of different subjects across the campus does not, in itself, tell us anything of substance about the propensity of the university as such to sponsor and to encourage modes of critical thought. It might turn out that some of these modes of critical thought are new and are taking off in spite of, and not because of, their institutional context. The development of the critical self or of the student as a critical actor represents a challenge to conventional modes of criticality. The argument could be that such modes of critical thought have their sponsors in the wider community, in the professions, or in the business and commercial sector. The university, as such, is at best indifferent or even, *sotto voce*, somewhat hostile to the encouragement of critical thought in its students. That is the argument that will be made here.

The university as organization

How could this be? How could it be that the Western university might have become indifferent and even antipathetic to the very theme that it has raised as its banner since the Enlightenment? It has not been a deliberate act, nor even especially noticed. Indeed, it is the absence of awareness that is significant. That blankness (to use one of Leavis's terms) is symptomatic of the wider societal and cognitive changes in which universities are involved. The changes in the university go unnoticed because it shares in those wider changes. This is less a case of indifference and more one of overlooking. But this situation cannot all be attributed to wider societal changes. The university is culpable. It is a player in its own right, to a significant degree. At least, the question has to be posed: Could the university be other than it is?

In *The Closing of the American Mind*, Allan Bloom (1987) saw the universities as bearing a significant responsibility for the closure he was identifying. His argument turned on an analysis of the changing academic culture. The academic community had been diverted into non-progressive interests, the path of truth having been forsaken for relativism and other false avenues. Missing from Bloom's argument is any real sense of the contemporary character of the modern university as a social institution. But that is of the essence. We cannot understand the intellectual culture of the modern university unless we also understand the university as an organization. The former is influenced by the latter. If there is a closure of the wider collective mind, in part that has to be attributed to, or understood as being influenced by, the organizational structure of the university. Structure does not necessarily beget culture, but it does put constraints around it.

The idea of the university as an organization is not entirely new, and it can be pressed too far in understanding the modern university. The mediaeval idea of the university, of a *studium generale* as distinct from a *universitas*, lay in the former being formally recognized as a definite place of learning with some kind of stability to it, whereas the latter was a looser form of association. Since then, through the nineteenth and the twentieth centuries, the university has gained more structure as departments and courses have developed. Indeed, in the contemporary era, it could be argued that the university has come to take on the characteristics of a post-Fordist organization, in which the structures are much more fluid and uncertain. Academic roles are more permeable with respect to the wider society: boundaries between the internal and the extramural can no longer be drawn tightly in any discipline. At the same time, departments give way to matrix structures in which staff's roles are more ambiguous and multi-faceted. In modular systems, courses give way to a near-infinite possible number of programmes. Students, too, have less of a definite academic 'home' as they frame their own learning sequences and combinations. So both historically and presently, the idea of the university as an organization has to be treated with care.

Nevertheless, the modern university – whether mass, multi or mega – has increasing characteristics of organization. Ever since its mediaeval origins, the university has been a state institution, but the state has been relatively benign. Now, expectations of the university are higher. State financial underwriting of the enterprise is heavy, even if it is being held static. But the point is not merely financial. There is an ideological investment in the university of a new order. Partly, this is the result of the university as a mass institution: there are, in a democratic society, more demands on the university to deliver services of wide appeal. Partly, too, it is a result of world economic competitiveness. For both of these reasons, the state plays a more dirigiste role in the work of universities. And this expanded role is experienced not only in financial probity and in accountability and even surveillance of the core activities – research and teaching – but also in a framing by the state of those activities. The framing is not necessarily a tight framing: both direct and indirect measures are deployed. Efforts are made to influence the curriculum both directly through state initiatives and indirectly through encouraging a student market.

The tightening of the relationship between the state and higher education – financial, managerial, evaluative, and in relation to the university's core activities of research and teaching – is only part of the wider environment in which universities are placed and to which they have to accommodate. A heightening interest in curricular matters on the part of professional bodies is a second factor. A third is the demographic point that a higher age profile of incoming students brings both a wider and a more articulated set of consumer expectations. The rise of intermediary bodies between the state and universities is a further matter, many of which are engaged in relatively intrusive forms of surveillance. The position in which universities have been placed, of having to raise an increasing proportion of their own revenues, is yet another dimension.

In such an environment, greater organization is inevitable. Transparency, accountability, efficiency and responsiveness all require it. The tight framing of the envelope of student formation, especially around a competency framework, requires it directly. And the move towards modularization and credit accumulation and transfer (which can be seen as a means of producing more efficiency, transparency and responsiveness) requires it indirectly. These dimensions of change interrelate. For example, the requirement that each curriculum unit should have an explicit set of stated objectives is an unintended consequence of modularizing the curriculum as offerings are made transparent to largely uninformed customers. At the same time, computerized management information systems have made possible new forms of accountability: it is relatively easy to establish at the level of discrete modules just who is teaching what and with what outcomes. An initiative to bring about more efficiency and transparency (although this is often more a hope than a realization) also produces an internal market. Modularization is a nice example, therefore, of greater systematicity and responsiveness on the part of universities.

Universities have to become organizations as rational responses to the environment in which they are placed. There is no conspiracy on the part either of the state and its agencies or of university management teams, either collectively or separately. There does not have to be. Neave (1990) suggested that Western universities have seen the rise of the evaluative state and so of the evaluated university. That is so, but the evaluative elements of the external environment are only part of a larger constellation of forces and interests acting in parallel. Ideologically and instrumentally, the university has to act in a responsive mode, and it has to become organizational in its operations. The *organized university* is a necessary feature of our age.

And academic freedom?

In such an environment, academic freedom is not taken away; rather, the opportunities for its realization are reduced. The difference is subtle but important. If academic freedom is the freedom of individual academics to pursue academic activities (such as teaching and research) in academic settings (such as universities) in a manner and to an end of their choosing, then we are not seeing academic freedom as such diminished to a significant degree. Despite the laments from within the academy (Russell, 1993), academics are not yet typically told what to teach or research or how to do so. What we are seeing are the conditions of academic work so tightly framed with reward structures that academics find it easy to read the signals. In this situation, the opportunities for the realization of academic freedom are effectively reduced.

That academic freedom is, in effect, being reduced in practice if not in intention could be felt to constitute grounds for a counter-resistance on the part of the academic community. Only a minority of academics are, after all, fully subscribing members of the postmodern fraternity; most, therefore, might be expected to have some minimal allegiance to the grand narrative of academic freedom. Surely, it is a theme that might still unite the academic community. And if there are few signs of resistance, then perhaps the story being sketched out here is overdrawn? Again, such a conclusion would not follow from the premises.

First, the drawing in of the boundaries of what are taken to be legitimate academic activities would not be felt as such if the incumbents knew no other. Natural levels of turnover in the profession would lead, over half a generation, to just that: a high proportion of staff who knew no other situation. Secondly, academic work is taking on many of the characteristics of work in the wider society, with more part-time and short-term contracts. Its insecurity is rising. Incumbents hoping for one of a decreasing proportion of permanent posts will wish to avoid rocking the boat. Thirdly, as universities become part of society, the new arrivals from other professional domains will enter with conceptions of work that are different from the resident incumbents; indeed, many will be surprised at the *low* level of surveillance and accountability.

One reading of this situation is that the culture is shifting. The dominant sets of values about, and conceptions of, academic work change among the academics themselves. They come to take as natural what might have been antipathetic to the dominant views within academic culture a century ago.

Such a reading has plausibility but it can be overstretched. It contains two assumptions: first, that there was a golden age of academic freedom, perhaps before the 1970s; and, secondly, that academics took full advantage of such opportunities. Academics were free *and* practised their freedom. Both assumptions bear scrutiny.

The first assumption is largely true. Until relatively recently, academics were extraordinarily free to practise their trade. Paid by the state and assured of a clientele, they were not even exposed to the disciplines of the market known to most – although not all – other groups of professionals. Universities did not have the organizational characteristics that they have recently acquired and the state had not developed its forms of surveillance. Nor were the clients (that is, students and research bodies) particularly demanding. So the academics enjoyed unusual degrees of freedom.

The problem lies in the second assumption. The academics enjoyed freedoms but declined to exercise them. They remained content to work within the tight framework of their own discipline, where they formed their own self-conceptions and professional identities. They played by the rules of their discipline. Neither bending those rules nor stepping outside the discipline to speak out on academic matters as such constituted their conception of academic life. Far from enjoying and exploiting freedom, academics were rather frightened by freedom. Fear of freedom was indeed a fair description of the academic mind (Fromm, 1960).

A contemporary quiescence, then, on the part of the academics does not indicate a change in academic culture as such. The academic mind was always rather compliant and pliable: the academic temperament is not so much that of seeking the easy life but of wanting to be left to pursue one's own interests within one's intellectual field. A heightened level of organization on the part of the university, therefore, is not problematic in itself. It will not be perceived as an attack on academic freedom, since academic freedom was never a dominant value. The arrival of organizational man (or woman) will only be seen as threatening if the core activities (and that means mainly research) around which the academic self-identity is framed are threatened. Since even the arrival of state initiatives in the UK, such as classroom surveillance – through the Quality Assessment methodology – and the Enterprise in Higher Education initiative, could not easily be construed as threatening those values, no resistance was forthcoming.

It emerges, then, that the organized university and the academic community can live with each other, if a little uneasily. For example, the new managerialism is unduly anxious about whistle-blowing. The new managerialism, being concerned to promote each university and to project the university beyond the competition from other universities, and being sensitive to market perceptions of negative publicity, is nervous about academics who speak out about university matters. Matters are, accordingly, labelled as internal and deserving of internal solutions before being made public. The range of matters on which academics can now speak out appears to diminish – and, formally, it has. The ring-fencing is real. Penalties will befall those who

break the organization's rules. But the restrictions are largely formal in character: they are hardly felt substantively by academics. Academics speaking
out on matters of general professional significance are unusual. They never
did it *en masse* when they had every opportunity to do so. Whistle-blowers
need not apply, but they hardly ever applied anyway.

The closing of the university mind

Academics may not sense a diminution in their academic freedom. The
space available to them for activities that could be construed as legitimately
academic may have drawn in without demur of any significant kind. The
culture of academic life, in the sense of the dominant values of its incumbents, may be shifting. That is not our immediate concern. What is our
concern is the character of universities as organizations: their structural
features and their attendant modes of communication. If the opportunities
for critical thought are closing, that is, in part, due to the changing structures and communicative processes that characterize the modern university.
This we have learnt from Becher and Kogan (1992): that structure and
process have to be understood as inseparable. But if these are two sides of
the coin, we still need an account of the direction in which the coin is
rolling and of the forces that are propelling it.

As an initial generalization, I contend that we are seeing in the university
the supplanting of a hermeneutic mode of communication by an instrumental mode of communication. These changing processes are supported
by the shift towards the university as an organization that we have been
noting. Process and structure work together.

By a hermeneutic mode of communication, I mean the mode of communication that is accompanied by a genuine attempt to understand the other
party. The term 'the academic community' has a quaint ring about it, but
its passing is symptomatic of this drift from communication for understanding to communication for strategic action. Communication for understanding characteristic of a genuine community requires mutual respect which is
structural. In a situation in which departments feel themselves in competition for scarce resources within universities, and in which they also compete
across universities, 'the other party' becomes less a partner in an open conversation than a rival attempting to seize the main chance.

Of course, this drift is neither absolute nor new. Priority disputes are
part of the growth of scientific knowledge but, even today, separate teams
worldwide can work in a collaborative spirit with each other. The point is
the more general one about the universities as organizations. They have
become organizations separately and they have become – in the formation
of a state-sponsored system of higher education – a kind of collective mega-
organization. Within universities, planning, management information, budgeting, target setting, efficiency savings, devolved budgeting and accountability
measures become taken for granted as aspects of managing a modern university. Vice-chancellors come to term themselves 'chief executives': they

are running a multi-million pound corporation (a large if not the largest employer in town).

In this situation, strategic reason is bound to grow. Whether it has to grow at the expense of communicative reason is a more open issue. The pragmatic envelope is such, however, that we see a colonization of the latter by the former: communication for effective results tends to drive out communication for understanding. Another way of putting it is that, in the managed university, vertical 'communication' supplants horizontal communication. There should be nothing surprising in this: higher education is simply reflecting epistemological and ontological changes in late capitalism. Postmodernism may celebrate difference and playfulness but, in state-sponsored sectors such as higher education, we are witnessing systematization, detraditionalization, operationalism and decisionism. Communication, understanding, genuine collaboration and consensual will-formation – which have characterized the idea of the Western university – are not outlawed as such; they are surplus to requirements in a university become organization.

In such a situation, critical thinking is not lost altogether. What is in evidence is, rather, a form of critical thinking that serves the operationalism and decisionism of the modern organization. The desired forms of critical thinking are precisely those that bring organizational change, evident results, improved balance sheets and appropriate outcomes. This is not, it should be noted, a point about centralized as distinct from decentralized decision-making: it is not that the desired critical thinking is confined to the central management team, meeting weekly or fortnightly in the chief executive's office. On the contrary, in the post-Fordist university, everyone is his or her own manager. The desired forms of critical thinking percolate downwards, ideally to be found in everyone: every member of the university should become iconoclastic in his or her thinking, providing it is kept within the bounds of the university's mission and is deployed to stated ends. Entrepreneurialism *is* wanted but only providing it is kept within limits. No moonlighters, please.

The critical thinking characteristic of operationalism finds a place in all the university's core activities. In relation to teaching, critical thinking engages in rationalizing the teaching programme both at the university level and at the level of discrete modules or units. New organizational structures arise, cutting across departments supposedly with the intention of encouraging academics to communicate with each other about teaching matters. The real drive, however, is not communicative but is operational: it is not a case of might we evolve a new course unit on topic x but, rather, can we teach topic y in such a way that it will do duty for several clusters of students on different kinds of programme in the modular system? In looking to the faculty to communicate in the design and delivery of modules, the underlying motive lies not in a belief in the intrinsic value of collegial cross-fertilization, but in the instrumental managerial desire to avoid 'unnecessary' overlap in modules and so drive up the total efficiency of the teaching effort.

What we take a university to be, therefore, in terms of its human trans-actions, is changing. The university as organization looks for results in the form of demonstrable outcomes. The bottom line – whether in relation to teaching, research or consultancy – is only one aspect, and not necessarily the most fundamental. The right kinds of judgement by the external agen-cies, the right kinds of student outcome in the form of labour market attractiveness, and the right kinds of course in the form of student enrol-ments: the strategic thinking of the corporation begets performative meas-ures of success and of value. Productivity is measured; students, indeed, become products. Critical thinking that brings about a changed culture of *this* kind is entirely welcomed.

Parochial thinking

The university likes to think of itself as cosmopolitan with its worldwide connections, its array of languages and lifestyles (across the disciplines) and its vision beyond the ordinary. In fact, the university has been a thoroughly rural community. Its international connections, forming so-called invisible colleges, are simply the rural community of a discipline writ large. The university has been a collection of rural communities. Even the much vaunted elaborateness of its codes has been misread. That elaborateness has never been made transparent: it was not a contrast to a condensed code but was a version of it. You had to be a member of the community to understand it. And any newcomer to the village who did not understand the language, the tolerated forms of critique and even (literally) the dress code would soon be spotted.

What we are witnessing, as the university becomes more an organization, is less a shift from rural to cosmopolitan as a shift from rural to urban. The rural dwellers have come into the city. In the UK, the shift is nicely caught by the difference between the founding of the 1960s' 'new universities' in green-field sites and the founding of the 1990s' 'new universities' in inner cities. The city demands a more organized and a more uniform way of life. Certainly, its size offers anonymity to a degree; but, sooner or later, the bureaucracy catches up with those who would rather not be noticed. It is a shift from Gemeinschaft to Gesellschaft: from person-oriented commun-icative processes to role-based interactions. Forms of reason are less idiosyn-cratic and more predictable. The university calls for organization not only in its structures and its operations but also in its thinking and its self-understanding. But for all its organization, the dominant mode of thinking is still parochial. It is a criticality within limited horizons, horizons of insti-tutional profile and solvency.

The academic self was invisible to the university as such. Now, in the university as organization, the academic self has become transparent as the academy's social relations have become less local and more institutional. Organizational man and woman become the new academic personae.

Community, therefore, dies; or appears to do so. Partly, this is a matter of time. In a setting in which the cost-effectiveness of transactions is judged by the incumbents themselves (since their own outputs are now being monitored), time is of the essence. Conversation without an obvious outcome falls outside the acceptable.

Critical thought, as we have seen, does not die but is fundamentally reinterpreted. Critical thought has to prove its worth by yielding outcomes that now fit into the revised mission. Critical thought that yields efficiency gains, a 'positive' public profile, high scores on the public judgements by external bodies, greater transparency of effort and an improved balance sheet will be welcome. Critical thought that yields greater understanding on the part of students or a heightened understanding among the public of a policy issue (especially where it runs against the grain of the dominant view), or which conflicts with an internal managerial policy, will not be noticed, be marginalized or be held to be injurious to the real mission of the university.

The argument should not be misunderstood. It is not that critical being is ruled off-limits on campus. In one sense, to the contrary: academic life is pulled into wider fora and is invited to be 'critical' of contemporary practices and policies in the wider society. Rather, it is that the structure and process of the organized university act together to induce a critical self which acts and thinks within the horizons of getting on, of offering solutions to pre-identified problems, and of ensuring a successful profile. The critical self is widened and reduced at the same time. The formation of a genuine academic community of mutual and open dialogue is not part of this outlook. The external world begets an internal structuring which, in turn, impacts on academic work (Smyth, 1995). The critical voice is reshaped into that which serves the paymaster.

Constructing a critical community

Can a critical thinking that is genuinely collaborative, open-ended and oriented to reaching real understanding survive? Can there be a genuine academic community – a critical academic community engaged, for and across itself, in open dialogue? There are three possible answers: no; yes, but only at the margins; and yes, but if it is to characterize the modern university as such, it has to be reconceptualized. Talk of academic community and critical thought implies that they were easily detected in an earlier golden age. We have cast doubt on such assumptions. So the present situation forces a rethinking of what a university as community and its appropriate forms of critical thought might be, and the forms of action that might encourage its instantiation on campus.

There is a double-bind here. Managerialism brings with it operationalism and strategic thinking, and a closing of the boundaries of critical thought within the university. And yet, managerialism of a kind is necessary if the structural features of the modern university we have been identifying are to be combated. It is its own form of criticality. In the modern age, sharp questions have to be asked of an operational kind: a university as community has to be managed.

Even so, if a management team can reduce community and critical thought, it can also expand these features of university life through the promotion of cross-disciplinary communication. If it can restrict the formation of the critical self on campus, it can also act to expand the space in which the critical self can develop. If the 'academic community' was never a genuine community built around critical but mutual dialogue, then a new challenge bears in upon the management team to work to build that critical community. The new managerialism has only just begun. It has in front of it an even greater challenge of helping the university become the academic community that it always claimed that it was.

This implies, first, effort to bring academics together from across the university to address large issues jointly; but it also points to the need for senior members of the university to build intellectual bridges in relation to the core activities of teaching and research. Secondly, it means a willingness seriously to engage in open communication processes in which the participants feel that they can speak out and do so with some potency: their voice matters and can have real effect. Thirdly, the range of issues on which communication is invited and encouraged should not be limited: participants will have their own agendas which have to be taken seriously.

These three conditions together impart a heavy challenge to university management teams. The communicative transactions being suggested here have to be worked at continually. Managers have to engage constantly with staff in the kinds of open conversation where the end is uncertain. Unless staff sense that they are genuinely engaging in such transactions, they will feel that they are being subject to a form of strategic communication. But the critical self requires communicative space in which to develop. Many university managers will, of course, feel uncomfortable, since control is then denied to them. Such continuing effort will be resisted because it has no obvious outcome: the cost–benefit returns will be poor, at first glance. Management for the university as organization will not feel that such managerial labour is either warranted or, indeed, proper within the role as conceived. The managerial role, accordingly, has to be reconceptualized as opening up the possibility of academic community.

Conclusion

In the reconstruction of the critical university, talk of vision, leadership and inspiration is dangerous. It implies either a technological fix or a charismatic approach to institutional change. Both are otiose because both run against the concepts of genuine community and critique. For those, something approaching a Habermassian ideal speech situation is required, in which all participants feel that they are able to take part freely without dimensions of power coming into play. The Habermassian ideal speech situation is more applicable to the communicative space of the university as a whole than to its pedagogical transactions; in that sense, it is the managers that have to become Habermassians even before the lecturers. But the ideal speech situation, construed in that way, has to remain an ideal: the features of universities as corporations that we have sketched are largely given. The question is whether, in parallel, a university as a critical community can emerge. That it has not so far been achieved is no reason not to attempt to bring it about.

Part 2

Towards Critical Being

5

Critical Being in Higher Education

Introduction

In Part 1, we saw that the academic community has framed narrowly its conception of critical abilities, confining them largely to critical thinking in the context of formal knowledge. That limitation is being challenged: critical being in the modern world has also to include critical self-reflection and critical action. Postmodernism and the idea of discourse together usher in a plastic sense of human being, the self and self-identity fragmenting to become a collection of identities reading a number of texts. A durable self can only be sustained, if at all, through critical self-reflection and authentic – and, thereby, critical – action.

The university is taking on a parallel message, but is acceding to a narrow interpretation of critical self-reflection as that of supplying self-monitoring capacities for the corporate world. In that vein, too, the university is accepting that it should be more oriented to the realm of action, but here critical action is understood as being critical of contemporary practices so as to bring off undisputed ends of economic well-being and organizational projection. The university's conception of critical abilities widens to include the self and the world but is held within limits, which threaten to thwart the attainment of the emancipatory promise of critical being.

In this chapter, I want to draw together and to develop these ideas into a coherent framework.

A trap for the unwary

I want, quickly, to dispatch a contemporary controversy on the topic which would be a blind alley to our explorations. That controversy focuses on the issue of whether critical thinking is a species of thinking *sui generis* or whether it is to be understood only as a form of thinking specific to particular cognitive frameworks. McPeck (1981, 1990) has been a particularly strident advocate of the latter view, holding that critical thinking has to be critical of something and that being critical of, say, a scientific theory calls for different cognitive moves from those required in being critical of a literary text. Siegel (1988), on the other hand, holds that we can still sensibly talk of critical thinking without qualifiers: there is a large measure of agreement between those in different disciplines as to what is to count as critical reason. In essence, this debate boils down to a context-independent or a context-dependent view of critical thinking.

This debate has occupied much attention in the philosophy of education over the past decade, but it is a debate that is going nowhere and which should not detain us. Certainly, in various guises, the issue has and will continue to bubble up through the surface of our explorations here. But, in the terms in which the debate itself is conducted, both sides are missing the main issue and, in doing so, demonstrate the narrow terms in which the debate has been cast.

The key issue in getting clear about critical thinking is: what is it for? This simple question eludes those in the context-dependent/context-independent debate because they take it for granted that critical thinking is conducted by individuals and that it has a necessary relationship with disciplines: their dispute is over the character of that relationship. Some believe that students possess a kind of critical thinking cognitive faculty in its own right, which can be developed and stretched, like some kind of mental muscle, and applied to the different epistemological situations that the separate disciplines present. Others believe, to the contrary, that the exercise of students' critical faculties takes its shape and its point from the presenting epistemological situation. Being critical is a rule-governed activity and the rules are the norms of a particular epistemic community.

Setting the terms of the debate in this way is entirely understandable if one's concern is simply that of the development of critical thinking skills by individuals. If one believes that critical thinking skills are especially worthwhile, the task of the educator becomes one of understanding those skills. Questions then arise about whether there is a single set of critical thinking skills that can be developed by educators, or whether they are so specific to the different disciplines and educational activities that their inculcation has to permeate the whole curriculum. Questions also arise over the mode of their transmission: if critical thinking skills are context-specific, then their acquisition is the responsibility of all teachers. If, on the other hand, they are generic to all subjects, then a cadre of 'experts' on critical thinking can take charge – problem solved.

Issues of this kind are behind the critical thinking movement in the USA. That movement has taken off in the context of a heterogeneous and near-universal higher education student population, general concerns about the level of cognitive achievement by undergraduates, and a particular concern that students do not understand or value the rules of evaluation, argumentation and criticism. In *this* situation, critical thinking – understood as logical thinking – takes on the burden of supplying a general culture of the mind to the whole higher education system.

Although it takes on a particular hue in the USA, an interest in critical thinking as argument has recently taken off internationally. This worldwide interest in critical thinking skills and their construal in technical terms has to be seen in the context of the ever-closer relationship between higher education and the world of work, especially in relation to the exponential rates of change. In this context, critical thinking appears both to offer the human capacities to cope with change and to provide the dispositions that respond positively to change. In turn, educationalists have been only too ready to fall in with the role demanded of them. The world of work wants critical thinking skills: very well, let us provide them (this sounds like the sort of function that we can legitimately offer, after all). All, then, that is left to higher education is to determine the character of critical thinking skills: are they *sui generis* or are they specific to the different disciplines?

It is hardly surprising, too, given this context and framing of the issue, that there will be those who will hold to a *sui generis* line. If we can show that there are general rules of critical thinking and that there are critical thinking skills that are independent of knowing contexts, then all kinds of new academic labour open up, both in clarifying those general rules and in introducing students to the acquisition and deployment of those general rules and associated skills. The sociology of the situation encourages a particular philosophical line.

What is being largely overlooked in this transatlantic debate over critical thinking is its purpose. If, instead of asking 'What is critical thinking?', we were to start by asking 'What is it for?', a quite new range of problems and, thereby, of ways of conceiving of critical thinking opens up.

The scope of critical thinking

Critical thinking has to have an object – to that extent, I agree with the context-dependent lobby. But the objects of critical thinking can be distinguished in terms of the fundamental human interests that they represent. There are three *domains* of critical thinking. One can be critical of:

- propositions, ideas and theories, especially as they are proffered in the world of systemic knowledge (CT1);
- the internal world, that is oneself (CT2), a form of critical thought that is demonstrated in critical self-reflection;
- the external world (CT3), a form of critical thought that is demonstrated in critical action.

This three-fold division parallels Popper's (1972) epistemology of three worlds: World I consists of the brute world of spatio-temporal objects; World II consists of the subjective world of human consciousness; and World III consists of the world of objective knowledge. My classification parallels but is not identical to Popper's. First, Popper made much of the notion of objective knowledge (as being constitutive of his World III), whereas my classification is in no way dependent on the notion of objective knowledge. Secondly, although Popper felt that relationships hold between the three domains, my view is that the relationships are more complex than Popper allowed. For example, under my third domain, that of the external world, I would wish to allow tacit, interpersonal and experiential forms of knowledge of the kind bound up in professional action as well as social institutions and social practices. Thirdly, I agree with Popper that our corpuses of systematic thought can illuminate our immediate understanding of my first and second domains and, in that sense, no sharp boundary can be drawn between them. But I also hold that it is possible to inhabit all three domains of critical thought *in the same act*.

What, then, is the point of my three-fold division, if no determinate boundary can be drawn between the three domains? The point is to highlight the varying objects that critical thinking can take *and the purposes it can fulfil*. The student standing in front of the line of tanks in Tiananmen Square was taking up a critical stance against the world and so, in a quite direct and dramatic way, was demonstrating critical thinking in action (CT3). *Indirectly*, he was also saying that this is where I stand. He was being utterly authentic, implicitly saying that this is the real 'me'. This act of defiance is a true reflection of my view of the world. Indirectly, therefore, this action was also testimony to the potency of (CT2) self-evaluations and self-critique. Perhaps, too, the student's view of the regime against which he was making his stand had prompted a heightened understanding drawn from the perspectives of political science, political philosophy and sociology and was, therefore, reflective of critical thinking of propositional thought (CT1).

There will be those who will say that critical action (CT3) is reducible to critical thought as such (CT1); that our critical actions in the world, especially if they are serious, will be dependent on our understandings derived from formal systems of thought. My argument as to the irreducibility of these forms of criticality will be turned on its head. It will be said that, if our critical evaluations of the world are expressed in action, they have to be grounded in the empirical evidence and perspectives supplied by the disciplines. Critical action (CT3) depends on critical thought (CT1).

This argument has to be repudiated. We do not have to have command over abstruse corpuses of knowledge to take up a stance towards the world. Admittedly, it is not possible to have an unmediated view of the world, but that does not mean that we only have access to the world through the disciplines. But even this rebuttal does not quite get to the heart of the matter. The main reason why the reductionist argument won't work – the view that CT3 is reducible to CT1 – is that it neglects the purposes of critical thinking. To take up a stance against the world, to evaluate a proposition and to attempt to understand oneself, these are three fundamentally different purposes of critical thinking. Each is worthwhile but none is reducible to either of the others. Being overwhelmed by a tank is not the same as being overwhelmed by an argument, and nor is it the same as being overwhelmed by a loss of one's own identity.

Respecting distinctions

Even if the substance of this three-fold distinction is accepted, no doubt challenges to it will be advanced. It may be said, for example, that forms of thought are not outside the world but are very much in it and are part of it. But the distinction that I am making is still valid: there is a clear difference between evaluating theories within political theory and contending in action against a particular political party or regime (to pick up the example of our Chinese student).

Alternatively, it may be said, following the work of Gibbons and his associates (1994), that knowledge is created in society and tested in it (mode 2 knowledge as distinct from mode 1 propositional knowledge). In other words, valid forms of knowledge are themselves rooted in action and are not just to be found in propositional knowledge. But this argument concedes the essence of just what I am pointing to: that the world presents a distinct epistemological set of anchorages for our critical engagements. What it adds is that action in the world can itself be a form of knowledge production and validation, but this much I argued earlier. The substance of the point I am making, that critical action in the world and critical thought in relation to organized bodies of propositional knowledge are distinct but equally valid forms of critical expression, remains intact.

It may also be said, and correctly so, that we may only be able to understand some human activities by taking account of formal bodies of thought. Technologies, social institutions and professional activities may themselves be conducted by those who are in command of formal or abstract ideas or even bodies of thought. This case is problematic for the distinction I want to make. It indicates that sometimes critical action (CT3) may *have* to embrace critical thought (CT1). But this is not to say that CT3 has entirely to assimilate CT1 or vice versa. We simply become adept at pursuing the two forms of critical thinking at the same time. To act with understanding in the world may require sophisticated technical understanding or conceptual insight. The act may not be intelligible in the absence of the knowledge and understanding. But the act remains a claim on the world or an intervention in the world in its own right.

Lastly, it will also be said that critical thought is a set of actions. Coming to an understanding, taking up a stance in relation to the encountered ideas and engaging with them, these are all actions. Critical thought, if it is of any seriousness, is purposive, intentional, nuanced and sensitive to its context. It is action of the most sophisticated kind. The name that Habermas has given to his project over the past twenty years, after all, is precisely that of the understanding of *communicative action*. Critical dialogue is a thoroughgoing form of action.

This is a powerful line of argument: serious thought is a form of action. Even to form a clear view of one's own calls for persistence, inner strength (in, say, taking on, in one's own mind, the acknowledged authorities) and determination. Certainly, in some circumstances, declaring where one stands can lead to torture or even the loss of one's life. The pen is not always mightier than the sword. But, to revert to our motif of the Chinese student, working out one's position within a university campus does not usually call for the same range of acts as acting it out in the wider world. Sometimes, there are no safe discursive spaces, even on campus. However, for the most part, in Western democracies, distinctions can be drawn between the communicative acts required in engaging in critical dialogue on campus and in carrying that dialogue into the wider society.

The distinction, therefore, between critical thought (CT1) and critical action (CT3) is fuzzy, but we should not abandon it. CT1 becomes CT3 when it is taken outside the propositional discourse and is subject to other discourses of the wider world (of political action and power, of economic interests and of instrumental reason). In those circumstances, the distinction between CT1 and CT3 becomes clear. It is also vital to maintain the distinction if higher education is specifically to promote critical capabilities that are likely to withstand a world of social and economic change, of ideologies buried in practices and of asymmetrical patterns of force and power.

The scope of higher education

Higher education has taken its dominant conception of critical thinking to be that of CT1, of critical thinking focused on formal bodies of thought. Synthesis, analysis, logical argument set within the permitted moves of a particular discipline: these are the kinds of critical thinking normally favoured within the academic community. The other two possible forms of critical thinking – critical self-reflection and critical action – have not been entirely neglected; but, while now appearing as definite features of higher education, they remain undeveloped.

As curricula have widened to embrace more action-based components, especially in programmes that have a specifically professional element, students to some extent have been exposed to the wider world and, to a limited extent, have been required to take up a stance in it. They have been expected to be able to size up a situation in which they are placed and to act appropriately in it. This is critical thought in-the-world (CT3). But this is a limited expression of the potential of that mode of critical thinking. It would hardly be usual for students on teaching practice, in an industrial placement on a sandwich course or in a clinical situation on a medical course directly to challenge, say, the aims of the organization as such; and still less, to assert themselves as critical persons with their own identities separate from the corporate culture. Problem-solving within narrowly defined situations is the normal range of permitted critical moves. Developing a minimal professional competence is the name of this game.

This is understandable. We want to see a minimal level of competence in our professionals, whether or not they are likely to end up in life-threatening work situations. But the opportunities presented by this exposure are insufficiently taken: a wider sense of the student's critical capacities and of the potential of the lived experience to generate that enlarged critical consciousness could often be developed. At stake here are issues of control and power: we want a critical consciousness but within limits. The equivalent of the Tiananmen Square student is not envisaged. The students had better know their place.

Even less well developed is CT2, critical thought focused on the student as an individual, although again it is to be found in limited ways. The expression 'critical self-reflection' is sometimes heard. In the value system of the academic community, there is a sense that students ought to develop the capacity to reflect on their own cognitive achievements. There are two agendas at work. On the one hand, it is understood that the academic life resides as much in an internalized dialogue within the individual as in a dialogue between consenting adults. On the other hand, there is in the Western university an attachment to the idea of personal autonomy. The one agenda speaks to a higher-order state of mind, and the other to a higher-order state of human being.

It is true that critical self-reflection has had some attention. For example, Western universities have begun to experiment in student self-assessment (where students are asked to come to a judgement about their own work, whether individually or, more often, in a group project). But, mostly, this aim has been realized tacitly. The ability to show that one is self-reflexive and is able, for example, to recognize alternative points of view to that to which one is attached would often be an unspoken element in the way in which work is assessed. It would be a rare set of course objectives that listed such a state of mind and it would be an even rarer assessment approach in which the course team gave a specific judgement on its achievement. Critical self-reflection has not been a significant element in higher education practices, much as it might figure in its rhetoric. But even where it is present, its interpretation has been restricted to the student's competence in a disciplinary context. The student's self-critical abilities on a wider front are even rarer as an educational aim.

We can now summarize, again, our first classification of criticality in higher education. We have distinguished three domains of critical thinking, to each of which attaches a specific form of criticality. The three forms of criticality together fill out the *scope* of critical being (See table 5.1).

Table 5.1 Domains of critical being and their associated forms of criticality

	Domains	Forms of criticality
1	Knowledge	Critical reason
2	Self	Critical self-reflection
3	World	Critical action

Figure 5.1   A higher education for critical being

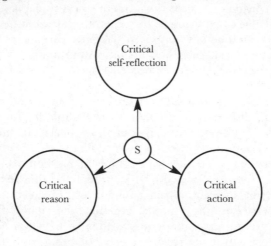

The key issue behind this classification of criticality is one of the purposes of critical thinking: Do I want to extend my capacity to act critically in the wider world, or to evaluate critically theories produced within bodies of thought or, indeed, to understand myself critically? These are irreducible separate human interests. Accordingly, a higher education that understands itself as the inculcation of a critical spirit will have to be sensitive to all three domains of critical being. Diagrammatically, therefore, higher education for critical being takes on the configuration in Fig. 5.1, with the student standing in a relationship to all three forms of criticality.

Levels of critical thought

If the domains of critical thought form one axis of our schema, another is formed by the levels of critical thought. For that, we have to develop one of the classifications set out in Chapter 1.

Critical thinking skills are capacities of making permitted cognitive moves of rational argument. Questions arise, as we saw, over whether those moves are context-specific or context-independent. The key point is that critical thinking skills tend to be understood in relatively narrow terms and, indeed, in technical terms. Given this cognitive situation, how might one appraise it? What are the permitted strategies of evaluation? These skills are techniques to be applied, whether within a discipline or body of thought, or as a more general set of cognitive skills.

As well as expecting students to acquire such skills, we can also hope that they would become aware of their own understanding of the topics that they are addressing. How secure is it? How deep is it? How wide-ranging are the connections that I am making with other topics? How much reliance am I placing on authorities and how much is this position the result of my own thinking? How original is it? How bold is it? How clear is it?

These reflexive capacities, which are part of what we might term *metacritical capacities*, are fundamental to higher education. (They should be distinguished sharply from metacognitive skills which are located in the field of student learning and refer to the capacity of students to interrogate their own learning styles.) *This* kind of internal dialogue indicates a self-monitoring capability which is an essential condition of human autonomy. These capacities to reflect critically on one's own understanding are part of a genuinely higher education: they call for substantive learning, say of a propositional kind, but they go beyond that to the development of the reflexive capacity to evaluate that understanding and its epistemological standing.

Such metacritical capacities point towards *critical thinking*. We are in the presence of critical thinking when a student comes to recognize the essential contestability of all knowledge claims. When that state of mind has been reached, the student understands not just that what she encounters in books and elsewhere, including the views of her lecturers, is contestable but that her own ideas are contestable too. There is no resting place; an inquiry after truth is never-ending. With understandings of this kind, with a sense that the next book, lecture or experiment is not going to yield all the secrets even on one small topic, a *critical stance* opens up. This is a critical stance of a radical kind. It is not a set of skills. This is a critical capacity oriented to the world of knowledge as such. All knowledge claims are understood to have elements of openness; they do not close off debate but, on the contrary, their being made serves only to open up debate.

This critical thinking is not to be confused with the growth of a relativistic attitude on the part of the student. Perry's (1970) stage process of the evolution of the student mind, in which the relativistic stage is an advanced stage but through which the student moves on the way to a stage of commitment, is only of passing interest here. That theory is a psychological theory of cognitive development. What is being posited here, in contrast, is a view as to what it is to be a student in the modern world. This openness, this propensity to take up a critical stance, is more a matter of the kind of person we look to our students to become. Criticality refutes thoroughgoing relativism for it relies on critical standards which relativism ultimately eschews.

Critical thought is a yet higher level of criticality. Whereas critical thinking is a capacity of students as persons, critical thought is an attribute of a body of thought. A body of thought can be 'critical' in two senses. First, an intellectual field can be said to be a form of critical thought when it has a high degree of openness. No intellectual field will be entirely open. That we have learnt from Foucault (1980); but we also see it every day in academic life. Groups of academics – whether on a corridor or worldwide – collect around united views of their intellectual projects. Their journals will purport to be critical but will contain a collective sense of the presuppositions of the project, including its forms of address, its opposition and its goals. But, provided that there is a significant level of public contestability about the knowledge claims made within the field and that, therefore, its evolution has a level of unpredictability about it, we can say that we are in the presence of critical thought.

It will be said that this is an empty point: all intellectual fields found in Western universities are forms of critical thought. But the level of openness differs considerably across intellectual fields. The degree to which counter voices are tolerated in the key journals is a crucial but largely unexplored feature of academic life. Journal editors are increasingly significant gate-keepers. Discipline is kept within the disciplines (Ball, 1990).

Secondly, we can call a body of thought or a discipline 'critical' when it takes on the character of illuminating social practices such that we become more aware that those practices could be other than they are. This critical capacity reaches its apotheosis when it reveals, perhaps through the use of concepts such as power, emancipation, ideology, discourse and empowerment, that the current state of play is the outcome of uneven forces. The description becomes critical; the actors concerned are now supplied with the conceptual tools to see themselves in a new way. Through such a critical theory of themselves, they are able to emancipate themselves. In principle, this critical capacity is available to all disciplines, since all disciplines are sites of power.

Critical thought, therefore, is a concept that works at the level of bodies of thought. It is a sociological rather than a psychological concept. Its application works when a body of thought does more than seek simply to describe the world. It comes into play when it affords genuine enlightenment, in unmasking the hidden forces at work. Certainly, awkward questions arise about the epistemic basis for such a critical theory. How can a body of thought both describe and evaluate the world? Isn't genuine knowledge value-neutral (Geuss, 1981)? We can sidestep those questions here. Critical thought works at the level of the deep structure of events and institutions, so providing the actors concerned with the wherewithal to comprehend themselves in new ways which, in turn, makes possible new modes of enlightened action.

Metacritique is the potential of a form of thought to comprehend itself. It is the claim of Critical Theory that science lacks this capacity, lacking the willingness to examine its own presuppositions but, instead, wishing to present itself as a form of pure and value-free reason. In short, science could be said to be ideological. We should, however, distinguish two forms of metacritique.

First, metacritique could mean the capacity of a form of thought to interrogate and reflect on its fundamental categories, concepts, tests of truth and presuppositions. Here, the very constitution of the form of thought is the focus. What marks it out as this form of thought rather than that? This need not be a transcendental critique: there need be no presumption that the categories, concepts, rules and even tests of truth to be laid bare are timeless and immutable. A sense of epistemological change is entirely compatible with this kind of detective work.

This metacritique has profound implications for the student's development since, where this epistemic self-monitoring has developed, the student is likely also to develop such a reflexive epistemic identity. It will be taken for granted that it is part of her higher education not just to become an adept practitioner of the discipline, proficient in the exercise of its critical thinking skills, but also to take on this more philosophical critical reflexiveness, understanding the structure of her mode of thought, its dominant concepts and frameworks and its tests of validity.

Secondly, metacritique can be evaluative. *This* metacritique seeks to place the form of thought, to understand its origin, its current societal functions, its inner ideologies, the way it acts to form human beings and the power it wields in society. Whereas the former metacritique was philosophical in character, this is largely sociological. I say largely because the ethical basis of the discipline can come into play here as well. Is the world treated as an object of its attentions, a subject of potential transformations that its knowledge makes available, or is the world revealed in a more sympathetic light, as a centre of moral claims in its own right? Is this form of thought a means of securing techniques for exerting power over subjects – human or material – or of giving some deeper insight into their worthwhileness?

For example, to what extent does tourism studies offer solutions to pragmatic business problems irrespective of the effects of the tourism industry on people or on the environment? Or, to what degree does history help us to interrogate contemporary social problems and issues through a historical lens, or is it a kind of technical hermeneutic analysis of texts in and for itself? Or, again, is engineering largely a matter of solving technical problems or does it introduce a sensitivity to the people whose lives are likely to be affected profoundly by its practices?

What is at stake in questions of this kind is the pragmatic and social constitution of a discipline. Implicitly, questions such as these are saying that things could be otherwise, that the discipline could embrace a wider range of interests and sensitivities. Foucault's (1980) insistence on the link between knowledge and power cuts both ways. As well as being a site of power, it is possible, in principle, for the form of thought to be practised differently. Whereas its epistemological basis is largely given (but still worthy of being revealed through metacritique), its sociological basis is positively up for grabs. At least, we have to believe that to be the case; as educators, we have to act as if it were the case that our *own* intellectual field is itself permanently under scrutiny, with not just its epistemic character but its wider social role being available for interrogation.

Certainly, the injunctions I am making can be turned on this text. For example, we can ask questions about the character of the (still embryonic) field of higher education studies. To what extent has the study of higher education come to offer 'solutions' to pre-given problems within the state's policy agenda (for example, in providing technical strategies for coping with reduced resources in a mass higher education system)? To what degree has it provided legitimations – 'stories' – which nicely describe in elaborate terms just those pre-given policies (in taking on 'concepts' such as quality, account-ability, the learning society and transferable skills)? More fundamentally still, to what extent has the internal policing of the field allowed such reflex-ive questioning about the character of the field? To what extent have marginal voices been tolerated? Whatever the answers, the example is illustrative of my general position. If the story of this text is to be believable, it has to apply to the text itself. There are no no-go areas for this critique.

Critical being in higher education

We have identified two axes along which criticality can be distinguished: its domains are concerned with its purposes; its levels are concerned with its epistemological standing. In summary, the forms of criticality that we have distinguished are as follows:

Domains
Formal knowledge
The self
The world

Levels
Critical thinking skills
Metacritical capacities
Critical thinking
Critical thought
Metacritique
    Philosophical
    Sociological

The temptation immediately presents itself to place these two axes against each other (the three domains and the six levels of critical thinking), thereby suggesting that we have potentially eighteen forms of critical being that the university can develop. We would then have a schema of the kind shown in Table 5.2.

But does it make sense to place these two axes in juxtaposition? If we have come to give unduly high marks to formal knowledge, and if our conceptions of critical thinking have been built around those values, then critical being in relation to the self and to the world has been given short shrift. This, indeed, is my argument and that, for the future of this planet and human society, more attention needs to be paid in our universities to those latter two domains of critical being.

In short, the vertical axis – the levels of critical thinking – has evolved in relation to only one domain of criticality, that of formal knowledge. Placing the two axes against each other is, therefore, illegitimate. But it is *suggestive*. It suggests that, if we are to do justice to the three domains of critical thinking – in relation to the self and to the world as well as to formalized knowledge – then we might usefully consider that those two domains are

Table 5.2 Two beguiling axes of criticality

	Domains		
Levels	Knowledge	Self	World
1. Critical thinking skills			
2. Metacritical capacities			
3. Critical thinking			
4. Critical thought			
5. Philosophical metacritique			
6. Sociological metacritique			

Table 5.3 Levels of criticality in the domain of knowledge

	Domains		
Levels of criticality	Knowledge	Self	World
4. Transformatory critique	Knowledge critique (reframing of knowledge)		
3. Refashioning of traditions	Critical thought (malleable traditions of thought)		
2. Reflexivity	Critical thinking (reflection on one's understanding)		
1. Critical skills	Discipline-specific critical thinking skills		

also susceptible to treatment at different levels. We can monitor ourselves on different levels, and we can engage with the world on different levels. A schema of the levels of critical being of the kind shown in Table 5.3 suggests itself. The schema shows four levels of critical being and shows them worked out for the domain of knowledge based on our discussions.

Conclusion

Taking on board the notion of levels of criticality and working it out in the domain of knowledge is only the first step in construing and practising an adequate form of critical higher education. Unless we subject the other two domains – self and world – to examination, we shall reinforce the truncated sense of critical being that we have today in higher education. At best, we shall end up by producing graduates who are able to be critical sufficient to keep the corporate organization afloat. They have their critical antennae and their self-monitoring capacities working in the service of those instrumental goals.

We are in danger of seeing just such a new kind of higher education emerge. Superficially, it appears to be doing even more justice to the idea of critical thought. Criticality spreads across the table, as it were. But, I shall argue, these developments are in danger of being arrested at the lower levels of criticality. As a result, we are ending up with a higher education that falls short of its potential to assist the constructive reshaping of our world.

The working through of those levels of criticality in the domains of the self and the world will, therefore, be our major task in the next two chapters.

6

Critical Action

Expanding critique?

At the heart of my argument is the contention that criticality has been narrowly interpreted by the academic community, being seen as a desirable set of accomplishments in the domain of formal knowledge. Critical being has been understood as critical thinking as such. Critical being in the other two domains of the self and of the world has, until recently, been neglected; in so far as they have been given any attention, critical self-reflection and critical action have been accorded a marginal place in higher education.

That is changing. Mass higher education, being more intimately associated with the wider society, allows a range of additional perspectives into the academy. Courses are being redesigned to include both action and self-reflective components. The contexts by which critical thought gains a purchase are widened. The new worldly orientations bring into the curriculum value conflicts, ethical dilemmas, design challenges, environmental (in the fullest sense) concerns and priority judgements as well as practice as such. It could, therefore, be argued that mass higher education generates *more* critical thought; it does not undermine critical thought.

In this chapter, I shall argue to the contrary. Alternative frameworks of action and thought can be helpful in generating critical thought (Brookfield, 1987) but they are not a sufficient condition of it. They may, depending on their character, limit critical thought if the criticality in these additional domains is held at low levels of critical being. In this chapter, I shall pursue the argument in relation to critical action and, in the next chapter, in relation to critical self-reflection.

Changing frames of critical thought

Within higher education, critical thought is a modern concept. However, it can be seen in weaker forms in previous ages. It has reached its modern apogee as the self-consciousness of academic disciplines. Through critical thought, disciplines can continue to reinvent themselves. It is a vehicle for cognitive reproduction but within the disciplines. As knowledge becomes differentiated, so a knowledge economy develops. Winners and losers, profit and loss, these are the signs of cognitive growth and decay. Critical thought is a necessary condition for staying in the knowledge game. In this sense, critical thought is a necessarily modern concept, characteristic of the knowledge society and of the growth and differentiation of knowledge games within it.

Following distinctions made in the last chapter, we may take critical thought to be the cognitive style characteristic of propositional forms of knowing, while critical thinking we may take to be the legitimate mode of appropriating a form of knowing. The two are not necessarily to be found together. Undergraduate students are often denied exposure to the fundamental theoretical conflicts that drive a chasm through the research community in a discipline. Critical thought around the key conflicts of the discipline or even its purposes may not be felt to be appropriate to undergraduate study. Nevertheless, for the most part, at least the rhetoric of the academics teaching in the disciplines is that of developing critical thinking among their students.

The modern concept of critical thinking derives from its anchorage in the disciplines. On the surface, a differentiated concept of critical thinking has emerged. Critical thinking takes different forms across the disciplines, partly because of the different cognitive interests produced by the varying objects of the disciplines. Graphic design, physics, management studies and sociology take up contrasting stances towards their objects. Accordingly, their implicit notions of what it is to be critical also differ. The academic community has cloaked these local codes with a rhetoric of universality: context-independent talk of analysis, synthesis, evaluation, judgement, application and even 'the general powers of the mind' is invoked. It is admitted that there are differences in critical thinking across the disciplines which we expect from our students, but they are still exemplifications of a global allegiance across the academic community to a universal code of critical thought.

Nevertheless, the differences in critical standards are a sign of the collective strength of the academic community in imposing its standards of right thinking. The dominance of the disciplines and the emergence of critical thinking as a desirable educational aim are bound up together. The reflexivity of the taught is a reflection of the power of the academic community to impose its internal interests in the social reproduction of the academics in their separate disciplines.

With a mass higher education system, with changing relationships between the academy and society, the disciplines are losing their grip. The university now offers undergraduate programmes in hundreds of fields of study, ranging far beyond programmes built around disciplines and the elite professions. Midwifery, accountancy, estate management, media studies and timber technology are only indicative of the range. In this context, critical thinking becomes a problematic category for higher education. It is not merely that programmes often contain explicit action elements; it is not merely that those action elements are both specific *and* generic in character. It is rather that the new pragmatic orientation in higher education curricula tends to take for granted – to some extent – the presence of the object of their inquiries (that there is a health service; that there are companies with accounts to be audited; that there are estates to be managed; and that there are timbers on which technologies should be wrought). There is, therefore, a *non-critical* element contained in many of the newer studies.

It will be said that there is nothing new in this, that universities are now returning to their mediaeval inheritance when they were much more a training for a profession, albeit the elite professions of law, medicine and state administration. Having been dominated for the last one hundred years by academic interests, universities are finding that the interests of the wider society are now reasserting themselves and programmes of study are now (and properly so) containing a worldly aspect. There is truth in the charge, but it is a feeble truth, for it simply describes the world we are in and only at a superficial level. It begs the question as to whether the linkages between academe and the world of work are the same as those in the mediaeval university.

The newer forms of study are not merely operational but are instrumental in character. That is, they are designed to bring about technical effects on a taken-for-granted world (or slice of it). They are built around a technical interest in the world in which the world is objectified and externalized, and is understood to be a suitable vehicle for instrumental operations to be wrought upon it. The action that they encourage can be said to be critical, but its critical component is arrested at the instrumental level. It is a critical action that accepts the world largely as given and seeks to produce more effective operations within it. Transformations are entirely acceptable *providing* that they produce greater profitability, power and security.

The mediaeval curriculum might, in the professional schools, have contained an operational character, but it was not instrumental in the sense suggested here. Not only were the studies framed in the larger curriculum of the Trivium (grammar, logic and rhetoric) and the Quadrivium (arithmetic, astronomy, geometry and music), but the Trivium, 'as exploration of the word', took precedence over the Quadrivium, 'as the exploration of the world' (Bernstein, 1996: 83). 'The construction of the inner was the guarantee for the construction of the outer. In this we can find the origin of the professions' (p. 86). But we have been seeing the abandonment of the inner world, except that the inner world is now finding its way back in the form of an instrumental control of the self by the self (in other words, *self-control*). As a result, 'knowledge, after nearly a thousand years, is divorced from inwardness and literally dehumanised' (p. 87).

One of the features of mass higher education is that students often present with a technical interest of just that kind. They have already taken on the instrumental identities presupposed by their studies. Usually, therefore, there is a fit between students and lecturers. But sometimes there is a difference. Students may present with an interest in, say, 'taking' business studies, which they take to be a form of *study for business* and see themselves as 'consumers' of such a set of technical competences. But they just may find themselves in the company of an educator who takes business studies to be the *study of business*, who wishes to engage the students and to develop their inner identities, their selves, as persons. Both studies may be said to be critical, but both the domains and the levels of critical thought in the latter far exceed those of the former.

The newer forms of operational study should be distinguished from their antecedents. As engineering and architecture are joined by social work and computer science and then by business studies and tourism studies, the attendant sociology alters. Less held captive by dominant professional bodies, and less governed by a weight of academic tradition in the field concerned, the new offerings have an overtly pragmatic character and even a practical character. It is not that the older forms of vocational education were devoid of such elements; rather, it is that they were overlain by other elements. We have here a slide from vocations to vocationalism, from the demands of a durable calling to the operational challenges of contemporaneous concerns. In the process, clients and a tuistic relationship give way to customers and a non-tuistic relationship (Downie, 1990), in which the claims of the client as an other are not seriously acknowledged. It betokens a shift from being able to act in the world with understanding to mere operationalism, from what is right to what is effective and from action to technical accomplishment.

The counter-claim

It will be said that to talk of operationalism is to invent a straw man. Higher education cannot seriously be characterized in such terms, especially if the term is intended to imply a lack of understanding or reflection. Three counter-claims in particular can be put. First, the new forms of curricula are likely to encourage critical thinking *more* than traditional curricula. Secondly, the older forms of curricula were always stronger on the rhetoric of critical thinking than on its reality. Thirdly, the new curricula overlie the older curricula; they do not supplant them.

The three arguments can be taken together. They can all be conceded without dislodging my central claim. It may be the case that new forms of self-monitoring are being required, that the discipline-based forms of curricula always interpreted critical thinking in narrow terms, and that a mass higher education system allows for a range of approaches to critical thinking (nothing falls off the edge), while still being the case that our forms of critical thought are unduly limited and are inadequate to the challenges of the modern world. The counter-claims hit their target but with such puny force that they leave no mark. They are an inadequate response to the issue.

One reason that they are an inadequate response is that they are empirical in nature, whereas the argument here is essentially conceptual in character. They tell us or remind us of the way the world is or has been. They do not tell us what we ought to do. They are a useful reminder of the range of forms of thinking that is being or has been termed 'critical', but they offer no imaginary resources for conceptualizing critical thought in the modern world.

Again, it might be said that this point is overdrawn. Assume, for example, that among a list of personal transferable skills we find an entry 'critical thinking skills'. Such an entry would amount to an injunction to the higher education community to incorporate such a core skill in all curricula. This, then, would be a forward-looking proposal, implicitly expressing a dissatisfaction with the current state of affairs. 'Graduateness' should embrace a number of sets of skills, one of which would be critical thinking skills. There might even be a personal record or profile of each graduate, giving the external world (including employers) an indication of the level of the graduate's skills under this particular heading. The future, and a wish to change current practices, would be part of the deep structure of such a bald list of transferable skills. It is wrong, therefore, to suggest that the advocates of the contemporary changes do not have the future in their bones or are uninterested in trying to reconceptualize our current practices.

The first response here is that, even though the lists of transferable skills being promulgated are numerous, critical thinking rarely appears. (It does appear, but rarely.) There is an ambivalence towards critical thinking among the proponents of transferable skills; and understandably so, for there is a tension deeply embedded in the concepts of critical thinking and of skills, whether transferable or not. On the one hand, skills are bounded repertoires of techniques which allow for effective responses to limited situations. Even if we allow that the presenting situations may differ enormously (the doctor may be faced with an emergency on board an aircraft), still there is a boundedness about the techniques which are brought to bear. On the other hand, genuinely critical thought has an unbounded quality to it. But this spells uncertainty. It makes our knowing efforts and our social encounters unpredictable in substance and in form. It is hardly surprising, therefore, if critical thought engenders mixed feelings. It is both welcomed and mistrusted.

The more significant point about the contemporary interpretation of the concept of critical thinking is that it incorporates a means–end approach to knowing the world. The 'critical action' that goes with it is being encouraged as a means to the ends of greater economic competitiveness, of securing economic and social change, and of debunking traditional and taken-for-granted practices and assumptions. Yes, this critical action stands for a different order, a new world, a world of continuing change (even if it is ambivalent about the unpredictability that might then be unleashed). But this critical action, for all its apparent radicalism and iconoclasm, is severely limited. It takes for granted that the aforementioned goals of economic

competitiveness and organizational change are worthwhile goods. And it
also takes for granted that critical thought is an instrument for achieving
those goals.

The irony of this situation will be clear. Critical action, which possesses
emancipatory potential and promise, is confined to a mere underlabour-
ing role. Also, its potential for furthering dialogue and communication on
the one hand, and self-understanding and self-development on the other,
is shunted into the siding since, here, it is called upon to serve only the
demands of technical reason. Real open-ended conversation and exchange
is not on the cards; nor even self-enlightenment. Rather than ushering in
new forms of light and self-understanding, this critical action is being asked
to compound taken-for-grantedness, closure, and an acceptance of particular and narrow forms of self-understanding and social development.

Sharp operators

So where have we reached? How might we conceptualize critical thinking
in such a way that it begins seriously to inform decision-making and action,
with all their exigencies and challenges? Can action in the modern world
be *critical action*? Is there an inevitable tension here between critical action
intended to bring about an effect in the world and critical thinking which
has at least a tacit intention of enhancing our mutual understanding of the
world and our own selves? There need be no gap here. There are pressing
reasons for attempting to bring these forms of critical thinking into a rap-
prochement with each other.

Key concepts currently deployed in social theory are globalization, detraditionalization, risk and manufactured uncertainty (Beck, 1992; Giddens,
1994). These concepts speak to transformations not just of an economic
order but also of our social and, indeed, of our existential order. We live in
a world of change; that much has been apparent for some time. What is
new is the sense that change is systematic and pervasive on the one hand
and, while being the result of our own cognitive and technological inputs,
is unpredictable on the other. Change takes on the formal character of
chaos, reaching into the most intimate aspects of our lives, our selves and
our identities (Beck and Beck-Gernsheim, 1995).

Post facto, the changes may be describable according to understandable
mechanisms. But for those experiencing the events, they are often unpredictable in their effects. This is, as a result, an unstable world. Traditions
are called upon to give an account of themselves before being consigned
to history; actions in one part of the world have an impact on more distant parts of the world (such as our choice to purchase or not to purchase
a commodity made with certain rainforest timbers); and our knowledge
of the world enables us to make more informed decisions but, when acted
out on a societal or global scale, may have major social consequences (our
understanding of the social relations underpinning marriage and of the

likelihood of divorce is having a recursive impact on the family and marriage as social institutions).

This is the world into which graduates will go. As graduates, they will be expected to make informed decisions and to take action, based on a proper appreciation both of the contemporary context and of the likely impact of their decision-making. But, it is clear that there can no longer be any such informed decision-making. We are always going to be in the dark to some extent. Amidst globalization, we have to make decisions without being aware of the full context; there simply aren't the resources or the time to unravel it. And we have to engage in action without knowing fully the likely consequences. The university has built itself on a knowledge project; but the world we now experience is *radically unknowable* in many respects.

And yet we have to move on. Decisions have to be made; action has to be taken. Dialogical critical thinking may be helpful in bringing to bear the fullest range of intelligence on a topic and in clarifying the potential result of its deployment in different ways. But there will always be epistemological gaps between our understanding, however consensual and enlightened, and our actions, however sensitive to context they may be.

Talk of living in the real world may be tempting here. The scholarly mind, it may be said, can only carry us so far. In the end, and even in the beginning, we have to get real. We simply have to operate in the real world. There is something in this line of thought but it can be pressed too far. We do not have to stray into the murky waters of the relationship between theory and practice, or of distinctions between praxis and techne, or of concepts such as practical wisdom and tacit knowledge, helpful as all these distinctions might be. The immediate question is: what is to count as operating effectively? Or, even, what is to count as the real world? The sharp operators know instinctively what it is, or think that they do. In higher education, for instance, the new managerialism can see its own overt and, perhaps, even immediate effects. The institution is more efficient, is streamlined, is leaner (its non-core activities 'outsourced'), is downsized without diminishing its apparent impact, is more cost-effective, or is simply – glory of glories – within budget and likely to remain so in the foreseeable future. The sharp operators can see the results of their handiwork. They have seen the future and realized it in their university, and it works.

Game, set and match, therefore, to the sharp operators. But before conceding as much, we should beware of the alternative trap: that of rubbishing this new hold on academic life. Effective operation of universities may run against the grain for many, but that does not constitute an argument against it. The management of universities, which have become large corporations on any judgement (the largest in the UK having recurrent budgets of the order of £200 million per year), is not to be dismissed lightly. Large resources, many of which are derived from the public purse, are at stake. No-one wants another Cardiff, in which a major institution of higher education came close to bankruptcy (Shattock, 1994). But the question remains and, therefore, deserves repetition: what is to count as effective operation?

So far as higher educaton is concerned, the question can only be answered within a sense as to what is to count as a university. The temptation, in an age of mass higher education, of consumerism and markets, and of postmodernism, may be to say that effective operation is what works in practice. Pragmatism rules, OK. This, in the end, is the logic of the position of a philosopher like Rorty (1989): there being no ultimate undeniable principles or hold on the world that we can identify, we simply press on with life with whatever values we have. Life then becomes a matter of texts or stories that we create for ourselves, as best as we may. The university, and the education it offers, becomes what we make it.

This is not an incoherent position. But it is a position of diminished responsibility, in the sense of a narrowness of vision and understanding of the potential role of the university in human affairs. It allows for 'effective operation' to be defined purely instrumentally, as that which works, which balances the budget, which secures a high proportion of graduates entering the labour market possessing a wide 'portfolio' of transferable skills, and with the university being run at ever-higher levels of efficiency, its public profile being projected ever further. Sheer pragmatism invites a strategy of operationalism, of effectiveness and of instrumental reason. *This* critical action allows for pretty well anything at all that fulfils the underlying instrumental agendas (and so we see the signs of sharp practice in financial transactions, and in the franchising of degrees to overseas markets). The sharp operators have the field almost to themselves, partly because those occupying other positions are not themselves sharp operators, despising that stance towards the world and its associated modes of understanding and human interaction, and partly because those others have no articulated alternative position of their own. The sharp operators have fun at the expense of those who would seek an alternative vision of the university.

Critique-in-the-community

In the domain of knowledge, critique is being arrested at mundane levels of critical thinking skills. Higher levels of critical thinking, of a critical frame of mind, of a sense of the conventional character of each body of thought, and of the possibilities of critiquing the body of thought itself, are brought into play less; and the highest form of critical reason, in which intellectual fields are themselves placed in the dock, hardly ever at all. In higher education, some frameworks of thought are taken for granted.

At least the move to modular systems of course provision holds out the possibility that students will have their own frameworks of thinking disturbed by the contrasting perspectives that different disciplines can present to them. But in a credit-based system, the motivation for cross-disciplinary reflection will hardly be forthcoming: the rewards are for assimilating this module and for banking its associated credit. Let's get this module out of the way and go on to the next one. Why pause to work out their possible interconnections and even their contradictions?

Parallel forces at work can be found in the domain of the world. Action elements are increasingly coming into the higher education curriculum, even where they have formerly been absent. And those action elements can be said to contain components of criticality. But the interpretation of those critical components is usually limited to instrumental ends. Action for social and personal transformation is not typically envisaged.

The action elements have not just increased; they have widened. They are not just to be found in professional or industry-related courses and, even there, additional components of action are evident. Especially, but not only, in the wake of the Enterprise in Higher Education Initiative, these developments have been widespread. Disciplines such as archaeology and history have taken on board action, in which, for example, students might help to set up an exhibition in a local museum, assisting with the design of the publicity material as well as engaging in the more disciplinary-focused elements. Characteristically, such elements would involve the sizing up of a situation, engaging with and evaluating clients' needs, talking to 'the public' and assessing their interests and responses, and determining an appropriate set of strategies. All these could be said to be examples of critical action: they all involve the students in evaluation, in identifying alternative courses of action, in choosing a course of action, in carrying it through, in self-assessment and in taking responsibility for their action.

This is all to be welcomed. It brings a significant widening of criticality into higher education: domains of the world and of the self. But this is not the critique-in-action of the Tiananmen Square student. Fundamental social and personal transformation is not on the cards here. Situations are taken as given: the actions are worked out against a horizon of givens (of social and economic institutions, of customers and of profit, of products and their having effects). There are limits, therefore, to the new inclusion of critical action in the higher education curriculum.

Certainly, many of the new action-based curricular components are more complex than that and expose the students to higher levels of criticality in action where, for example, they are confronted with real-life dilemmas, whether in a clinical situation (as in law or social work) or in the commercial setting (through complex business scenarios). There are even examples to be found that approach or even reach the kind of exposure to transformatory possibilities that I am urging. There would be no substance to the present argument if there were no examples that could count as testimony to it. But my general argument remains: action elements often fail to fulfil their potential for developing students as critical persons.

By way of a knock-down example, consider study service. Brought into higher education over the past twenty years, it has developed apace despite its often marginal place in the curriculum. Characteristically, an enthusiast will fight to ensure that it wins a place in the undergraduate curriculum in an institution and the academics in their discipline-based courses will shrink at the prospect, declaring that their course is already overloaded and has to accommodate their own topic. Study service exposes students to the wider community, and calls upon the students to develop personal resources in applying their cognitive skills and their knowledge to community settings. The settings may be non-profit-making, the task may be fuzzy, and human engagement of the most demanding kind may be required. When brought off in ambitious ways, students may well be encouraged to reflect on their experiences, drawing upon a range of disciplinary perspectives.

At its best, therefore, study service approaches the kind of critical action being urged here. It stretches criticality across the three domains of knowledge, self and the world. It involves integration of those domains, within them and across them; the students are required to engage in a critical interdisciplinarity which hooks up with their own self-understanding and their construal of their actions in the world. And the action it calls for goes well beyond mere behavioural repertoires to reach higher levels of critical being, involving the handling, in action, of ethical dilemmas, of judgement and of multiple discourses.

But for the most part, so we might conjecture, the equivalent of the Tiananmen Square student is not envisaged even here. If the action is situated in an urban setting, or a commercial setting, to what extent are the presenting situations critically examined in terms of the power structures and ideologies that they reflect? Social institutions, practices and ideologies just might be examined critically, but to what extent would such critical explorations be reflected in action?

The students develop as persons, they have some insight into the human condition and they are enabled to develop their critical capacities in each of the domains of knowledge, self and the world. But this is 'study *service*' and not critique-in-action. The students supply a doubtless much-needed service to those that they encounter. Their education is all the wider for it, and the people that they encounter will benefit. But this service is liable to end up as an amelioration of the social conditions in which the students find themselves. For all its undoubted educational value, for all that it enables students to reach relatively high levels of critical action, still the highest levels of envisaging, and of working to bring about – in all its messiness – a radical transformation of the world they are in, is not expected; and it will not be forthcoming.

A critical disposition

But in the domain of the world, what might the educator hope to see emerge in her students? It is rather a stance towards the world, a critical stance. 'Stance' is a term used by Squires (1990) and it suggests an orientation towards the world on the part of the individual. It implies a sense of the world, but also of the possibility of standing apart from it and of taking up a view of it that is not given entirely by the world itself. The trouble with the idea of 'stance' here, however, is that it is too static – and in both directions. It can too easily convey the sense both of a static world and of a static orientation towards it. The world is given and the critical stance is given.

Instead, I suggest that educators look for in their students, in all the domains including that of action-in-the-world, a critical *disposition*. This term implies a much lighter-footed approach, an ability to size up the world in its different manifestations and the capacity to respond in different ways. What is secure is the willingness to evaluate the world, howsoever it appears. A disposition, after all, is deep-seated. It suggests that we are in the presence of a person of a certain kind. The critical spirit, therefore, involves persons fully; it involves and takes over their being. The critical spirit is not to be caught by talk of skills; by images of mere behavioural accomplishments, of techniques to get by with. Fundamentally, it is about the kinds of people, of persons, that we are trying in higher education to help to bring about.

On living in the real world

The acquisition of the critical spirit looks three ways. It looks to the world and it looks to the self, as well as looking to frameworks of analysis and comprehension by which the world and, indeed, the self may become increasingly intelligible. The critical spirit can only get a purchase that is adequate to the contemporary world when all three of these domains – world, self and knowledge – are present and come into a relationship with each other. There has to be an attempt on the part of students seriously to come to know the world, and to understand the self as a constituent of that world; there has to be a propensity to form an evaluation of both the world and of the self; and there has to be a willingness to engage in the world so as to effect changes that are not purely instrumental. When all three exemplifications of the critical spirit are together – thought, action and self – we are in the presence of critical persons.

This is why taunts of 'you are not living in the real world' are especially otiose when aimed at instances of the critical spirit at work. The critical spirit takes the real world seriously, really seriously. However, it does not kowtow to the real world. It does not take what counts as the real world as given. It stands apart from that givenness and tries to show, *in action*, that there are other ways of understanding and living in the world. Clearly, the real world will find this disposition unsettling; it does not relish what might be forthcoming. It does not know which of its frameworks of understanding or of action are going to be scrutinized and are going to be the subject of potential change as individuals realize themselves as critical beings.

The real world is sure of itself. It is sure that it is the real world. It may be happy to have its practices, technologies and hold on the world tweaked a bit, brought up to date; and it may even talk of transforming them. But it has too much invested in this world seriously to allow total transformation; and so its toleration of critical thinking and critical action will have definite limits. It will want to keep criticality within bounds, even though it knows that such discursive limitation is to deny the possibility of any critical thinking worth the name. And even though it knows deep down that we are now in a world of such fundamental, unstoppable and unpredictable change that radical critical thinking, and critical action, has become – paradoxically – instrumentally necessary. But the operationalists do have a point. Some traditionalists do appear to want to deny the real world. There is a strand of thinking within the university that refuses seriously to acknowledge that universities are institutions having to operate in the real world and that most graduates will want to earn a living in the real world.

Of course, the critical spirit will wish to challenge the notion of the real world, and rightly so. The critical spirit will want to offer and even to supplant received notions of the real world with alternative conceptions. That is part of the essence of a proper higher learning. It is in that way that the university acts out its responsibility. This is a continuing responsibility which only deepens with the passage of time, since received notions of the real world are urged ever more powerfully and the university puts itself in danger of uncritically falling in with those definitions.

However, there are three problems with this position. First, it betokens a parasitic relationship with the wider society. It amounts to: support me so that I can critique you. I have no responsibility other than that. This is not a dishonourable position for would-be intellectuals, as Julian Benda (Stryker, 1996) made plain. But it is a limited view of critique: it shrinks from assisting in reconstructing the world that it critiques. Further, it all too easily becomes froth without substance. Secondly, not being overly concerned with the pragmatic challenges of living with the operationalism of the world, it renders students vulnerable precisely to that very world that it would critique. Thirdly, and picking up the schema I am proposing, this position neglects the challenges of acting critically in the world to positive effect, with the further consequence that the potential for personal self-criticism and personal self-development are, thereby, thwarted. This critical spirit prides itself on its purity and on its being thoroughly educational, but ends up consigning students to becoming flotsam amid the challenges of the real world that they will face.

Conclusion

Just as we can identify different levels of critical thought (Chapter 5), so too can we identify different levels of critical being in the domain of the world. In essence, in our discussion, four levels of critical action have been distinguished (to set against the levels of criticality we identified in Chapter 5) (See Table 6.1).

Table 6.1 Levels of criticality in the domain of the world

Levels of criticality	Domain of the world
4. Transformatory critique	Critique-in-action (collective reconstruction)
3. Refashioning of traditions	Mutual understanding and development of traditions
2. Reflexivity	Reflective practice ('adaptability'; 'flexibility')
1. Critical skills	Problem-solving (means–end instrumentalism)

Students are increasingly being encouraged to incorporate action components in their programmes of study and those components can usually be said to contain elements of criticality. But the tendency is for those developments to be held at the lower instrumental levels of critical being in this domain. It is clear that operationalism cannot be allowed totally to frame our definitions of critical action. If critical action is to achieve its full potential of encouraging the student to come forward with imaginary and emancipatory possibilities, it must reach out to the received definitions of the world and engage with them. But in engaging critically and constructively with the world, it has to maintain some critical distance from the world. The new operationalism cannot be permitted to frame the limits of critique-in-action. Imaginative reconstruction for emancipatory ends calls for a higher education that is critical of the so-called standards that the new operationalism would impose.

Critical action has to be added to critical thought. But we have so far left out the student as an individual with her own self. The construction of a critical self is, therefore, the subject of the next chapter.

7

Critical Self-reflection

Introduction

Reflection is increasingly being called upon in rationales for higher education. Is it a synonym for critical thinking, or is the term doing some extra work? I shall argue that the idea of reflection carries important connotations which can help us fill out our concept of criticality in higher education. In terms of the schema for which I am arguing, reflection is to be found in all three forms of critical being – critical thought, critical action and critical self-reflection – but comes into its own in the third of these. Through critical self-reflection, students develop their *selves*. The self is not just or even mainly an intellectual self, but is a much more encompassing hold on life. Critical self-reflection is a necessary, although not sufficient, condition of critical being.

Two fundamental questions arise: What is to count as critical self-reflection? And to what extent is it legitimate to incorporate such a notion into our modern conception of higher education? The modern era of higher education can be understood as a phase of epistemological hegemony in which the academic class has imposed its own limited notions of critical thinking on the university, notions that for the most part have extinguished the sense of personal formation that characterized nineteenth-century English higher education. Only now are we seeing a resuscitation of the personal dimension (captured, for example, in the notion of *personal* transferable skills). But how is the dimension of the personal to be justified in our contemporary conception of higher education? And what might it entail?

Before getting started on that essentially philosophical task, however, we can note something of the sociological background. The contemporary interest in reflection is not happenchance. It is explicable as an educational response to the reflexivity that late modernity is calling for and, indeed, which is characteristic of late modernity. The immediacy with which events in one part of the globe can have an impact on quite distant parts, the loss of the authority of traditions, and the generation of risk through human knowledge and technologies: these phenomena generate a questioning of fundamental categories of knowing and action. This questioning is radically reflexive: one's own categories and assumptions inevitably fall under the microscope – *one's own microscope.* This reflexivity is not purely reactive, however. It has a major formative function, since it provides the potential for new orderings, new insights and new sources of action and knowledge. In critiquing one's present understandings, new understandings can emerge.

The appearance, therefore, of the idea of reflection in educational discourse can be seen as a means of embodying and furthering this social reflexivity. This reflection on reflection, however, cuts two ways. On the one hand, it alerts us to the point that reflexivity is a necessary condition of personal survival in late modernity. A higher education designed to further reflexivity becomes, therefore, critical to that project of personal survival. On the other hand, this reflexivity speaks to the external world. It provides society with resources for coping with a world characterized by radical uncertainty and, thereby, for social survival.

Criticism and reflection

In higher education, criticism is giving way to reflection; we hear less of the one and more of the other. The emergence of reflection is, I have suggested, readily explicable in terms of the self-monitoring and self-reflexive qualities apparently demanded by the modern world. 'Flexibility', 'adaptability', self-education through the lifespan: these meta-qualities point to the capacity on the part of individuals to be ready to jettison their taken-for-granted world and take on another. This postmodernity is one of temporary personae, in which individuals are charged with the responsibility of continually reproducing themselves so as to be effective in, and so as to contribute to, a world of unforeseeable change. To adapt effectively to – and even to bring about – a world of unknowable change requires self-referential capacities of a high order on the part of individuals. What knowledge of the world there is has to be taken on board so as to inform the self about the self, disturbing and challenging as that may be. 'Reflection' thus becomes an educational codeword for this set of reflexive and self-monitoring challenges.

'Reflection' thus points to the ability to move oneself forward. There is at work, however, an instrumental agenda. One is being asked to move oneself forward by oneself but not *for* oneself. Goals of economic competitiveness, of organizational efficiency and of institutional responsiveness come to the fore. What appears on the surface to be an agenda about the fulfilment of the individual's life-world, about empowerment and even about emancipation, is being driven by an agenda of instrumental reason. The internal 'life' reproduces the external life.

In taking on the vocabulary of reflection, higher education is liable to be sucked into this agenda of economic reason. Worse still, it will convince itself that all is right, that its own deep agendas of personal development, enlightenment, empowerment and emancipation are being fulfilled. Without continuing vigilance, reflection will take on the form of an ideology in higher education, a social project masking its real intent; a wolf in sheep's clothing if ever there was one.

Adding value?

As higher education becomes incorporated ever more into the projects of the state, in particular the requirement that it orient itself sharply to the world of work and economic competitiveness, criticial thought is not vanquished but it changes. What is called for is a capacity that can size up a pragmatic situation, can suss out conventional practices, and can sense where the main chance lies. This is a worldly form of critical thought, oriented to the world and towards changing it.

This situation amounts to nothing less than an assault on the traditions of the Western university; and not before time, so some will say. We cannot live on propositions alone, nor even their critique. If we are to survive in the world, both as persons and collectively in society, critique has to turn both outwards to the world and inwards to ourselves. If higher education is to offer knowledge services for the modern age, if it is to be meaningful in that sense, these wider senses of critique had better be taken on board. And so it has come to be. But in the process, a double jeopardy results. First, conventional knowledge is shorn of its critical element and is reduced to the garnering by the undergraduate of mere information. Secondly, as we have just observed, the newer forms of critique are confined to fulfilling mere instrumental agendas. In keeping with Jurgen Habermas, we can accept that instrumental agendas are not to be faulted in themselves. We do have to live, survive and prosper in the real world, and academics forget that too often. But instrumentalism can never be enough, even for the modern world of instrumental action.

This point has two sub-plots. First, the self-referential and critical abilities that the modern world is calling for require an open-endedness that transcends instrumentalism. Reflexivity and critique cannot, at peradventure of their undermining, accept constraints. They rely on open dialogue (reflexivity relying on an open *internal* dialogue) in which no point of view is ruled out of court, *a priori*. Instrumentalism takes the world largely as given and attempts to find means of living ever more productively and efficiently in it. The ends have to be taken on trust; a radical critique of them might bring paralysis when what is on the agenda is the task of getting on and prospering, within given values. Secondly, instrumentalism works within a horizon of ontological assumptions. The world is objectified: the task is that of securing effects in it and on it. Objects, events, situations, technologies, knowledges and persons are valued so long as they have a use value. Higher education is valued for the relevant added-value wrought in students.

Weak reflections

We can here return to the two axes of critical being, of domain and of level. The three domains (knowledge, the self and the world) can each be critiqued at different levels. Because the academic world has focused its energies on knowledge, critical thinking has been delineated most fully in that domain. Critical thinking skills, critical thinking, critical thought and metacritique are understood as cognitive operations wrought on cognitive texts. But parallel modes of critical reason can be delineated for the other two domains of the self and of the world.

There is a tendency for critical being to be confined to operational and instrumental forms *in all three domains*. Critical being as a form of skills, understood as operating with positive effect on presenting situations (in all three domains), is prized. Critical being as processes of reaching profoundly new understandings is mistrusted (whether in thought, in action or in one's self-understanding): one can have too much of a good thing. Such a conception of critical being might, after all, bring in its wake emancipation and empowerment. This critical being will hardly be in the interests of any party. Not only will it be anathema to the operationalists, by definition, but it will also be otiose to the academics and to the students. It would spell a diminution in the power and control of the academics, and it would presage the challenge of authenticity and self-realization for the students. All parties, therefore, are in league together to prevent radical forms and processes of critique getting a foothold.

As critical being in higher education widens to embrace the domain of the self (CT2), these new curricular components tend to be skill-oriented. In the promotion of self-reflection we see, for example, exercises such as the keeping of logs or diaries which are reduced to sets of skills (such as the recording of critical incidents). As the exercise becomes a summing or recapitulation of events, memory traces and responses, an agenda of surveillance and control is not far away. The use of a reflective text as a means of generating *new* meanings, totally new interpretations, and thus a means of creating a totally new self, is eschewed. These are weak forms of self-reflection.

It might be tempting to claim that, as higher education embraces wider tasks of acting in the world and of promoting self-reflexivity, so instrumentality overruns an otherwise emancipatory conception of critical thinking for which the university would stand. But that claim should not be accepted. Despite its protestations, the university remains an independent player in this creeping instrumentality. What we can say in the academy's defence is that it is being encouraged along the path of instrumentalism by the big battalions in the wider society. If critical thinking skills are attractive to the wider society, then the academy will readily fall in with this demand. It can satisfy its conscience that it is fulfilling its historic mission and deliver the goods now required by the paymaster. Unfortunately, in so doing, it becomes the dupe of an instrumentalism that it would normally hesitate to countenance. The banner of critical thinking flies over the university but, in reality, the university has been delivered uncritically to uncritical forces.

The student widens

So far, we have reached the position that the idea of reflection draws its power from being construed as reflection-on-self but is being held at limited levels of criticality. Fulfilling its potential, reflection is self-reflection; it is a form of critical thinking about self (CT2).

Reflection works in all three domains of critical thought and is, therefore, a polymorphic concept. But its use in the two domains of knowledge (CT1) and the world (CT3) is hardly distinguishable from critical thinking as such; if it is, it is the weaker concept. It contains resonances of a particular kind of mind at work: the reflective mind is rightly prized in higher education and is to be worked for. But it falls short of critical thinking as such in those two domains. Reflection indicates that we are in the presence of a mind that does not take for granted what appears as real but which wants to go beneath the surface to arrive at a deeper understanding. Critical thinking in these two domains (of world and knowledge), however, looks to go further, to evaluate, to analyse, and to produce an alternative – and, by implication, a better – construction.

In the domain of the self, reflection comes into its own. The very act of reflection-on-self is a claim for autonomy, for personhood and for self-actualization. Reflection does not exhaust critical thought, even in this domain. 'Critical self-reflection' is a legitimate construction and can be heard among academics as a description of the qualities they are hoping to develop in their students. The term 'critical' indicates that the self-reflection is accompanied by a range of alternatives. The student interrogates her own thinking or her actions, recognizing that other thoughts or actions might be even more worthwhile. In the process, new thinking and new acts may emerge. The self-reflection is accompanied by self-criticism.

There are, admittedly, problems with the idea of self-reflection in higher education. The British and especially the English view of higher education has been singular in its sense that higher education involves the development of students as persons. The nineteenth and early twentieth century idea of improving the student's 'character' has given way to a more subtle sense of the student as a person in the making. The notions of 'the student experience' and even of transferable skills bear traces of the more than cognitive development that higher education is expected to impart. But, even so, higher education is only one institution in society. It could not seriously be claimed that it had a responsibility towards every worthwhile facet of a student's personhood (Reeves, 1988). Talk of self-reflection, therefore, has to be qualified.

Characteristically, it is the knowing self that matters in higher education. However, what counts as the knowing self is currently being dramatically widened as more experiential, action-oriented and situationally specific forms of knowing are coming to be prized. Problem-solving, knowing-how and even personal knowledge are coming increasingly into the lexicon of higher education. The result is that, even if the idea of self-reflection is limited to the knowing self, that self is now very wide indeed. Students are increasingly being invited or are even required to develop a repertoire of communication skills, to handle situations with clients as embryonic professionals, to cope with value conflicts, to engage cooperatively with other students on projects, and to experience social and civic responsibilities within study service.

The self within higher education, therefore, is widening. The meaning of 'student', accordingly, also widens as, even in relation to knowing activities, the self is widened. More of the student as person is included under the construction of student-as-knower. Higher education offers less of a hiding place: more of the student, even as knower, is yielded up for development, surveillance and assessment. The scope of self-reflection is widening as a result, or ought so to do.

Unless self-reflection is present and is adequate to this widening of the self within higher education, higher education will take the form of pure social control. Sociologically, higher education is expanding its function as a means of social production. The self is constructed in higher education and in ever-widening fashion. Only through an accompanying widening of self-reflection can the spectre of higher education as a form of social manipulation, of the technical manufacture of personhood, be avoided.

As the curriculum takes on more action-oriented components, the self is situated and constructed in the world, through the curriculum. Correspondingly, as mode 1 knowledge (of the world) is joined by mode 2 knowledge (in the world), the student's self is also widened and created through ever wider forms of knowing. If the student's self is being pulled in new ways, operationally in the world and epistemologically through a wider range of knowing activities, self-reflection becomes not just a curious effete add-on, marginal to the main enterprise. It becomes a crucial component in stabilizing the educational, personal and cognitive disturbances that the student faces. Self-reflection takes on a central role in an education for the modern age.

Eight forms of self-reflection

There is no abstract self on which to reflect. In higher education, two domains of criticality – of knowledge and of action – are especially available for reflection. Both knowledge and action have public aspects. There are, in addition, more private aspects of the self on which to reflect, even in higher education. We can distinguish eight forms of reflection.

1. *Self-reflection on the student's own disciplinary competence.* This self-reflection takes its form from the norms of the disciplines. The conversation of the discipline becomes an inner dialogue of the individual student. The

rules and the voices of the intellectual field are internalized. The student embarks on a continuing interrogation and critique of her own understandings.

Where this self-reflection is significant, higher education is an initiation into a discipline. Purity of perspective is important. Self-reflection, therefore, is a means of forming a disciplinary person who comes to see the world through a particular set of cognitive spectacles. Its dominant position in higher education, even if waning, is indicative of the extent to which the academic corps hijacked the Western university to its own ends over the last one hundred years.

2. *Educational reflection.* Educational reflection is picked up in such terms as liberal education, *Bildung*, general education and even interdisciplinarity. It is also implicit in the idea of academic community, for that notion rests on there being general ideas of education, communication and human development which transcend the disciplinary differences. This self-reflection ushers in self-control, breadth and tolerance of perspective, mutuality of understanding and an appreciation of the limited character of one's own vantage point.

The encouragement of this form of reflection in higher education would be evident in efforts to promote cross-disciplinary educational aims. A concern for truth, a precision in communication, a scrupulousness in analysis, a willingness to search for synoptic overviews, a determination always to go on searching deeper and a disinclination to be satisfied with a particular understanding, and a preparedness to step outside one's immediate viewpoint to see things from another perspective: these are dispositions of a non-specific character. Reflective powers of this kind beg all sorts of questions: do they exist or are they, in the end, only to be filled out in discipline-specific ways? Could there be, in modern higher education, a genuinely cross-disciplinary effort to bring them off?

Doubts over the basis for self-reflective powers of this educational kind must be recognized. But such powers should not lightly be set aside. They are not just cognitive in character but offer the prospect of the development of persons. The dispositions, and qualities of tolerance to which they point, are not even simply constitutive of what it is to be a rational person. They betoken wider human virtues of wisdom, of vigilance, and even of empathy. Liberal education and *Bildung* are umbrella terms for just such personal forms of development. Reflection here carries cultural connotations too, since it looks to the formation of at least a stratum of society that understands itself as embodying these human qualities, essentially of a reasonableness deployed with generosity. Yes, reason is valued, but it is not the only value in this form of reflection.

3. *Critical reflection.* Here, the sense of reflection is caught by terms such as emancipation, transformation and liberation. A theoretical underpinning

is offered by Critical Theory. Through self-reflection, we can free ourselves from ideological delusion. Or, at least, we can start the process. The full process points to social action, to the removal of the deformations of the surrounding distorted discourse which had produced that ideological contamination.

With this sense of self-reflection, higher education becomes a process of stimulating a self-learning, leading to a new way of perceiving oneself. This is challenging to the educator, since ideology – against which this aim contends – generates resistance. Students are unlikely to buy into this form of self-reflection. It will be too painful, bringing with it the challenge to divest old conceptions of the self, of the world, and of the self in relation to the world. Students will resist the personal responsibilities and rediscovery that such a transformatory reflectiveness requires. Educators have, therefore, to address students' self-concepts if this idea of self-reflection is to take off.

4. *Reflection as metacompetence.* As higher education becomes drawn into the state's projects, so it is asked to respond to instrumental agendas marked out by such terms as competence, skills and value-added. In a sense, this role amounts to an abandonment of reflection. Sheer technique, getting things done and with increasing efficiency, is what matters. Even the idea of understanding is downplayed.

Yet there is a sense of reflection at work here. Transferable skills, for example, look to a metacapacity to size things up and to identify units from one's repertoire of skills which will serve in the new situation. This metacompetence, this ability to read situations and call forth appropriate competences, is fundamentally a self-reflective power, and it is implicated in terms such as adaptability and flexibility. There is a contradiction at work. Understanding is marginalized on the competence model, but the notion of transferability relies on understanding. One cannot size up a situation, and determine appropriate competences, without understanding. This operationalism would deny reflection but reflection is implicated in it, even if, as a form of instrumental self-monitoring, it is a stunted form of self-reflection.

5. *The reflective practitioner.* In this conception, self-reflection is seen as residing in the concrete practices of professional life. Indeed, it is constitutive of professionalism, as Schön's (1987) notion of reflection-in-action indicates: a continual interrogation and imaginative reconstruction of one's actions as they are unfolding. The self-reflection takes place in action. What appears as behaviour is, in reality, the residue of discarded possibilities for professional action. The professional world is a multiple world, full of alternative possibilities of strategy, action and communication. It is reflection-in-action that brings order into this potential chaos and determines the course of action.

Self-reflection here has a double aspect. It calls forth a chosen action from the myriad of identified possibilities (now evaluated and discarded by the professional self) and it puts that choice into effect. The two moments – of evaluation and execution – appear indistinguishable, but they are formally separable and constitute important components of professional action. Neither is sufficient without the other. To go beyond Schön, this is reflection-*for*-action.

6. *Reflection as self-realization.* This reflection is individualistic in character. It has affinities with critical reflection (3) and the reflective practitioner (5), being oriented towards the self in the world, but it is unconcerned with theoretically based self-enlightenment and is not boxed in by paradigms of appropriate action in the context of a client–professional relationship. What matters here are the individual's own projects, in and for herself.

On this account of reflection, our educational practices will begin from personal experience, will celebrate it and will encourage a self-belief in it. We become ourselves by becoming more aware of our own projects, and being secure about ourselves as pursuers of those projects. We define ourselves through our personal projects. More than that, projects hitherto classified as attempts to understand the world are re-constituted as projects of self-discovery. Action research and qualitative research in the social sciences sometimes take on this form.

Mature students in particular live out this form of self-reflection. For them, higher education is often a vehicle for realizing their own projects in which they wish to develop as persons. Higher education becomes a form of personal action research in which the student's hopes and ideas are tested. Self-reflection, understanding and action are integrated.

7. *Reflection as social formation.* Here it is recognized that the reflective self alone cannot bring about self-realization but has to draw on others. Not far away are considerations of the life-world: sedimented traditions which are available for critical reflection and reinterpretation, but which offer the basis for social growth. Traditions are essentially local in character and are kept alive through reflection. Such communitarianism is a debating society sense of reflection. It assumes that all members of the group understand the particular rules of its debates, can communicate with each other through those communal rules and are prepared to play by those rules.

There are clear links here with disciplinary reflection (1), for disciplines are local communities with their own rules. But to come into its own, this reflection would anchor in communication as such. Study service, action in the community and peer tutoring could be said to engender this form of self-reflection, because the students are required to divest themselves to a large extent of their academic personae and go openly into the language and perspectives of those that they encounter in the community. This is no pure cognitive exercise, invest themselves in these activities and so deve ing accepted in communities. This is an imm ing for self-reflective powers of a demanding that springs out of the inner disturbance th tions can bring.

8. *Societal reflection.* This sense of self-reflection is rec starting point that the world is susceptible to purposive interve Problems are set by and within the world and their solutions are to be found in the world. It is recognized that problems are specific to situations and that particular sets of skills are needed appropriate to those situations. Policy studies in its most general form comes increasingly to form the core of some subjects, such as tourism, transport, management and accountancy. What is at issue here is the development of strategic thinking oriented to a class of identified problems. But it is also considered that more general kinds of reflective capacity can be identified in the world. Specific and transferable skills, although they are normally put against each other, here stand together. They are both redolent of an attempt to drive higher education towards reflective capacities oriented towards control in and on the world. A pragmatic epistemology is at work. The test of truth here is: does it work?

Note that even transferable skills, despite their apparent generality, are specific in the following way: they objectify the world such that it becomes a stage on which human skills can be wrought. Even intellectual skills, such as problem-solving, can all too easily embody this assumption. Problems are assumed to have solutions, and higher education becomes a vehicle for developing this form of reflection. The self introjects the stated demands of the world and, here, critical self-reflection becomes a mere self-monitoring for pragmatic value-added.

Missed opportunities

Self-reflection comes in different forms, and higher education takes on many of them. That higher education takes on some forms rather than or in greater measure than others is crucial. Behind the eight forms of self-reflection just sketched out lies a hinterland of late modernity. But our eight forms do not find equal favour.

We can place the eight forms of reflection against the three domains of criticality in the way shown in Table 7.1. There are a number of points to make about Table 7.1. First, students are being encouraged to be self-critical but the dominant modes of reflection are those in the domain of the world. Metacompetence, reflective practice and active problem-solving: these are the favoured forms of self-reflection; in effect, a self-monitoring of one's performance in the 'real world'.

Eight forms of reflection in the three domains of critical being

wledge	_Self_	_World_
Disciplinary	2. Educational	4. Metacompetence
	3. Critical reflection	5. Reflective practitioner
	6. Self-realization	7. Social formation
		8. Societal reflection

Secondly, self-reflection on the student's more personal self – her own projects and the way she situates herself in the world – is largely neglected. The dynamic of this situation is that the position is worsening. A generation ago, when the process of higher education was more relaxed, there was space for the student to be able to take a wider view and to see higher education as an opportunity for personal development. Now, that path tends to be restricted to mature students.

Thirdly, the instrumental forms of self-reflection oriented towards the world do not just marginalize the more personal forms, oriented towards the individual's own hopes and sense of self. They bring about a restructuring of the student's self. The student's inner self is constructed more by external agendas – largely of the world of work – than by the student's own personal aspirations, values and hold on the world. We are in danger of moving, in higher education, into a valueless world, in that it is devoid of the student's own personal values.

Lastly (and to pick up our other axis of criticality), the levels of self-reflection that are being encouraged engender relatively low levels of criticality. Self-monitoring to given standards and norms is supplemented by reflective practice within local frameworks of action. Less in evidence is the development of the student's self through engaging with a range of cultural settings, while there is no sign at all of a deliberate attempt to foster a critical self-reflection leading to personal reconstruction.

In short, higher education – in taking on self-reflection as a key theme – has taken on a large idea but is giving it short shrift. Significant connotations of the term are underplayed or even neglected. As a result, the curriculum lacks its full self-reflective power. This is a set of missed opportunities.

Conclusion

Just as with critical thought and critical action, critical self-reflection turns out to be susceptible to different levels of approach. The key distinctions are summarized in Table 7.2. Just as with critical thought (CT1) and critical action (CT3), the interpretation given to critical self-reflection (CT2) is held at relatively superficial levels. Self-monitoring for ego maintenance and for instrumental ends are the order of the day. The self sorts itself out: the appearance of autonomy is safeguarded. But the fulfilment of extramural agendas dictates the formation of a self only at low levels of self-reflection.

community. This is no pure cognitive exercise, for the students have to invest themselves in these activities and so develop themselves by becoming accepted in communities. This is an immersion in community calling for self-reflective powers of a demanding kind. It is a self-reflection that springs out of the inner disturbance that unfamiliar social interactions can bring.

8. *Societal reflection*. This sense of self-reflection is recent. It takes as its starting point that the world is susceptible to purposive interventions. Problems are set by and within the world and their solutions are to be found in the world. It is recognized that problems are specific to situations and that particular sets of skills are needed appropriate to those situations. Policy studies in its most general form comes increasingly to form the core of some subjects, such as tourism, transport, management and accountancy. What is at issue here is the development of strategic thinking oriented to a class of identified problems. But it is also considered that more general kinds of reflective capacity can be identified in the world. Specific and transferable skills, although they are normally put against each other, here stand together. They are both redolent of an attempt to drive higher education towards reflective capacities oriented towards control in and on the world. A pragmatic epistemology is at work. The test of truth here is: does it work?

Note that even transferable skills, despite their apparent generality, are specific in the following way: they objectify the world such that it becomes a stage on which human skills can be wrought. Even intellectual skills, such as problem-solving, can all too easily embody this assumption. Problems are assumed to have solutions, and higher education becomes a vehicle for developing this form of reflection. The self introjects the stated demands of the world and, here, critical self-reflection becomes a mere self-monitoring for pragmatic value-added.

Missed opportunities

Self-reflection comes in different forms, and higher education takes on many of them. That higher education takes on some forms rather than or in greater measure than others is crucial. Behind the eight forms of self-reflection just sketched out lies a hinterland of late modernity. But our eight forms do not find equal favour.

We can place the eight forms of reflection against the three domains of criticality in the way shown in Table 7.1. There are a number of points to make about Table 7.1. First, students are being encouraged to be self-critical but the dominant modes of reflection are those in the domain of the world. Metacompetence, reflective practice and active problem-solving: these are the favoured forms of self-reflection; in effect, a self-monitoring of one's performance in the 'real world'.

Table 7.1 Eight forms of reflection in the three domains of critical being

Knowledge	Self	World
1. Disciplinary	2. Educational 3. Critical reflection 6. Self-realization	4. Metacompetence 5. Reflective practitioner 7. Social formation 8. Societal reflection

Secondly, self-reflection on the student's more personal self – her own projects and the way she situates herself in the world – is largely neglected. The dynamic of this situation is that the position is worsening. A generation ago, when the process of higher education was more relaxed, there was space for the student to be able to take a wider view and to see higher education as an opportunity for personal development. Now, that path tends to be restricted to mature students.

Thirdly, the instrumental forms of self-reflection oriented towards the world do not just marginalize the more personal forms, oriented towards the individual's own hopes and sense of self. They bring about a restructuring of the student's self. The student's inner self is constructed more by external agendas – largely of the world of work – than by the student's own personal aspirations, values and hold on the world. We are in danger of moving, in higher education, into a valueless world, in that it is devoid of the student's own personal values.

Lastly (and to pick up our other axis of criticality), the levels of self-reflection that are being encouraged engender relatively low levels of criticality. Self-monitoring to given standards and norms is supplemented by reflective practice within local frameworks of action. Less in evidence is the development of the student's self through engaging with a range of cultural settings, while there is no sign at all of a deliberate attempt to foster a critical self-reflection leading to personal reconstruction.

In short, higher education – in taking on self-reflection as a key theme – has taken on a large idea but is giving it short shrift. Significant connotations of the term are underplayed or even neglected. As a result, the curriculum lacks its full self-reflective power. This is a set of missed opportunities.

Conclusion

Just as with critical thought and critical action, critical self-reflection turns out to be susceptible to different levels of approach. The key distinctions are summarized in Table 7.2. Just as with critical thought (CT1) and critical action (CT3), the interpretation given to critical self-reflection (CT2) is held at relatively superficial levels. Self-monitoring for ego maintenance and for instrumental ends are the order of the day. The self sorts itself out: the appearance of autonomy is safeguarded. But the fulfilment of extramural agendas dictates the formation of a self only at low levels of self-reflection.

Table 7.2   Levels of criticality in the domain of self

Levels of criticality	Domain of self
4. Transformatory critique	Reconstruction of self
3. Refashioning of traditions	Development of self within traditions
2. Reflexivity	Self-reflection (reflection on one's own projects)
1. Critical skills	Self-monitoring to given standards and norms

Higher levels of self-reflection, implied by notions of *Bildung* and even liberal education, let alone emancipation and self-empowerment, are not seriously on this agenda. Students on professional and industrial place-ments are asked to keep a log of their activities and are even invited to offer rational reconstructions of their chosen repertoire of actions; but all this is in fulfilment of given – and non-criticizable – external agendas of the cor-poration or even (as in teacher education) of the state. Self-censorship and self-surveillance is the logic of this game.

Certainly, some of the forms of self-reflection that we have identified go beyond this limited agenda. Students in study service and in the better forms of professional education are exposed to a wide range of situations in which they are bound to develop as reflective persons. But, even there, the strategies that students adopt tend to be coping strategies: the disturb-ance to the ego is minimized, and the self is stabilized. These self-reflective powers are worthwhile but they fall well short of enabling the self to go on reshaping itself through the lifespan. And less still do the contemporary conceptions of self-reflection aim at enabling students to embark on an emancipatory self-construction, in which the self comes into possession of itself, assured of itself and able to take on the world. And yet that is what the modern world requires of higher education: to provide the basis of an emancipatory process in which students, by means of their own powers of self-reflection through their lifespan, come increasingly into themselves, maintaining their critical distance from the world around them while acting purposively in it.

Reflection, then, is on the agenda of higher education in expanded form. But the permitted forms of self-reflection are arrested at superficial levels. The self is revealed and exposed and is asked to take on given external agendas. It can hardly be termed *critical* self-reflection. This self-reflection rates only one cheer.

8

A Curriculum for
Critical Being

Only connect

My argument is that criticality can be distinguished through two axes: first, its levels, ranging from narrow operational skills to transformatory critique, and second, its scope, consisting of the three domains of formal knowledge, the self and the world. Drawing together our analyses in the past three chapters, in summary they take the form shown in Table 8.1.

Against this background, a curriculum for critical being presents itself immediately. It has to be one that exposes students to criticality in the three domains and at the highest level in each. Our task in this chapter, therefore, is clear: to examine in broadbrush terms what it would mean in a mass higher education system to construct a curriculum that gives full rein to criticality at all its levels and in its three domains. But, while necessary, that task cannot be sufficient to sustain a higher education in the modern world. For that task would amount to an identification and a bringing together of elements. Still in front of us would be the task of supplying some means of holding the elements together, conceptually and practically.

Unless we can supply an account of how these different critical tasks can be held together, the danger looms that we might produce students who are adept at critically evaluating, say, literary texts or other works of humanistic culture in one way, but who adopt quite different powers of critical evaluation in relation to the world. This is the nightmare with which Steiner (1984) presents us: a world in which the Nazis might appreciate Schubert or Picasso and then turn to their critique of the Jewish community in the Final Solution.

Such a schizophrenic realization of critical powers has to be avoided by the Western university. Yet just that prospect beckons as we see it: on the one hand, widening its application of critical thinking to embrace domains other than the world of formal knowledge but, on the other, tending to confine that development to operational demonstrations. A new kind of final solution cannot be ruled out, even if it seems a remote prospect (Bauman,

Table 8.1 Levels, domains and forms of critical being

Levels of criticality	Domains		
	Knowledge	*Self*	*World*
4. Transformatory critique	Knowledge critique	Reconstruction of self	Critique-in-action (collective reconstruction of world)
3. Refashioning of traditions	Critical thought (malleable traditions of thought)	Development of self within traditions	Mutual understanding and development of traditions
2. Reflexivity	Critical thinking (reflection on one's understanding)	Self-reflection (reflection on one's own projects)	Reflective practice ('metacompetence', 'adaptability', 'flexibility')
1. Critical skills	Discipline-specific critical thinking skills	Self-monitoring to given standards and norms	Problem-solving (means–end instrumentalism)
Forms of criticality	*Critical reason*	*Critical self-reflection*	*Critical action*

1991). Largely, after all, universities in Germany acquiesced in the activities of the Nazi regime: they were accomplices in the domination of instrumental reason over more humanistic forms of critical reason (Nash, 1945; Stryker, 1996). At the least, the Western university must strive to avoid producing the fragmented critical consciousness that would again support such a situation. And it can only do so if, through our universities and in our institutions of highest learning, we develop whole persons who integrate all their critical capacities, across all three of the domains and at all their levels.

Students as persons

The emerging determination to see students performing is not totally worthless. A higher education for the new century has to have an eye to the students as actors in the world, not just as thinkers. But the contemporary fragmentation is reducing action to mere performance. We see this in sandwich courses, in which the training element is not properly integrated with the student's core studies; in teacher education courses, in which the new insistence on classroom effectiveness drives even further a wedge between theory and practice (when the school-based regime was intended to unify them); and in the inculcation of so-called transferable skills, such as pre-sentational skills, where attention focuses on the overt performance.

These are all signs of the performativity to which Lyotard (1984) was pointing in his diagnosis of contemporary society. Lyotard's analysis is both fruitful and incoherent. Supposedly the seminal text on postmodernity, it actually points up trends that are signs of an excessive modernity alongside those of postmodernity. On the one hand, we are told that postmodernity exhibits an 'incredulity towards metanarratives' and, instead, celebrates local discourses. We can see this tendency in mass higher education, which shirks from any attempt to offer a grand overarching account of higher education. Now mass higher education is encouraged to sustain multiple 'meanings' and to eschew unifying aims (Halsey, 1992; Goodlad, 1995; Scott, 1995). On the other hand, Lyotard points to a performativity, shorn from a proper interpretation. But this is the technicism to which Critical Theory has long objected, and has done so as an attack on modernity and its narrow inter-pretation of reason. This separation of reason from morality and under-standing led, for Critical Theory, to Auschwitz and the Gulag.

Understanding, therefore, has to be reunited with performance so as to produce action. Critique in the domain of knowledge has to be brought into a relationship with critique in the domain of the world. Indeed, it is only by being shot through with analytical insight, intentionality and a wisdom born of the weighing of alternatives that we can talk of action at all. Our students – in a higher education worthy of the name – have not merely to perform competently, they have to have an account of what they are doing so articulate that they can offer a rationale for what they are doing and for the discarded alternative actions.

Many lecturers will say that they do this in their courses. However, such reflection will hold students at the lower performative levels of critical-ity unless those reflections situate the action in the wider world of social arrangements, policies and public interests, and students are invited to envisage alternative structures, systems and possibilities for collective action. Unless reflection rises to these higher levels of reflection, the student's reflec-tion would amount to decisionism and operationalism. Simply being able to identify a range of alternative courses of action and to supply reasons for the chosen course of action does not attain the higher levels of criticality. At the highest levels, these powers of imaginary reflection call up critique in the domain of the self, to accompany critique in the domains of formal knowledge and the world. When we are in the presence of critical being which connects critical reflection in the three domains of knowledge, the self and the world (Fig. 8.1), then we are in the company of critical persons.

It is the concept of the student as person, therefore, that supplies the conceptual and practical glue in a higher education for critical being. Tak-ing students as persons seriously is a formidable challenge to put to our higher education institutions: not merely the development of critical being in each of the three domains but, crucially, their integration, and within a mass higher education system. And yet, if universities do not bring off this

Figure 8.1 Critical being as the integration of the three forms of criticality

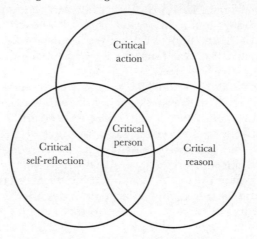

challenge, they will be falling short of their responsibilities in the modern world. To anticipate the next section of the book, this would not just be an injustice towards their students, it would be failing society. In modern society, saturated by 'manufactured risk' (Giddens, 1994), in which our knowledge systems act recursively on society, we shall only be able to purchase some small space for informed and controlled action and for the attainment of a durable self through a critical disposition integrated across all three domains. Otherwise, the world will inevitably run away, since the means to bring it under critical control will have been surrendered.

It will be noted that a conception of higher education of this kind, which seeks to integrate the three domains of critical thought, runs counter to the three dominant contemporary models of higher education. The academic model over-concentrates on critical thinking towards formalized knowledge (CT1); the competence model is so focused on effective performance in the world (CT3) that it does not warrant the title critical action; and reflective practice seeks to unite action and self-reflection (CT2) but often downplays formalized knowledge if not disparaging it altogether and, as a result, surrenders itself to an over-localized and operational view of professional action. Students as persons don't get a look in on any of these accounts.

Even before we attempt to fill out this idea of unification, three objections can be envisaged.

Purifying purity

First, it will be said from the traditional wing of the academic community that to widen critical thinking to embrace the domains of the self and the world would be tantamount to weakening and dissipating the force of higher education. The proposals offered here would spell the reduction of academic standards, since they represent a dilution of the purity of the intellect as the overriding value and concern of the university. The university gains its special status and function in society through the critical standards it upholds, precisely in relation to formalized bodies of knowledge. That is what the university is for. Anything else represents 'the degradation of the academic dogma' (Nisbet, 1971).

The objection holds no water. The so-called purity of the academic calling is a very recent idea, spawned of essentially a post-Second World War period which has seen the academics come to exert monopoly power over the academy and the definitions of education that it entertains. Both the mediaeval universities and the nineteenth-century newcomers were founded to provide the realm with useful skills, Cardinal Newman notwithstanding. The main objection to the purity ideal is not historical but is of the moment.

We cannot understand higher education today unless we situate it in some understanding of modern society – to that extent, Peter Scott (1995) is right. That a mass higher education system, born of a welfare state and now intended to meet the challenges of late modernity, should repudiate legitimate expectations of it to have some sense of the wider society is an incoherent position, to put it charitably. The liberal idea of higher education, in so far as it is being called up to justify a purist definition of critical thought, can be turned against itself: purity does not bring liberty but abandons any such prospect.

Paradoxically, late modernity poses problems not essentially of knowledge, since the world is unknowable both substantively and in terms of the tests of validity by which we come to know the world. Instead, amidst discursive challenge and even discursive contradiction, late modernity poses problems of *being* and of the constitution of the self (Giddens, 1991). Accordingly, critical thought in relation both to the self and to the world has to be brought into play. A liberal education resting on critical thought solely in relation to formalized knowledge is no liberal education at all.

The second riposte will be heard from the world of work. It will be said that the main business of business is business. Action, change, profitability, competitiveness, customer satisfaction, just-in-time quality systems, imagination and creativity, these are the key attributes. Critical reflection, accordingly, is to be valued just so long as it generates these characteristics. This is not to disparage critical thought in relation either to formalized knowledge or to the self: those two domains of critical thought are worthwhile but only in so far as they promote change in the world itself. They are residual domains, brought in only where necessary to shore up the worldly focused forms of critical thought.

This view must also be rejected. It not merely produces a diminution in critical thought in the two domains of knowledge and the self, but it also truncates critical being in the world. Critical action in the world is logically different from critical thinking in the context of formalized knowledge, but it can be enhanced by that form of critical thinking. So, too, with critical thinking in relation to the self. Critical action becomes action rather than mere performance when it is an authentic representation of the self; when it is the self-in-the-world. Graduates will do their professions or their organizations no service if they simply live out, however reflectively, the roles assigned to them. Critical action demands that persons fully inhabit their actions; that they are brave enough to live out their understandings in the world. Without this bravery, without this living out of one's comprehensions, a person's life is diminished; but so, ultimately, are our institutions. Despite itself, the corporate world ultimately requires real selves, three-dimensional selves inhabiting all three domains of critical being.

A third critical voice on the project before us – the unity of critical thinking and action in the three domains of knowledge, self and world – can be heard from reflective practice. The objection from this quarter would deny that the world of formal thought is significant in its own right. Such a view amounts, we are informed, to a form of 'technical rationality' (Schön, 1987). Formal knowledge comes into play, if at all, to assist in the reflective action as part of the armoury with which to interrogate action.

Reflective practice is the most sophisticated of the three critical voices since, in its more subtle interpretations at any rate, it finds a place for both understanding and the self. In particular, the self forms an important component of reflective practice, since it has to be a self that both engages in reflection and is, in part, constituted by it. The main problem lies in reflective practice giving prominence to 'practice' even if reflective in character and downplaying knowledge as such. The very possibility of an integrated and coherent unity between critical thinking in knowledge, the self and the world is outlawed by the notion of reflective practice. Reflective practice denies the possibility of unity by denying a serious role for knowledge. The pass is sold at the outset and has to be reclaimed.

All three of these contending voices have their own kind of purity which they would hold onto. But, paradoxically, the upshot of purity in the modern world is fragmentation. A higher education for critical being can only be achieved by accepting the multidimensionality of the task. The three domains of criticality have each to be respected *and* they have to be integrated. Otherwise, we shall see students emerge whose criticality either is stunted in one or more of the three domains or is fragmented or, more probably, is both. We have, simply, to purify our educational ideas of the belief in purity.

For critical persons

What, then, in general terms would a curriculum intended to develop critical persons look like, a curriculum in which critical thinking in the three domains of knowledge, the self and the world was brought together at all their levels?

At once, the question rules out modes of thinking that over-emphasize the different domains. Didactic lectures reflective of an excessive concern with formal knowledge; performance reflective of an exaggerated interest in having effects in the world; self-reflective activities, which stamp in a self-monitoring according to external norms: all of these have to be jettisoned. They have to be jettisoned not just because they represent a lopsided approach to critical thinking, concentrating overly on one of the three domains. They have to be jettisoned not just because they fail even to realize the potential human development in each of the three domains (so that we end up with rote learning, sheer performativity and introverted reflection, devoid in each case of broad understanding and critical insight). More searchingly, they have to be jettisoned because they fail to offer even the beginnings of a unitary approach to criticality and, thereby, fail to develop critical persons and critical being as such.

Much, therefore, of our contemporary approaches in higher education has simply to be set aside. Quite different pedagogical relationships are required. Students have to be given the space to become themselves, to bring their understandings to bear on situations and, in the process, make them *their* understandings; to understand themselves in relation to situations requiring some insight and learning, *including their own limitations*, and to develop the capacity for critical insight in action. A vocabulary such as student-based learning, problem-based learning and independent learning does no justice to the magnitude of what is required. On the contrary, their development as a strategy for resource economies will produce – unless otherwise checked – a narrowness both in the domains and in the levels through which critical being is realized. If the human learning and development of the kind sketched out here is to come about, we have to dispense with notions not just of teaching but even of learning ordinarily conceived. We need a different vocabulary.

The vocabulary to which we need to have recourse would include terms such as self, being, becoming, action, *inter*action, knowing, understanding, risk, exploration, emotion, interpretation, judging, insight, courage, exposure, daring, authenticity, collaboration and dialogue. A cluster of concepts of this kind is necessary if we are to do justice to an education conceived as the fostering of critical persons. We do not have to call up the dramatic picture of the student in front of the line of tanks in Tiananmen Square; we simply have to have in mind the challenge of professional life. If students are to prosper in the modern world, if they are to carry their world forward in worthwhile fashion, then they have to become critical persons in which they embody critique in the three domains of knowing, of self and of the world at the same time.

The riposte may come, but what is the cash value of all of this? What does a course look like which incorporates such abstract ideas? The riposte is not without substance, but it scuppers itself to some extent. It is right to be asked to indicate the practical significance of educational ideas and to map out in general terms what a curriculum might look like if it is to carry off a proposed programme. But the demand as stated falls foul of just the kind of thinking that I am challenging. If we are to produce critical persons, a course in physics or in English literature or even, shall we say, in timber technology or in landscape architecture will be unlikely to do it.

The problem lies not in any subject or discipline *per se*, it lies in the preposition 'in'. A course *in* physics or even *in* landscape architecture does not promise to produce critical persons of the kind I am proposing. Landscape architecture could come closer to it than physics, since the former willy-nilly will expose the student to some form of critical reflection in each of the three domains of knowing, self and the world. Physics, in contrast, does not compel a student to engage with the self or the world except in severely truncated ways. English literature and timber technology both occupy intermediate positions, with English literature inviting critical self-reflection on one's personal values and timber technology requiring engagement with productive processes.

What has to be faced is that a higher education anchored in a discipline, in which critical being is restricted to the domain of formal knowledge *and* is restricted in its scope to technical operations within a single field, cannot supply critical persons for the new millennium. Both the domains and the levels of critical being have to be incorporated and those three domains of critical being have to be integrated. Critical persons are precisely those individuals who exert some unity of critical power over their experiences in relation to knowledge, themselves and the world.

Keep it simple

So what, in general terms, would it be for higher education to develop critical persons, in which there was some integration of critical thinking in the three domains of knowing, self and the world? The first point is negative in character: there are no generic forms of criticality appropriate to the three domains to be incorporated into curricula. Academics in the disciplines do not have to turn themselves into educationalists who have identified realms of pure critical thinking, independent of a disciplinary base or a site of professional action. What is required is both simpler and much more complex.

Simplicity comes into play because, in the first place, what is called for is for academics to live out their own identities fully and utterly. Rather than imagine afresh a process that we call teaching and learning, the first requirement is that academics reveal themselves to their students as the hardpressed inquirers that they are. In a genuine process of inquiry, they have to engage in a struggle to formulate their thoughts, to labour to develop their thoughts (whether in the laboratory, the clinical situation or in the library), to expose their thoughts to others, to encounter critical evaluations of that thinking, to engage in risky undertakings and to move on in the light of those critical comments. These are not purely cognitive processes. They require of scholars and researchers to give of themselves, to develop themselves as persons, and to engage – albeit in truncated form – in critical action.

The propositions, theories, findings, proposals, creations, technologies and methods that they propose embody their *beliefs*. Belief in turn requires commitment and personal investment: publicly expressed, it is a way of constituting the self (although a limited academic self). But to this existential moment of self-declaration is coupled intersubjective processes of engagement according to the rules within which that academic discourse works. And that process calls both for courage, integrity and authenticity on the one hand, and for the qualities of intersubjective patience, sensitivity, respect and reciprocity on the other.

The simplicity, therefore, of getting students embarked on the road to a critical consciousness lies in academics avoiding concepts of teaching and learning as such, and setting aside the thought that there are institutionalized roles and relationships captured by conventional terms, such as teacher and student, which do justice to higher education. To put it another way, rather than hypothesizing a conceptual distinction between research and teaching (which then have to be brought together in some way), teaching may be seen as an insertion into the processes of research and not into its outcomes. What is required is not that students become masters of bodies of thought, but that they are enabled to begin to experience the space and challenge of open, critical inquiry (in all its personal and interpersonal aspects).

What is being suggested here is the abandonment of teaching as such (Sotto, 1994). But this is not to open the door to lecturers to construe their task as one of introducing students to the latest research findings. The educator's task, for a critical consciousness, is to set up an educational framework in which students can make their *own* structured explorations, testing their ideas in the critical company of each other. This is a highly structured process, in which the students are subject not only to the local rules of the particular discipline but also to the general rules of rational discourse as such. Turn-taking, acute listening, respect for the other's point of view, expression of one's ideas in ways that are appropriate to the context, and even the injection of humour: the critical consciousness can be too serious for its own good. More than that, there would have to be elements of genuine openness such that students can feel that their own voice and their own existential claims matter. This means that the lecturer's own position can and will be challenged.

So the simple task of educators adapting their own approaches to scholarship and research to their educational settings turns out to be complex. Pedagogical roles and relationships become uncertain, and necessarily invite risk into the proceedings. If students are to be given the space genuinely to form their own critical evaluations, and to engage in critical acts, the educational process has to become uncertain. A looser framing of the pedagogical relationship between lecturer and students is imperative. An uncertain world requires an uncertain education.

Levels of a critical education

The idea of levels of criticality points to an ever-changing horizon of perception: as the epistemic level rises, the object is viewed against an ever-wider context. Does critical thinking just limit the student to deploying set logical moves on the material in front of her? Does it enable the student to evaluate the text or the data in the context of an understanding of the field of study as a whole? Does it invite the student to place the topic in a wider context, such as its implications for our understanding of the world? Does it allow the student to come at it from a variety of critical perspectives, such that the field, with its presuppositions, is itself susceptible to critique?

Take, for example, a student taking a degree in tourism studies. Tourism studies is a complex field, potentially incorporating sub-fields as diverse as finance, accountancy, marketing, business studies, economics, the study of tourism itself as a social phenomenon, geography, history, cultural studies, politics and ethics. The key word in that sentence is 'potentially'. Very few degree courses in tourism studies will encompass that range: all will draw on studies of basic business functions such as finance, accountancy and marketing, but few will draw on the more human and social studies to any significant extent. Accordingly, a higher education for a critical consciousness in tourism studies immediately invites the question: what is the scope of critical thinking which informs its study on this particular course?

The lecturing staff, when interviewed, are likely to say that they warmly endorse the notion of critical thinking as a feature of their course, but what does it mean in practice? Are the students simply expected to acquire elementary skills ('critical thinking skills') of knowing how argument works, of forming valid inferences from the available and, in this case, often incomplete or rudimentary data? What is the range of perspectives through which they are invited to view tourism? Are they encouraged to see tourism purely as an economic matter, including its employment characteristics, or are they invited to explore tourism through a range of perspectives and considerations (such as its effect on indigenous cultures, its ethical components, its impulses towards globalization and its postmodern character, not to mention its effects on world health with the spread of AIDS). Even more significantly, are the students given the wherewithal to place their own programme of studies, to understand its limitations and its emphases? Are they able to critique that? And yet more fundamentally, are the students offered an educational experience that challenges them to develop their own critical stances in a non-threatening environment, so that they acquire the dispositions of critical thinking to sustain them beyond their immediate educational framework into their future careers?

There is a double difficulty here for many academics. First, talk of dispositions will be discomforting. How are dispositions to be developed? Academics may feel that they have challenges enough in mastering their own field without having to pause to work out how they might foster dispositions. Secondly, critique works – as we have seen – by exposing one framework to the critical interrrogation of another, or by allowing frameworks to collide (in tourism studies, the cultural with the economic, for example). But that means that academics have to acknowledge the limitations of the very framework in which they have developed their own intellectual identity. They have, if critique is to be fostered, to become other than they are, to pretend that their own framework is not that important after all.

These two difficulties can be addressed at the same time. What is required is an inversion of self-understanding on the part of the academics as educators. The development of dispositions and the capacity to bring into one's understanding a range of frameworks are, ultimately, a responsibility of the student. The role of the educator is to provide the educational space in which those developments are likely to occur. Compiling an agenda of issues that draw upon multiple frameworks, structuring tasks, getting students to collaborate on projects, positing imagination and intellectual range as criteria, and drawing students' attention to a range of relevant literature (not just in one's immediate field): strategies of this kind rather than teaching *per se* are necessary elements in producing critical persons. But they are not sufficient: for that, students have to take on their own responsibilities for their own continuing explorations. A curriculum for a critical consciousness requires real curriculum space for the students; but it is an existential space in which students can, interactively, form their own critical evaluations from this perspective or that, without any sense of intimidation or of being ruled offside.

The domains of critical being

This sketch, however, only points to necessary conditions of a critical education and, in itself, falls into the trap of embellishing critical thought in relation to formal knowledge. It is the kind of educational approach that many lecturers might feel they can easily accommodate. But much more is required of a critical higher education. A higher education for critical being has to extend across the other two domains of the self and the world. What might this mean in practice?

The most problematic domain is that of the world. What does it mean to take up a critical stance towards the world? How might we bring into our story the image that has formed this book's leitmotif, that of the Chinese student halting a line of tanks? Was that simply an example of an individual expressing himself as a citizen and his being a student was immaterial? In other words, the argument might be that the university, *qua* university, has no responsibility and even no place in developing a critical stance towards the world among its students. I have argued to the contrary. The university precisely has a responsibility, *qua* university, to develop the capacity within its students to take up critical stances *in* the world and not just towards the world.

The first question is whether the argument will be general to the university or will be specific to particular fields. It might, prima facie, be more legitimate to develop a justification for a critical stance towards the world built around tourism studies than around mathematics, for example. The argument, however, if it is to work with any force, has to be general in character. It has to be a condition of higher education that all its students are enabled to develop a critical capacity in the domain of the world, if the university is to fulfil its responsibilities towards criticality. But this consideration, that the argument has to have general applicability, only plunges us into further difficulty. What argument might suffice to work across tourism studies, mathematics, history and archaeology? What would such an education for this critical thinking look like?

An immediate answer is, perhaps surprisingly, straightforward. Every form of thought, every field of inquiry, every subject has a place in the modern academy because it has some form of social legitimacy. In most fields, there are all kinds of sites of their application in the world, both in school education and in the corporate, professional and industrial worlds. That, in some fields and disciplines, following the professionalization of knowledge, the links have become buried should not detract from the point. This is not a case of finding spurious 'relevance' but of recovering the social interest in each intellectual field (where it is not apparent). An extraordinary feature of modern academic life is that the veil separating knowledge from practice has been drawn down even in relation to professional fields. Intent on winning their intellectual spurs, academics take delight in declaring that they are not in the business of professional preparation.

But even if the dormant social interest in each form of thought could be brought explicitly into the curriculum, we would still be short of a fully critical stance towards the world, much less giving an account of our student in front of the tanks in Tiananmen Square. Did it matter whether he was a student of politics or history? Could he equally have been an engineering student?

At this point, we need to draw in the third domain, that of the self. If students seriously begin to reflect on themselves, to understand their own thinking, they might characteristically begin by gaining insight into the frameworks that they typically deploy. Do they enjoy just working things out according to the rules of the game, or are they prepared to be more adventurous by looking at things in different and even in new ways? In this way, critical thinking in relation to the world of knowledge (CT1) and in relation to the self (CT2) can come into a relationship with each other. But this could still remain a cerebral activity. Skills come into play but internally, within the rules of the local form of thought. However, once the student is placed in situations where those skills and understandings are exposed to pragmatic situations in the world, then the potential for critical thought to widen to embrace the world arises (CT3). This critical thought in the world, critical action, is not an add-on; it could never be, for example, the demonstration of 'enterprise' as such. Rather, it becomes part of an integrated critical being, in which critical persons in the three domains of knowledge (CT1), of self (CT2) and of action-in-the-world (CT3) are constituted and, through their integration, *the possibility of transformations in each domain arises.*

We have briefly to backtrack here. It only makes sense to talk of bringing into the curriculum critical thought in relation to the world (CT3) if and when critical thought in the other two domains – knowledge and the self – is present. We get to CT3 through CT1 and CT2. This seems to run counter to the point made earlier that the three forms of critical thought are independent of each other. But the two positions are entirely compatible. CT in the world (CT3) is *sui generis* and is not to be reduced to either of the other forms of critical thought. However, it is enhanced by critical thought both in the domain of knowledge and in the domain of the self. If students are to act authentically in the world, they will need to draw on both their imaginary insights in the domain of knowledge and their own self-understanding. In this integration of the three domains of critical being, they become persons, acting autonomously in the world and taking up a critical stance towards it.

Conclusion

Criticality can be achieved in three domains, those of knowledge, the self and the world. A curriculum intended to develop critical persons necessarily, therefore, has to find some way of developing critical thinking in the three domains so as to develop critical thought, critical self-reflection and critical action. However, these three exemplifications of the critical life have also to be brought together, if a unity of the critical outlook is to be achieved and if creative criticality is to be developed. The integration of criticality in the three domains calls for nothing less than taking seriously students as persons, as critical persons in the making. Students come into themselves as persons, in command of themselves.

The concept of person, in other words, supplies the conceptual and practical glue required if fragmented critical being is to be avoided. This sounds simple enough, but it calls for students to be given the cognitive, personal and practical space in which they can develop in all three domains, yet be guided in such a way that the three domains are brought into a relationship with each other. Understanding, self-reflection and action have to be given the space to take off, such that the prospect of independent persons can be present. But the educator's task is not complete unless the student is challenged continually to make connections between her knowledge, self-understanding and actions at the highest levels of criticality (as in Fig. 8.2). Then, and only then, in this integration at the highest

Figure 8.2 Critical being as the integration of the three forms of criticality at all of their levels

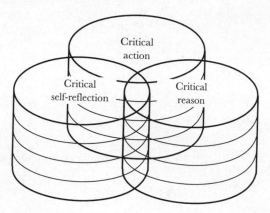

levels of creative critique, would we have the prospect of higher education becoming a site where critical being adequate to the wider world might be fostered.

Part 3

Critique in Society

9
Critical Thought in a Corporate World

Introduction

The corporate world is beginning to sense that it has need of critical thinking capacities among its graduate labour force. But what might this intuition, as yet vaguely articulated, amount to? What could it mean for the way in which we construe and practise higher education in the modern world? Is this a malign, a benign, or a progressive influence on the development of higher education? It could be any of these.

Working it out

Just at the moment that universities are becoming organizations, the corporate world is reducing its organized character. Organization is giving way to fluid structures, work practices and modes of being. Companies identify their core activities and 'outsource' those activities on which they still depend but which are better handled by those organizations specializing in them. Even the core activities are scrutinized such that, for example, periodic cycles of activity during the week are met by part-time staff. At operational levels and at executive levels, staff are hired to meet particular demands. As a result, the 'permanent' full-time staff shrink rapidly.

At the boardroom level, this appears to be a win–win situation. Less staff, fewer activities and fewer components of the organization have to be managed while, at the same time, both the quantity and the quality of the final product or service rises. There are problems of staff motivation among the part-time employees or problems of identification with the company's mission among the companies to whom work has been subcontracted but, in principle, these are containable. Contracts are drawn up in a tighter way, staff development and appraisal embraces all the part-time staff, and considerations of the quality of the service become explicit elements in the relationship. So success seems assured.

But if the company keeps changing, if it can easily slough off activities that it had long conducted, what becomes of the company? Handy (1995) talks of the 'inverted doughnut', with the core activities seemingly intact. But what counts as core is itself under constant scrutiny: why, then, should *any* particular activity count as core? Turning his gaze to education, Handy observes that even teaching could be outsourced (so that specialists are hired to offer particular educational services). But on this reading of the general idea, why *should* anything count as core? Especially in the corporate world, traditions cannot be allowed to establish themselves: there can be no assumption that any particular activity is essential to the identity of a company.

If, structurally, the ground keeps shifting, so it will in terms of individuals' hold on work. Companies and the employees themselves might talk blithely about individuals transferring their loyalties and work identities as they move from one organization to another, as their own segment of the product is put out to or is bought by another company, or as their status as an employee changes to part-time or to bought-in consultant. But, deep down, things cannot be as they were. The durability of relationships which allowed individuals to understand themselves as belonging to such-and-such company has gone. In the process, the work identity of employees also changes.

We are in the midst of a largely unremarked transformation in which the relationship between individuals and companies is being inverted. If there is a doughnut, its core lies within the individual and not within the organization. *If* there is any stability, it is that of the individual as a unitary self in managing him or herself through a never-ending series of work identities and working relationships. But in such a world, there may be no inner identity either. The working person in the modern corporate world has no self. The self becomes an assembly of components, some of which may be useful in this environment and others in a different environment. In this milieu, identities, practices and assumptions are easily discarded – they have to be. After all, the new organization may have a quite different culture and either one adapts or one goes elsewhere.

Handy (1995: 146 *et seq.*) talks of a 'portfolio', of an individual having elements of salaried work, consultancy, unpaid work, charity work and scheduled leisure time; and with the balance of the different elements changing through the lifespan. But the idea of the portfolio can have a deeper, existential, resonance in referring to the skills, qualities, values and dispositions that the individual has available at any one time. Here, too, the unitary self vanishes. For the skills, qualities, values and dispositions that find favour in one situation will not match those that find favour in another. And nor are these differences to be found only across companies. For all the talk of mission, the adept employee knows that the one company can have quite different expectations in different parts of its decentralized operations. Even in the one company, the unitary self fragments.

You will be self-reliant

Companies as organizations dissolve, structures dissolve, work dissolves and employees as unitary selves with known work identities dissolve. This is the logic of the corporate world being opened up to us. One result is that the relationship between company and individuals is inverting. If the company is not given, if the work is not given, and if the pattern of human qualities and capacities that are desired is not given, then the company can no longer be responsible for supplying those conditions of the good life. If they *are* to be found, they will be found through the individual and her or his own efforts in managing her or himself.

Hence, a call for 'self-reliance' emerges (AGR, 1995). It was personal transferable skills that were going to save the day and provide some assuredness of reliable performance from individuals in the workplace. But, now, it is beginning to be recognized that there can be no succour from that quarter, that if situations and expectations keep changing, then there will be nothing to transfer. What we want are extra-clever chameleons who can change not just their colours but their whole working selves, and in an instant if necessary. And so the idea of self-reliance is born.

Core skills (or transferable skills) remain superficially attractive (Assiter, 1995; Hodgkinson, 1996), and we are still getting used to that idea anyway. But the notion of self-reliance springs from a radical agenda in which it is recognized that there are potentially no similarities between the situations of working life such that any skill could be transferred. Instead, the onus falls on individuals to develop the widest repertoire of skills, aptitudes and kinds of understanding so that they can be effective in different milieux. The milieux may have *nothing* in common: there just may be no skill – core or otherwise – which can be transferred between them. The juxtaposition of the two agendas of core skills and self-reliance (AGR, 1995) may sound as if they are entirely compatible (indeed, made for each other), but there is a fundamental incompatibility between them.

The onus of ensuring any reliability or even appropriateness of performance falls, then, on the individual. Companies may hold on to the notions of staff appraisal and even employee development, but these have to change. No longer is it simply a matter of what the company can do for individuals to help to evaluate, develop and redirect them, for all of these responsibilities now also reside with the individual. Enlightened companies understand this in making available virtually unlimited possibilities for self-development. It is the self that has to develop and not any particular cluster of skills or understandings. And it has to be up to individuals to determine how they will develop themselves as selves.

The world of work is continually reshaping itself into new configurations. Even its geography changes as the Internet makes possible not just work at 'home' but work on the move. (The computer and the fax can be on the car seat.) Responsibilities devolve downwards not just for the completion of the work but also for its quality and its development. Everyone is his or her own manager, own quality controller and own staff developer: 'self reliance' *is* the name of this game. But self-reliance spells the individualization of work, in which individuals rely just on themselves. That would be literally an unworkable situation. However fragmented, however unstable, however much individualized, work will continue to contain interpersonal components. Indeed, in a globalized world of work, the elements of trust and dependency multiply across countries (as recent financial dealings by individuals in trading banks have demonstrated).

In this situation, work becomes a new kind of contract between individuals and companies. Companies need to trust the individuals they employ (on whatever basis they are employed). The conditions of that trust will vary enormously: trust can be betrayed in quite different ways. Ultimately, the issue is one of damage limitation: can the potential damage to the name of the company be minimized? But, more typically, the issue is one of delivery: can she or he be trusted to deliver the goods (literally)? If the work is outsourced, if the work is part-time, if the work is produced by a former executive turned consultant, the company's leverage is limited. These individuals will turn elsewhere for a better deal. Even inside the company, the individual – having demonstrated her wide portfolio of skills – may be a liability in one function but may be almost indispensable in another function. No-one can do it as she can or knows as much about it as she does. So the company's room for manoeuvre is lessened.

Corporate self: Moral self

'Self-reliance' thus takes on moral overtones. It is not just a matter of managing one's work operationally or even of monitoring oneself according to performance indicators; it is also a matter of taking on the human virtues sought by this fluid corporate environment. Companies look to individuals to handle themselves in ways that are appropriate to the company concerned. But they also look to such human virtues as truth-telling, reliability, empathy and understanding. Perhaps they always did – although that is uncertain – but now these human virtues have become crucial to the survival of the company. In this free-floating environment, individuals can bring companies down. Self-reliance, accordingly, has to be read as 'You should rely on yourself', but also as 'We rely on you to monitor youself to ensure that you are acting appropriately at all times. The price of your autonomy in your work for the company is that we can rely on you'.

Work dissolves, then, to be replaced by moral virtue. Well, not quite. What are wanted are not moral virtues of all kinds in and for themselves. What are wanted are moral virtues with a use value, moral virtues that are going to help the bottom line. Tell the truth both to us and to our customers, and don't just be economical with the truth either. Tell the full story to our customers, warts and all. That can help the bottom line, after all. We, as your employers, have to be able to trust you, but our customers have also to be able to trust us.

These, then, are fickle virtues for they are dependent on the market-place. MacIntyre (1990) would insist that real virtue is anchored in traditions and in a background of a collective sense of what is right and sound. But this new virtue denies traditions. It is the virtue of a 'detraditionalized' world (Giddens, 1994). It eschews larger allegiances or loyalties. On the other hand, amidst globalization, this new virtue has to be capable of being universalized. Globalization calls for a sensitivity to local traditions *and* it calls for the deployment of common standards and operations. In the 'McDonaldization' of the economy, not only the employees' attitudes but also the customers' attitudes are universalized. We are all Kantians now.

Trust, reliance, truth-telling, allegiance and empathy: virtue finds its way into the world economy. The corporate self survives, if at all, through the individual offering a moral self to the (temporary) employer. Inner direction arrives as a result of the introjection of external agendas. But, unlike the externality of moral traditions, this morality has no view about moral persons as such. It is a moral self for work. This is an inside-out morality: the inner moral self is called up for external purposes in the world of work. This is a conditional morality: it is a morality on condition that it works in work, not because it is believed to constitute moral persons as such.

It is not to be sniffed at; it is a morality. Truth-telling is truth-telling. But it *can* easily turn into being economical with the truth. The full truth may not be immediately harmful, but it can just get in the way. It is surplus to requirements. Time is money, after all. So this is a conditional truth. If it ain't broke, why fix it? Why even question it?

Questions have to be asked

The answer is that questions are not just desirable but are necessary if the company is to survive and to prosper. Pascale (1990: 16) points out that, of the forty-three 'excellent' companies identified by Peters and Waterman (1982) in their bestseller, *In Search of Excellence*, 'only five years after the book's publication, two-thirds of the companies studied had slipped from the pinnacle', with some being in serious trouble. For Pascale, a crucial determinant in the fate of companies is the way in which they manage conflict. That might imply that the well-run company is one without conflict. Pascale, however, turns the point on its head into a commentary on – as he sees it – the virtuous properties of conflict.

By conflict, Pascale has in mind not interpersonal conflict but a conflict of ideas. Conflicting ideas can come in all shapes and sizes. They might be alternative ways forward, rival views over the significance of separate internal operations, or differences of priority to be accorded to company goals (such as quality or cost control). Contention is not to be orchestrated out of the company: it is its life-blood. Properly channelled, this kind of conflict ensures that the company does not become trapped into established paradigms of self-understanding and practices. It fosters constructive change and enables the company to go on moving forward.

The orchestration of contention sets in train two conditions. First, there has to be a genuine climate of openness. It is not enough for employees to feel that they can ask questions; they have to sense that their questions are being taken seriously. (Following Chapter 4, we might ask to what extent our universities are currently living up to this challenge.) Secondly, and crucially, the orchestration of conflict requires a higher-order level of reflection in the company. If paradigms of understanding and practice are to be put under continual scrutiny, higher-order frameworks of interpretation and insight have to have a place. New paradigms or 'mindsets' (Pascale, 1990: 25) are only going to emerge through alternative and higher-order perspectives coming into play which can interrogate the current ways of thinking and action.

In this 'transcendent' approach to management (Pascale, 1990: 25), 'the essential activity for keeping our paradigms current is persistent questioning'. This collective questioning Pascale terms 'inquiry', which is nothing less than 'the engine of vitality and self-renewal' (p. 14).

In these notions of persistent questioning and of alternative frameworks of thinking, we can gain an insight into the 'learning organization'. A learning organization is not one that just learns from its mistakes, or sees how the competitors are doing things or is able to do things differently. It has the resources to step outside its contemporary frameworks to understand itself anew. It is an organization in which new things are done but also in which those new things are subject to evaluation from a variety of *alternative* frameworks. Or, more formally, it is an organization that has embedded in it 'double-loop learning' (Argyris and Schön, 1974): the learning is itself subject to interrogation and that is only possible if other frameworks of evaluation are available.

All of this raises questions that we can sidestep. Are the frameworks of evaluation necessarily higher-order or are they just different? (They can be both.) How are alternative frameworks of thinking and action to be generated, since by definition they are not part of the established ways of going on? (Companies have to provide discursive and structural space for the unthinkable to be valued.) To what extent does such counter-thinking have to be institutionalized across a company? (The more this kind of counter-thinking is spread across the company, and the more everyone feels the spirit of inquiry, the more success is likely.) The point is that the corporate world understands that there is no stable state (Schön, 1971), that change has to be embraced and that that, in turn, calls for the embedding of a spirit of mutual inquiry.

Peters and Waterman (1982: 37), in pointing up 'the tyranny of reason' in business life, mention a 'Honda worker who, on his way home each evening, straightens up windshield wiper blades on all the Hondas he passes. He just can't stand to see a flaw in a Honda!'. But 'the age of unreason' (Handy, 1995) calls for unreasonable people. A double-think arises. We want people to work for us with whom we can do business; we want people on the inside of our values. But we also want people who can think the unthinkable, who can engage in 'upside-down' thinking (Handy, 1995). We want iconoclasts but they must be homely icononclasts. *Our* iconoclasts think the unthinkable but are sensitive to the kind of organization we are. This critical thought, therefore, has its limits despite all the talk of paradigm-breaking.

The company accordingly becomes a resource for ideas, perspectives on the world and changing self-understandings. The modern company is an epistemological holding company, generating alternative ways of knowing – albeit within limits – and subjecting them to continuing evaluation. The company becomes a university at the same time as the university becomes an organization.

Critique in the corporate world

Critical thinking in the corporate world is an aid to corporate survival, if not corporate growth. But of what kind? How far, in other words, across our two axes of critical thought – domains and levels – does criticality in the modern corporate world extend? The dissatisfaction of employers with the 'products' of higher education can be seen as a sign that graduates are *insufficiently* critical of the world around them. However, some forms of criticality are more equal than others.

Critical reason *will* be in evidence. The company might even understand itself as trying to encourage new paradigms. But there will be limits to the range of alternative paradigms that will be *seriously* entertained. Searching critiques of the company's mission, of its tacit values, and of its total effect on society and on the lives of its employees are unlikely to be entertained unless they appear to be relevant to the company's well-being. Or, if such revolutionary thinking is permitted, then it is only wanted from a desig-nated unit or stratum. For the most part, the levels of critical thinking are likely to be limited to operational and strategic concerns.

Critical self-reflection, as we have seen, will also be encouraged. In a culture of total quality management, or just-in-time management, perhaps involving quality circles, each employee is expected not only to take respons-ibility for his or her actions but also to engage critically with the immedi-ate environment of his or her work practices. Prizes or other awards (a write-up in the company newsletter) may even be on offer for constructive, efficiency-gaining or cost-saving suggestions. Individuals are also expected to monitor their own actions according to the stated quality standards. But these forms of self-reflection remain at the instrumental level.

Critical action, as we have articulated it here, is mistrusted. A few eccent-rics may be tolerated 'to keep everyone on their toes' but the company, as a set of systems (Senge, 1990), will see in critical action the prospect of anarchy. The critical component of action, accordingly, will also be held at operational levels, such that action is monitored and refined to achieve stated goals more efficiently. Communication, for example, is understood as a system for downward and, at best, lateral communication, rather than as a means of injecting discursive opportunities for employees collectively to act decisively in modifying the total character of a company.

Accordingly, the suspicion must be that the critical self that the corporate world calls for is bounded by the strategic interests of the corporate world (Touraine, 1995: 141). Give us critical mind but not too much of it. And yet the corporate world has to live in the wider world. If the world is unknowable in many respects for individuals in the world (that is, for its customers), so is it for the corporate world. The possibility arises, therefore, that the corporate world underestimates the value of a fully critical mind and of a fully-fledged critical culture among its employees. If the world is problematic epistemologically, culturally, socially and personally, then those are matters that the corporate world will have to acknowledge sooner or later.

What is necessary for long-term organizational survival is critique in action; that is, nothing short of the imagination to redefine situations and the practical accomplishment collaborately to work for and to carry out the new vision. New frameworks are called for, in which conventional work practices can be comprehended anew, with alternative values and concepts. Effort has then to be spent in persuading the doubters as to these new views and in bringing them off.

It's all in the balance

In his book, *The Quest for Quality*, Goodlad (1995) points to heresies that result when activities in the university take on an exaggerated form. For Goodlad, exaggerations arise out of a tendency to favour the poles of two superimposed axes: self and society, thought and action. The schema raises questions which can be put to the corporate world.

In commercial life, is the theory underlying the company's development to be that of 'right first time', with an adherence to specified external rules, or is it to be one of 'total quality management', in which responsibility is placed on individual staff to demonstrate their responsiveness to the customers? Is society to be taken to be the company's shareholders or is it the wider society that might experience the effects of maladministration of the company's funds? Is a responsibility to staff as individuals to be understood as assisting them in their work effectiveness or their future careers or their total lives? Is the self simply the self that presents in the work situation, or is the self the totality of the inner experiences of individuals, which might be given space for expression?

Self and society, thought and action: the logic of our analysis is that a balance has to be found between these elements not only for the sake of society or individuals or a set of ultimate values, but even *for the sake of company survival*. Amidst globalization and an environment of uncalculable risk, the parameters of informed decision-making widen virtually to infinity. As the company as organization dissolves, so more onus descends on individuals to construct themselves as reliable workers, and that calls for the recovery of a self – even if a truncated self – in the world of work. As the need for company responsiveness grows, so too does the need for all staff to be brought within a culture of critical inquiry.

These considerations call for critical thought both at the individual and at the corporate level. Practices and presuppositions have to be analysed and evaluated and new possibilities identified which hold in balance the considerations and the contending parties. Logically, this may be impossible: principles and actions may conflict. It may not be possible to hold easily together a sensitivity to employees as individuals and (in a multinational corporation) to the interests of governments around the world. The play cannot always take place in all directions at once. So critical reason is required rigorously to assess the counter-claims and definitions against each other and in working out a coherent plan of action.

But for this critical reason to be conducted seriously, it would have to embrace considerations going wider than the organization's immediate interests, and even the consumers of its services. In the service sector, for instance, a decision to close an accident and emergency unit in a hospital raises issues not just of the immediate locality and the accident and emergency provision on hand. It also raises issues of priorities in the health service, the use of public funds and the division of responsibilities between general practice and hospitals. More broadly still, it raises issues of the processes of decision-making in the health service.

From critical thinking to critical thought to . . .

A critical consciousness for corporate prosperity will be willing to keep picking away at an issue, exposing the onion rings of deeper problematics. In that continuing exposure, critical thinking in relation to the immediate presenting problem turns to critical thought; that is, the sedimenting of a collective willingness to engage critically with work practices and thinking. In turn, too, as wider and more profound issues of national or even – in an age of globalization – international policy are raised and larger alternatives are glimpsed, so critical thought turns to critique. For example, it might be suggested that an entirely different set of arrangements might be adopted towards medical treatment, of a less intensive and technological character and which at least shared the responsibilities for decision-making much more with patients. To what extent such fundamental problematizing can find a place in the corporate world must be an open question.

The exposure of ever-deeper problematics, the willingness to subject tacit presuppositions to critical scrutiny, has no end. But action is required. Decisions have to be made and, usually in commercial or professional life, based on inadequate evidence. In complex organizations, those making the decisions (that is, pretty well everyone) may not carry out the resulting actions themselves but they have to take responsibility for those decisions. Critical reason has to be accompanied by critical action, which also calls forth the critical self. Unless employees are prepared to subject their own presuppositions to critical interrogation, unless a critical self is united with critical reason and critical action, the stability and reliability of performance and product will be in jeopardy.

In the corporate world, the three spheres of criticality – critical reason, the critical self and critical action – have therefore to come together. Together, they form a nigh impregnable force; they produce, at their centre, critical persons, capable not only of combating the vicissitudes of commercial and business life, but also of acting effectively and with insight and wisdom in that milieu. And, institutionalized into a process of collective inquiry, they can provide a corporate resilience that just might have a chance in a world of unknowable risk.

This, then, is the scope of criticality to be striven for in the corporate world and is the prize to be won. In understanding critical thought in that milieu, we have to posit a continuing dialectic between critique in the domains of knowledge, the self and the world. There can be no simple cobbling together of the three domains: each is crucial and none is reducible to the others, but each is in a dynamic momentum with the others. The critical self offers resilience to critical action in the world, critical action is informed by critical thought, and critical thought is tested in critical action. The three forms of criticality interlink, imparting strength to each other. And, together, they produce critical persons, capable of working collaboratively in the corporate world to effect positive change.

Give and take

The corporate world is imparting new possibilities to higher education in living up to its own belief in criticality. The world of work of late modernity calls for forms of critical being, in self-reflection and in action, that higher education has been neglecting. In calling for capacities of critical thinking that can break through to new paradigms of understanding, the world of work is even challenging higher education to live up to its own rhetoric in the domain of knowledge and to enable students to attain the level of critique there too. But, in facing up to those challenges, higher education – by fully living up to its agenda in terms of critical reason – can in turn offer to the world of work additional capacities for criticality that are going to be helpful to the corporate world as it faces up to its own challenges.

The Western university has a self-ideal of keeping its critical distance from the world, the better to understand it and to offer it new insights. Critique-in-action in the corporate world calls upon the university to live up to that ideal, since critique-in-action calls for alternative frameworks to come into play. The university can act as a meta-epistemological resource in enhancing the capacity in the wider society – including the corporate sector – to generate new frameworks of thinking and action.

There are challenges in front of the university in developing in its students such a capacity for producing extra-mural frameworks. If there are no clear undisputed criteria by which matters of substance (in thought and action) can be resolved, the basis for critique in the world is problematic. And yet, the matter is crucial. If the university is to have a rational purchase on the world through the capacities for critical thought that it imparts to its graduates, then it has to go on reflecting on and working at its own basis as an epistemological centre in society.

The matter is more complicated still. The challenges facing the university in developing critique-in-action are, in part, concerned with ontological questions of what it means to be a self in the world, and about the relationship of the self to the world of work. Work is only part of life, although – especially through the power and influence of multinational corporations – the two are becoming increasingly intertwined. The education of the critical citizen, accordingly, is fast becoming a matter of the education of the corporate employee. The corporate employee is also a citizen, with an eye on the impact of the corporation's policies and activities.

The world of work in general is implicated here. What it is to be a banker, a chief executive, a doctor, a journalist, a military officer, a midwife or a university vice-chancellor is unclear, assaulted by multiple and changing definitions. The enduring character of these questions in the modern age calls for continuing critical inquiry and self-reflection if effective action is to result.

The art of the impossible

Corporate life calls for reflexive persons. The corporate world is coming to understand this: its practices and assumptions and blindnesses – about its products, services, technologies, clients and unintended consequences -- have to be kept under critical scrutiny. But it is not enough for individuals to take on the responsibility for this capacity. Reflexivity has to be institutionalized; it has to be genuinely collective. Practices and assumptions are only going to be changed through social reflection and ensuing action. Responsiveness has to be understood collectively, not as the sum of individuals bearing the load of social and economic change on their lone shoulders. Ultimately, enlightenment has to work collectively: the learning organization has to be an organization that learns collectively about itself and not just one that encourages and even supports the efforts of individuals to take responsibility for their own learning.

The corporate world, therefore, offers backing – of a kind – to the general argument of this book. On the one hand, critical being has to be understood in terms of the three domains of criticality, of knowledge, self and the world. The corporate world now demands critical selves of its employees, who are knowledgeable about the basis for their actions and are able to engage in critical action that takes the organization forward. The axis of domains (of critical being) is, therefore, endorsed. But the axis of levels is also endorsed. The corporate world, although it is uneasy in saying so, inwardly recognizes that criticality, if it only means operating reflexively on the immediate task or role, is insufficient. Critical reason that is prepared to think the impossible, to offer imaginative scenarios that emerge from new frameworks of comprehension (about the organization's 'mission'), is required. Critical thinking skills are irrelevant: what are required are capacities for paradigmatic change; in short, critique.

The two axes of domain and level (of critical thought) are, therefore, endorsed by the corporate world. But the corporate world adds three further riders. First, critique, if it is to have any chance of carrying the day, had better have some positive elements about it. This, indeed, is one of the virtues of critique: coming at a phenomenon with a new framework of understanding, it is bound to yield positive results. It says, look at the problem this way; jettison the old ways of comprehending the problem. The new framework is pretty well bound to generate new possibilities of comprehension and action. The trick is to see that the negativity of criticism becomes the positivity of critique.

Secondly, critique, if it is to be effective, has to be collective. Transformations of institutions, organizations and corporations call for collective transformations of understanding. One implication is that our higher education pedagogies should be much more collective in character, encouraging students to engage critically but in supportive ways with each other. But it is important to see the logic of this point. It is not: engage in collective critical reflection because that is what the world of work requires. It is that critical reflection has to have a significant element of the collective in it. Critical reflection has to be tested in critical dialogue. Does this person's point of view hold water? Do these proposed ideas or actions seem sensible? Do we give our assent to them? Critique has to justify itself; it has to find fellow-travellers.

Thirdly, and extending the last point, critique has to be political. It has to be the art of the impossible. The Chinese student in front of the tanks was presumably prepared to die for his convictions, shared as they were by several thousand other students. Even so, the critical act of standing in front of the tanks was part of a collective effort to change the course of events (a collective effort that included trying to change the framework of understanding of the soldiers of the acts in which they were engaged). That the student radicalism of Tiananmen Square came to nothing in the short and even in the medium term does not dislodge the point; on the contrary, it confirms it. If critique in the corporate world is to be effective, it has to be political in the sense of containing an analysis of its likely reception, interpretation and outcome. Critique has to marshall its forces.

Conclusion

Critical action in the corporate world has to be accompanied by critical thought, interpretation and insight, but individuals engaging in these efforts have to be resilient, maintaining their own integrity; they have to sustain themselves as critical selves. And when critical thought, the critical self and critical action come together, then we are in the presence of critical persons. The plural 'persons' is necessary, since critical persons can come about only through the critical company of other critical persons. The critical capacities of individuals for critical thought, for critical self-reflection and for critical action cannot be understood apart from a collective critical capacity.

The corporate world is vaguely aware of these points; they are not new to a world of work beset by change and challenge which strike anew each day. Notions of the learning organization have to be seen, in part, as efforts to articulate a sense of critique in the world of work. But the world of work understandably shrinks from spelling it all out for, if it did, it would have to understand that there can be no limits to critique. Genuine critique, born of an equal dialogic situation, carries the possibility of revolutionary challenge from within. And that may be even tougher to handle than revolutionary challenge from without. In this case, better the devil you don't know than the one you do.

10

Critical Professionalism

Introduction

The term 'critical professionalism' is tautologous, or it ought to be so. The idea of professionals contains the sense of persons able and willing critically to evaluate the professional practices with which they are identified. The practices will include those of others in the profession; but, in the first place, it includes those of themselves. We look to professionals critically to evaluate their own activities.

'The reflective practitioner', therefore, is also tautologous. In that respect, Schön (1983) was telling us nothing new; he was not giving us an empirical finding but reminding us of a conceptual truth. Professionals simply are reflective practitioners; that is partly what we mean by the term 'professional'. To that extent, my term 'critical professional' and Schön's 'reflective practitioner' share common ground. However, in this chapter, I want to distinguish mine from Schön's.

Briefly, I shall argue three things. First, that Schön's conception of the professional is unduly individualistic, neglecting the extent to which professional life is *necessarily* social and inter-subjective. Secondly, his conception of reflection underplays the theoretical components. Thirdly, underplaying the theoretical leads Schön to a limited view of the critical thought and action that constitutes professionalism. To pick up the two axes of our schema, Schön's professionals are limited in both the levels and the domains of their critical capacities.

On speaking out

Professionals have to be able and willing to speak out. But, in saying that, issues arise immediately about what constitutes being professionally *competent*. There is a silence in Schön's work about this characteristic of professional life. Is the competent professional one who just gets on with the work to hand? On this view, competence would be a matter of responding in uniform ways to similar situations, to the requisite standards. Through this predictability, we can invest trust in professionals; and modern society, in all its cognitive complexity, could not function without a high degree of trust (Giddens, 1991). Through trust in those whom we rely upon as being competent, we may hope to reduce the element of risk in modern life.

Predictability, reliability and acting according to predetermined standards: these, then, seem to be the ingredients of competence. Where, in all this, is there room for the professional as such to speak out on controversial matters? There isn't. Even if we extend the notion of professional to include the idea of professional as expert (Eraut, 1994), we are still no further forward. The idea of expert implies a person not just able to deliver a response to a situation, albeit a complex and an appropriate response to a demanding situation, but also having at her disposal a wide range of conceptual and action-based resources such that creative solutions can be forthcoming. The expert is able to deploy her repertoire of resources to effect. The professional is an artist, mixing her colours on the palette to produce a quite new combination of results.

But still, the notions of competence, expertise and even reflective practice supply an unduly restricted set of ideas of professionalism. In some senses, they deny professionalism. They neglect what it is properly to profess. To profess implies precisely the capacity to hold forth with authority on a subject. The idea of professing is not restricted to interactions with clients; it can and should embrace the idea of speaking out on one's subject. If one is an authority, and is judged to be so, then one is an authority *tout court*. Provided one remains within one's sphere of competence, one not only has the right to speak out; one has a duty to do so.

Two issues are now before us. First, the disjunction between the restricted notions of competence and reflective practice on the one hand and professionalism as entailing a duty to speak out on the other has yet to be explained. Secondly, we have to give an account of how it might be that one could have a duty to speak out.

Members of key professions owe their status and social legitimacy to the wider society. Professions are socially sanctioned sites of power, a power built on the deployment of knowledge in the service of society. Principally, that service is provided through direct interaction with individual users ('clients'). But given that the professional's legitimacy is granted by society (many professions having Royal or state-backed charters, for instance), responsibilities to the wider society come into play. Consequently, when issues arise on which professionals can speak with authority (in relation to legal, health or architectural matters, for example), they have a duty to do so. As professionals – as members of recognized professional bodies – they are recognized in a substantive sense by society; they are given a licence to practise. There can, therefore, be no arbitrary limit to their professional responsibilities. If there are public inquiries, debates or controversies, on which professionals have a legitimate voice, then they have a duty to speak out.

Not to speak out would be to deprive society of a voice that has authority. A silence of that kind would lessen the extent to which society might be informed on important matters; it would reduce the possibility of the achievement of a learning society. To the extent that professionals remain silent, to that extent the civil realm is underdeveloped. Professionals have the cognitive and intellectual capital with which to advance citizenship through the understanding that they can impart to the wider society. Their authority being sanctioned by society, they have a responsibility to advance the well-being of society wherever they can within the limits of that authority.

Professional knowledge is given a standing by society because of its potency in social settings. It is, to coin a phrase, knowledge-in-society, a knowledge found to be valuable by the wider society. But, then, two things follow. First, its value lies in its being put to use, in its being deployed, acted on and taken up. It is valueless if it is seen as a formal and inert body of thought. To that extent, Schön has been helpful in insisting on the action and pragmatic elements of professional knowledge. Secondly (and here Schön has been less helpful), the stage for the deployment of professional knowledge has to include the whole of the wider society itself. The clients of professionals' services, in other words, are potentially the entire citizenry, not just individuals who present at the professional's door.

The professional's clients are the citizens of the wider society; the professional has been given a licence to pronounce on matters within her purview; and it is desirable in a democratic society that public understanding is enhanced. Together, these three points support my claim that a professional has a duty rather than a mere right to speak out. There is another point to be made, however. Having been licensed to practise by the wider society, there is an obligation on the professional to maintain a loyalty to the profession itself. This allegiance can turn into professional inertia and defensiveness, but the point is that the professional does not act in his or her own interests. She or he does not act solely according to the wishes of the client, but places the client's wishes in the context of her or his professional knowledge and values (which are sometimes reflected in a code of ethics). In speaking out, therefore, or in becoming involved in a public controversy, there is *some* degree of disinterestedness in the professional's utterances. In hearing the professional speak, the wider society can place some degree of trust in what is being said.

What is at stake here is what is meant by 'professional'. Just as individuals as clients turn to professionals because they can be trusted, so the element of trust extends across all professional activities. To say that professionals can be trusted in their transactions with individual clients but not when they are active in a larger societal context would arbitrarily truncate what we mean by 'professional' and would sow the seeds of mistrust in all that they do.

So professionals have a *duty* – not just a right – to speak out in virtue of their having socially sanctioned authority to pronounce within a particular domain of knowledge and action, their voice contributing to the growth of understanding in the public domain. Left unattended, in this account, is the distinction that I drew earlier between competence and reflective practice on the one hand and professionalism as entailing a duty to speak out on the other.

Professing-in-action

Competence and reflective practice are drawn from overlapping discourses. Or, more accurately, while competence is currently dominated by a performative discourse, reflective practice is currently housed both within that discourse and within a humanistic discourse of self-development and self-empowerment. The notions of competence and reflective practice inhabit contrasting discourses, but they also overlap. I want, therefore, to bracket together those two notions and to distinguish them from professionalism, and to do so in the context of this issue of professionals having a duty to speak out.

Both competence and reflective practice have elements in common. First, they take their point of departure from particular actions or activities. Competence has meaning within a bounded 'range' of events and responses; reflective practice operates on events and responses as they are encountered. The two terms are based on a sense of professionalism as being situated in a series of separate locales.

Secondly, there is a givenness in both terms. Their current definitions are both built on a sense that professional life is a matter of responding appropriately to events and situations as they are experienced. They differ in their strategies: competence implies that we can broadly work out in advance what is to count as an appropriate response; reflective practice says that things are more complicated than that and that the professional herself has the responsibility to work out appropriate responses (plural) and to choose a particular action from them. But both terms have this sense of professionalism as residing in the adeptness with which professionals respond to events with which they are faced. The events are given: the question is, how do we respond?

We have to reject this way of looking at professional life. Professionals are persons licensed to practise their trade, which is that of professing-in-action. This simple idea – professing-in-action – as the core of what it is to be a professional has large consequences, consequences that rule out both competence and reflective practice as adequate construals of professional life. In *professing-in-action*, a professional is given a licence to profess within the bounds of her calling and, as we have seen, has the duty to do so. That is why she has that authority bestowed on her by the wider society. [A professional is in authority, irrespective of any further authority she acquires as an authority (Peters, 1967).]

Professing-in-action is analogous to the role of a professor in the academy. Just as we expect a professor to be self-motivating, and not waiting for students to appear before he practises his calling, so the professional does not have to wait for individual clients to turn up. Certainly, that clients do turn up, and repeatedly, would suggest that the professional has substance to her authority, and her standing in speaking out on relevant social issues and controversies will be enhanced. But the transactions with clients do not define the limits of her responsibilities.

In professing-in-action, the professional is attuned to the relevant public debates and is authorized by the wider society to contribute to them. To that extent, we have presenting situations and events analogous to those characteristic of competence and reflective practice. And the professional will feel a responsibility to speak out where she has something she feels will assist the debate, including the public understanding of it. Yet, often, the professional will detect an issue not yet seen as such by the public or even by the profession itself. In that case, the event does not present itself. The situation is framed anew by the professional.

Drawing on the distinctions made earlier, we can term the professional's response to the former situation a form of critical thought in action. The situation is one of a public controversy and the professional exercises her critical thinking in responding to it. In the second case, however, there is no given situation on which the professional can exercise her critical thinking. Here, we are in receipt of a creative framing of the world by the professional. She is saying, here is a matter deserving public attention. In so doing, in exercising her imagination, intellectual powers and judgement, she is demonstrating *critique-in-action*. Critique, it will be recalled, comes into play when new frames of reference are deployed, such that the world (or a significant portion of it) can be seen anew. Old frameworks are jettisoned and a new pattern of understanding is offered to us. Professionals have not just the right to engage in this form of action; they have a duty so to do. Professionals, as professionals, are not entitled to keep their heads down.

This point requires a small qualification. One cannot have a duty to imagine the world anew, to conceive of a fundamentally different way of structuring the profession, or to see a new means of providing the services of the profession. (A professor cannot have a duty to win a Nobel Prize.) Professionals, however, have a duty to maintain and develop their critical powers, such that they are asking themselves radical questions. At least, then, they will be well-placed to contribute to the significant debates as they arise, even if they do not produce their own rewriting of their professional world. Also, the action required to bring a new ordering to general attention will take persistence, courage and political nous. These are not qualities to be found in all professionals, but they are the desiderata of the functioning of professionals in a changing world.

Professionals, we can conclude, have not a right but a duty to speak out. In speaking out, they will exhibit critical thought in the sense of critical thinking, of analysing and commenting on public controversies. And they may well offer a form of thoroughgoing critique-in-action, helping not only the profession but also the general public to comprehend the world anew, in so far as it concerns the profession. Professionals thus live up to their billing of professing-in-action. In so doing, they demonstrate the inadequacy of competence and of reflective practice as construals of professional life. Both concepts would confine professionals to local situations, would diminish the potency of professionalism, and would limit the levels of critical thought within the profession.

Professionalism has the potential to assist in bringing about a learning society and a more democratic society, in which citizens are better informed and in which the framing of the world is continually under informed interrogation. The forces at work that would confine professionalism to efficient and effective actions for clients should be resisted.

The trouble with reflective practice

The notion of professionalism is currently being emasculated. Seen as knowledge-in-use or even reflection-in-action, an undue emphasis is given to the action components and, in the process, the *action* elements are diminished. Providing a suitable corrective to an overly theoretical notion of professionalism is one thing; robbing the notion of professionalism of proper theoretical components is another matter. It is not that we should just lob in a fair dollop of theory, so as to balance theory and action. What is needed is a new notion of professionalism altogether.

I propose a conception of professionalism that draws upon the triple schema of critical reason, critical self and critical action for which I am arguing in this book. Specifically, I shall argue that the notion of professionalism lies in the critical deployment of multiple discourses. The full-fledged professional is adept at engaging with different audiences (clients, professional peers, managers and other professionals) through integrating critical reason, self and action. As a professional, one has a duty to speak out to inform the public domain. Being a professional cannot be a matter solely of professional–client transactions. The professional has to engage with a wider set of discourses that generate, in turn, wider responsibilities. In the fulfilment of those responsibilities, critical reason, critical self and critical action are united. The extended professional is necessarily a critical person.

The difference between my view and Schön's can be put in this way. It is not so much a matter of knowledge-in-use as critical frameworks-in-action. In rightly repudiating a theory-based conception of professionalism, Schön has overfocused on action and, as a result, has diminished the potential of professional action. What we receive from Schön is a truncated view of professionalism.

In my notion of critical frameworks-in-action, the schema that is at the heart of this book comes into play. That schema points to critical being residing along two axes, of level and domain. The levels of criticality refer to the extent to which it draws on narrow or wider frames of reference. The domains of criticality are three: knowledge, self and world. Professionalism, where fully and properly developed, will extend across both axes, of level and domain. At its fullest extent, professionalism involves – as we have just seen – critique, through injecting new frames of thinking and understanding so as to understand the world anew (and so will operate at the highest *level* of critical thought), and will extend the professional not only in the domain of knowledge itself but also in the domains of the self and the world. Where exhibited by the professional, we are in the presence of critical frameworks-in-action.

Professionals, as licensed authorities in public life, have a duty to maintain and extend their critical powers. In an age of performativity, dominant voices – even within some professions – would resist such a public service conception of professionalism and restrict critical thinking (if they found a role for it at all) to critical thinking skills; that is, deploying known rules of inference on presenting situations to arrive as quickly as possible at the most secure solution. In reaching a secure solution, truth is at best only one consideration, alongside those of efficiency, cost and political outfall. The notion of clinical reasoning is receiving just such a truncated interpretation.

To be sure, other voices are to be heard pressing for a wider interpretation. The notion of reflective practice is itself an example. It contains a sense of a limitless repertoire of actions and interpretations that professionals can bring to the presenting situations. Professionals, on this definition, are critical thinkers-in-action. They are continually involved in sizing up situations, testing their interpretations, formulating hypotheses that are a mix of theory and practice (they are practical hypotheses), and coming to judgements. This is critical thinking of an advanced kind. But it is more than critical thinking for it involves action, and it involves the self. Strangely, for all his talk of reflection-in-action, Schön's story gives us an underconceptualized account of action. It also neglects the self. I shall come to these matters in a moment.

The point is two-fold. Reflective practice offers a space for a critical thinking wider than competence, but the sense of critical thinking made available by reflective practice is still limited. First, reflective practice gives priority to practice: the critical frames that the professional uses to interrogate her professional experience are somehow generated by the practice itself. Unfortunately, Schön does not tell us how the critical frames are derived. His notion of reflection-in-action implies that the critical frames are just supplied by action itself, the deposit of the professional's accumulated experiences that have been subjected to continuous evaluation by the professional. Secondly, it imports and implicitly celebrates a pragmatic definition of truth. Truth is what works. There can be no extra-professional validation of the professional's truth claims on Schön's account, for that could – on his story – let in pure theory; and that would never do, since that would open the door to an overly rational view of professional life. Thirdly, missing too from Schön's account is a sense of the ethical strand in professional life. The aesthetic is present, the professional now having become an artist-in-action; but of the ethical, a sense of any principles or an ethic that might inform professional–client transactions, we meet a silence on Schön's part.

Both the second and the third considerations would allow extra-situational criteria of validity, but that is just what Schön eschews. They would also let in validation of professional knowledge-in-action by the professional community. But here, again, we receive a silence from Schön: peer judgement and the sense that the professional receives her authority partly from her standing in her profession do not sit easily with the notion of the individual reflective practitioner.

My main target in all this is not a debunking of Schön as such, but is that of professionalism seen in the wider context of an unknowable world, a world of change, of contested accounts and of reflexive knowledge. We need a larger account than that offered by Schön.

Bridging the gaps

The conceptual resources for the account of professionalism that I want to develop were flagged earlier and have three components: (1) the dual axes of critical thinking that form the core of this book's argument (that critical thinking can be understood in terms of levels and domains); (2) the idea that professional life can be understood as that of deploying and advancing general well-being through multiple discourses; and (3) that professionalism consists of deploying critical frameworks in action: professional knowledge is critique-in-action. These three components provide, as we might term it, critical professionalism.

It is a truism that the foundations of professionalism are provided by knowledge. Every profession has its distinctive knowledge base. We may argue over the nature of that knowledge: Schön, Hirst and Eraut want to drive up its action components but do not deny that there is still a knowledge base to professionalism. But that simple observation having been made, a set of issues opens up which professionalism in the modern world has yet to address.

First, knowledge has an open-endedness to it such that there can be no resting point. It is not just that knowledge is continually growing and that, therefore, professionals have to 'keep up to date'. It is not even that professionals have to have a sense of the contestability of all knowledge claims and that, therefore, their own claims and actions are always contestable. It is not even that knowledge is ultimately indivisible (despite there being different sets of tests for truth) and that, therefore, professionals' competence must always be limited. Rather, it is that putting knowledge into action is inherently problematic. Schön's way of addressing this matter is to collapse knowledge into action; but this is an entirely inadequate response. Bringing Hume up to date, we can say that there is no secure act from knowing: from knowing, no particular act follows. But that cannot mean that professional action is devoid of knowledge; it just means that the connections between knowledge and action have an infinite open-endedness about them.

There are three gaps here. There is an epistemological gap, since professional action contains knowledge but the situation does not define in advance the knowledge that should be brought to bear. There is a praxis gap, since the presenting situation does not define the action that should follow, either. And there is an ontological gap, since the presenting situation does not totally structure the professional identity – the professional being – that is to be offered to the world.

Practising epistemologists

Professionals, we can say, have to be *practising epistemologists*. They have to be able to interpret the world through cognitive frameworks and be adept at handling those frameworks in action. There can be no arbitrary limit to either of these dimensions of professional life. In a world that is subject to rapid and global change, where professional roles themselves are under scrutiny and where actions have unpredictable repercussions, there can be no limit on the frameworks that professionals might deploy to make sense of their world. Equally, there can be no *a priori* restriction on the scope of action that a professional might choose to take. It is not, in either domain (knowledge or the world), that anything goes. The knowledge drawn on must be relevant, even if the professional is showing us new patterns of relevance. And the action taken must be appropriate and justified, even if its like has never been seen before. The professional, as a practising epistemologist, is continually creative in the domains of knowledge and the world.

There is no end to the character of the critical frameworks that the professional might deploy. What set of concepts is fruitful? Are the concepts purely technical, representing a sub-culture of the academic world? Are they pragmatic, representing a sub-section of the professional community? To what extent do they draw in frameworks from the wider world, whether, say, of efficiency, of equity or of ecology (in its widest sense)? The frameworks by which the professional can understand her own professional life can multiply not only in range but also in scope. To what extent does the professional have a sense of her own profession, its historical development, its relationship to other professions, its shape and functioning compared with the profession in other parts of the world, and its responsibilities, its challenges and its potential amidst the changes faced by society and by the global economy?

Far from professional life being given, it possesses a triple openness: a cognitive, self and action openness. It is an openness about how we understand professional life, about what we take it to be. It is an openness of action. And it is an openness of understanding and developing a professional self-identity. It is an interpretative openness born of a changing world, of there being multiple discourses through which we can interpret professional life (such as care, efficiency, service, empowerment and transformation), and of there being no limit to the ways in which we can act through those interpretations. A shorthand term for some – but only some – of these conditions of openness is postmodernism, which underwrites the multiple interpretations that are available in the world. But *that* interpretative openness underplays the real, worldly, multiple discourses with which professionals are having increasingly to grapple in securing their livings in a complex and ever-interdependent world.

In such a world, a pragmatic openness arises alongside this epistemological openness. If interpretations of professional life are not given in any sense, still less are actions. What is an appropriate way in which doctors should interact with their patients (and vice versa)? What are pedagogic relationships in a university to look like? With what voice and with whom should the engineer speak in working on a major project with social implications (such as the design of the Channel Tunnel)? The potential range of actions even in a 'given' situation is infinite. The actions are infinite because the potential interpretations are infinite. Actions and interpretations, therefore, are intertwined, the professional weaving her way in thought and action through the multiple discourses that confront her.

All these are signs of critical frameworks coming into play, frameworks being critical in offering alternative horizons of meaning and of possibilities for action. In bringing such frameworks to bear on her interpretations and actions, the professional is a critical professional. It is not just a matter, therefore, of whether to act in this way or that, but also of: within what framework shall I act? In fulfilment of what set of principles shall I act? What understandings, what perspectives, what theories and what key concepts might offer a way forward? The potential frameworks will be critical *of each other*: they will have tensions between them and may be incommensurable. The key challenge of modern professionalism is just this, of trying to make sense of disparate discourses in one's professional actions. It may be that, on occasions, the discourses collide such that one cannot act under them coherently. One cannot easily treat a patient both as a consumer of expensive services and as a patient in need of personal attention.

The challenge, then, that faces the modern professional is the management of incoherence. Not just competing demands on their time but also competing demands on the way that they might live out their professionalism: this is the challenge that faces professionals on a daily basis. The contending frameworks that confront them both supply the challenge of potential incoherence and provide the resources with which to grapple with the practical and conceptual dilemmas that face them. Frameworks may be internal or external to those within the professional sub-culture; they may be instrumental or dialogic in character; and they may spring from endorsing or critical ideologies. But all these frameworks are critical in that they reside in alternative discourses and, therefore, are implicitly critical of each other. The art of the modern professional lies in handling these multiple discourses in thought and action.

Seen in this way, action can become a means of inserting into society critique through professional action. Through taking on frameworks with large narratives – of freedom, equity, empowerment and emancipation – professionals can intervene purposely in the world. Professional thought and action, accordingly, are limitless in their interpretations. The professional both is the interpreter of new discourses and can enable society to understand itself through new discourses. The professional, through her critical thinking and her action, is a discursive creator.

And what of the self?

So far in this chapter, professionalism has been drawn out along the two axes of the levels and domains of critical thought that lie at the centre of this book's argument. Professionalism can include a fundamental critique of frameworks of thought and action. What has so far been underplayed is the third domain of critical thinking, that of the self. Without this third strand being injected, we have an unstable picture of professionalism. And, left on just the two pillars of knowledge and the world, it would topple over.

Actually, the ground has already been charted. In invoking unusual frameworks of comprehension and action, in understanding one's professional responsibilities anew, in conceiving of new ways of going on and in granting substance to alternative value systems, the professional is necessarily bringing her *self* into play and in different ways. But she is also recreating her self. Her professional being develops. She is in the business of ontological reconstruction.

First, the professional is saying, 'This is how I would wish to construct my professional identity'. These, now, are the abiding concepts, frames of reference and value systems that I recognize as having legitimate claims on me, on my professional self. Secondly, since we construct our selves only with the assent of significant others (including those who wield symbolic power, such as professional bodies), in saying 'This is how I would wish to construct my professional self', one is also making a claim on the profession itself. One's peers are being enjoined to take on that way of construing professionalism. Thirdly, in holding out a new way of understanding the professional role or its values, the professional will require qualities of fortitude, steadiness and integrity of self. Critical professionalism calls for considerable personal qualities: the self will be put under considerable pressure to withdraw the offending frame of reference. It marks the professional out as 'not one of us'. The professional self is not given but is continually negotiated.

Sustained or undermined by the power of the dominant frameworks, the professional self cannot remain unchanged. The professional self becomes a distinct professional self, in and for itself, sure of itself. This sureness is a sureness *not* of self-conviction, but of resilience and successful negotiation in different milieux. The modern professional, we said earlier, has to handle multiple discourses. This is a sureness, accordingly, that is brought about through the professional engaging with multiple audiences and through the different discourses that they comprehend.

There is no single text of the professional's life: whether, in postmodern vein, we want to say also that there is no single self to the professional is a moot point. The successful professional, it could be said, is adept at presenting separate selves to the different audiences. Sometimes, of course, the different audiences are literally present at the same time (as readers of the newspaper article or as participants in the public conference). And then the real adeptness shines through in the manufacturing of a text that can be read in different ways and at different levels by multiple audiences. But, whether we read it as different presentations of the one self or as different selves more or less integrated in the one act, a self or even selves there has to be. The professional is not just staking out claims about the world – about the kinds of services to be offered or the professional–client relationships – but is making claims about herself. She is constructing her professional self and is looking for its validation from her audiences. Of course, some audiences may be more ready to underwrite that particular self than others. In turn, the professional will be making judgements: how significant is this audience? What power does it wield? The construction of the professional self requires calculation in an uncertain and even unknowable environment. But who said that the construction of the professional self was easy?

Conclusion

Professionalism is being shorn of its critical components. It is being diminished, its critical edge being reduced to problem-solving in bounded professional situations or to reflecting 'critically' on one's professional practice. Far from injecting liberating elements into professional life, this is liable to play into the hands of the operationalists. Critical thinking fulfils, here, an instrumental agenda, so that 'professionals' become self-monitoring autodidacts, able to engender greater efficiency in professional work. Indeed, professional life here is reduced to professional work, with critical thought the mere handmaiden of a heightened technique.

This rationality is not to be downplayed, as Habermas has insisted. But it imports an unduly limited view of the scope and range of critical thought in professional life and, in so doing, reduces the role of professionals and surrenders their autonomy to instrumental voices. Professional life has to be reinterpreted in modern life. Understood as critical professionalism, not just the right but the duty opens up to keep continually under review the character of that life and to project new understandings to the wider society. Professionals have the duty to profess. But professing in a postmodern age calls for the capacity to be open to multiple discourses and to engage, albeit critically, with them. This calls for criticality at all the levels of critical thought so as to embrace fundamental critique. It also calls for an integration of critical thinking in the three domains of knowledge, self and world. Proper engagement with multiple discourses demands no less. In this process of critical professionalism, professional persons develop.

There will be no easy or happy point of integration: the multiple discourses are incommensurable. But these are professional persons able to help to sustain a rational society. The babel of voices is only apparent. Citizens still have to form their own conclusions on difficult issues: the professionals – who dispute amongst themselves – do not sequester those civil rights. The citizens are empowered, able to make informed decisions about their own fates. No wonder that there are voices that would emasculate professionalism. Endorsing Friedson (1994), we can say that professionalism can be and should be reborn.

11

Academics as Intellectuals

Introduction

The notion of 'academics as intellectuals' gains its point from a sense that academics might *not* be intellectuals. Academics in the modern world are often not intellectuals in the fullest sense; indeed, they are not even academics in any straightforward sense. However, while difficult, the fulfilment of the intellectual role is both possible and desirable. For the conceptualization of that role, we shall draw upon the general schema of criticality that lies at the centre of this book. The dual axes of the levels and the domains of critical being apply not just to the education of students or to wider professionalism, but also to the academics themselves. The realization of the academic as intellectual cannot be comprehended or practised as a role internal to the academy but has to embrace a sense of active engagement with the external world. Academics as intellectuals have to engage in critical action and so become critical persons.

On being an academic in the modern age

There are problems over what it is to be an academic in the modern age. Indeed, to what extent might those who are paid to teach in higher education today recognize themselves under the banner of 'academic'? In a mass higher education system, the category of 'academic' becomes problematic. An immediate explanation might seem to be that of an increasing split between research and teaching. But this is unconvincing: under the press of research evaluations and in the absence of a clear differentiation between research and teaching universities, there is more research and scholarship being undertaken. The journals proliferate. In a formal sense, there is more academic work being conducted, not less. And yet the category of academic remains problematic.

This reflection also rules out another candidate by way of explanation, that of the organization of academic work within the universities, in which staff are given teaching-only contracts. Although there might be exceptions, such as teacher education, for the most part the staff in universities are expected to teach and to produce research or scholarly publications. There remains, for the time being, a general expectation that many of the overt practices of being an 'academic' should be fulfilled. But, somehow, the category of 'academic' sticks less easily now despite the sheer amount of academic work being accomplished.

The cause lies not at the levels of policy or in the internal organization of the universities. It lies in larger influences. Peter Scott (1995) has recently argued that the rise of the mass university has to be understood amidst wider social changes. The mass university system is part of a response to changing patterns of work. In a post-Fordist era, computers and robots offer more consumer-responsive modes of production. The new 'mass production' has the nice characteristic that, in theory at least, the consumer can have any colour she wants. As a result, in this opening up of infinite worlds of consumption, planners, designers, analysts, managers and advertisers are now required; people, in other words, who can tell stories, who can redescribe our world. The university, accordingly, is in the business of redescribing rather than of understanding the world.

In this situation, the category of academic becomes problematic. It spoke of the study of texts produced by other academics. Those texts were about the world but there was a separateness from the world built into their character. The academics spoke to other academics. Now, the boundary between academic life and the wider world is dissolved. The 'strong classification' that existed has been broken, as the dominant sources of educational power have sought – with much justification – to bring the academic world into a closer relationship with the wider world. In the process, too, the tight framing of the pedagogical relationship has been reduced, the category of 'student' being now a preparation for the world of work rather than a set of experiences with point derived internally from the academy (Bernstein, 1996).

The category of academic, therefore, is dissolving, since the boundaries between the academic and the wider world *and* between the academic and the student are both weakened. In turn, the authority possessed by the academic is diminished. Hitherto based on a mastery of a canon internal to an academic sub-culture, the pedagogical relationship was buttressed by the academic as *an authority*. Now, with new forms of educational transmission being urged on lecturers (reflecting agendas of performativity and efficiency), with new modes of educational realization (reflecting an ideology of operationalism), with new patterns of institutional organization (in which staff become human resources) and within a world of social and economic change, that authority dissipates. New sources of legitimacy are urged on staff, hinged on information technology, knowledge-in-action, so-called transferable skills, standards of competency and the process of learning. In research, the academic is now required to demonstrate, before a project commences, its impact on the wider world. No longer is it sufficient to conduct research that is well-founded and which produces significant advances in our understanding of the world.

The substantive definitions of the practices of the academic are now made elsewhere, the task being reduced to enacting that predetermined role. The role has become a hybrid, straddling different and even competing frames of reference. To that extent, academics can be accounted professionals. Being a professional in the modern world means handling multiple discourses, and academics have joined the club. The price – which *had* to be paid – is that the purity marked by the category of academic is now irreparably gone, and not before time.

The diffidence, then, that many members of staff of universities have in seeing themselves as 'academic' is understandable. The diffidence represents an accurate sociological reading of the situation faced by would-be academics, quite apart from the existential awkwardness it reflects. The boundary between practices marked as 'academic' and those marked as worldly is now fuzzy; and so the academic role is unclear. The diffidence, however, is misplaced. It is misplaced historically, philosophically and sociologically (despite what has just been said). To develop the argument in this way, I shall widen it to include the category of intellectual.

The loss of the intellectual

Historically, the sharp separation of the academic function from worldly concerns is recent, being certainly twentieth-century in its introduction. In Victorian England, academics in the sciences and in letters saw a role for themselves in engaging with the wider society and, indeed, in carrying their thinking directly to the wider society in public lectures and debates (Gordon and White, 1979; Heyck, 1982). It has only been with the largely mid-twentieth-century academic control of universities and the academicization of knowledge production in the universities (Scott, 1984) that the role of academic has been drawn more narrowly. Indeed, the point can be put more strongly. It was with this narrowing of the responsibilities of the university lecturer that the academic was born. The idea of the academic had point at a time when the role was separated from the wider society, when the production and dissemination of knowledge – now become academic knowledge – was in the hands of the lecturers (or 'dons').

The generous way of reading all this is as a process of professionalization. In staking out academics' own forms of knowledge, in securing control over its production and dissemination, not just the academic role was born. The academic life collectively became a kind of profession, in charge of its own affairs. But the cost was considerable. The category of academic might have been born but the category of intellectual was extinguished. The weakness of the one is a direct corollary of the strength of the other.

The idea of the intellectual-on-campus cannot be understood apart from a sense of relationships between the universities and their host society. Whether as conservative intellectuals, endorsing and articulating the dominant ideologies of society; as would-be critical intellectuals, supposedly

securing an independent vantage point from which to critique society's institutions and frames of thought; as organic intellectuals, allying themselves
to emancipatory forces or classes; or as utopian intellectuals, standing apart
from society but imagining and proffering to society large visions of what
might be: all these roles of the intellectual point to wide responsibilities
aimed at maintaining or, indeed, developing value in society (Mannheim,
1960; Gouldner, 1979; Gramsci, 1980). The role of the intellectual is normative and imaginary, even when seen as endorser.

The callings, therefore, of academic and intellectual are different. The
academic looks inwards, to the peer community, to the internal norms and
values of the academic sub-culture. The intellectual looks outwards to the
wider society. Depending on how the role is conceived, the intellectual may
identify with restricted elements of society (largely, the dominated or the
dominant), but the extramural character of the role is a necessary part of
being an intellectual.

The key question is: are these separate callings conflicting? Is it possible
to be both an academic and an intellectual in the modern world? On the
analysis just given, the question is misplaced. The role of the academic has
been dismantled in any case and, in the UK at least, the role of the intellectual has never been institutionalized. However, I remarked earlier that
the diffidence that lecturers feel about 'academic' as a self-description is
untoward historically, sociologically and philosophically. The argument seems
to be moving in different directions. The category of academic has been
displaced in the modern world, but there is life left yet in the idea.

I have said something about the historical misreading: historically, those
living in the academy understood that they had obligations to the wider
polity. The trickier argumentative challenges are those of the sociological
and of the philosophical misreadings.

Too clever by half

It is often remarked that, unlike other countries in continental Europe, the
UK has never had an intelligentsia. It has not possessed a group with a collective sense of its having a relationship with, and a responsibility towards,
the wider society to offer a source of cultural and cognitive challenge. The
humanists might have enjoyed more cultural capital than the scientists
(although that was doubtful in the Victorian age), but their role was that
of cultural endorsers rather than as supplying a source of critique, a means
of injecting alternative frames of reference into the polity. In so far as the
academics of Victorian England understood that they had an intellectual
role (and they did), it was to inform the citizenry about the world as it
was coming to be understood. Public lectures were a form of extramural
liberal education, of public enlightenment rather than of public liberation
or emancipation in a radical sense.

On offer from the academics was a demonstration of the power of critical thought. Darwin and Freud supplied new ways of understanding man's

relationship with the world and new self-understandings, although this new thinking was marginal to the universities. Missing entirely was a sense of self-empowerment through personal and social action. The historical base, therefore, for a proper realization of the intellectual role is not auspicious, it has to be said.

However, coming up to date, opportunities for realizing the intellectual role are now opening just as the academic role is being weakened. Certainly, the current alignment of forces is not conducive to a realization of the intellectual role. A state-driven performativity, coupled with the marketization of higher education, rightly dissolves the inner-directed academic role but also surrenders it to pragmatism and operationalism. The exclusivity of academicism is exchanged for the tight control of the new operationalism. Performativity rules, well, if not OK, it just rules.

But the emphasis on performance, on instrumental pay-off, cuts two ways. On the one hand, the power of academicism is broken, and thankfully so. That was never going to supply a social epistemology that would engage with a world of economic, social and ecological disturbance. But, in the breaking of the academics' monopoly power, the academics are offered even greater forms of influence, if not power. The academics are no longer a caste distinctive in society.

Plough, sword and book were separate in traditional and mediaeval society (Gellner, 1988). But now, as book is supplemented by the personal computer, knowing the world is intimately linked to social and economic reproduction. 'Book' may now take the form of a consultant's report, of a new design, of an analysis of economic trends, or of a code of practice in professional life. Even as written text, 'book' now takes many forms. Academics can practise their trade in different arenas. 'Visiting professors' are testimony to the hybrid role that knowing the world has become. University courses are offered jointly by universities and commercial and professional organizations. Higher education is to be found on different sites. Society has come into the heart of the university, its pedagogical and its epistemological practices. In the process, the potential for academic influence over our knowledge of the world does not diminish; it multiplies.

It seems that the category of the academic must diminish, and the category of the intellectual has no site for its purchase. I implied earlier that such readings are sociologically understandable but that they are also a misreading. The remarks just made about the new hybrid role of the academic go some way towards demonstrating the misreading, but there is a little more to add.

Mixing the modes

We are desperately (to use a term of Leavis's) in need of a new conception of academic; and one that embraces the category of intellectual. The sense of desperation is justified because the potential about which I spoke a moment ago is largely just that: unrealized potential. Our contemporary conceptions of the academic are too limited. Currently, they take three forms. First, there remains a strong internalist conception, tying the role (Oakeshott-like (1989)) to the maintenance and, indeed, the development of academic forms of life. Secondly, the instrumentalists fall in naively with the recasting of knowing as performativity: student outcomes, skill development and immediate employability leave their pedagogic mark, while impact, usage, technological transfer and patent possibilities leave their mark on research. In both spheres, finding solutions for given problems is significant. Thirdly, the operationalists recast the academic role as a set of operations to be wrought directly on the world, with demonstrable effects. The rise of the academic-as-consultant is the crucial example here (to which I shall return in a moment), in which the hybrid character of the modern academic is accepted with alacrity.

In sum, the three dominant conceptions of academic are (1) a fading academicism, where value is judged by the knowledge producers themselves; (2) an ever-stronger instrumentalism, where value is judged by the external community; and (3) a newer operationalism, where value is produced by the producers acting directly in the world, subject to criteria of the wider world. The rise of mode (2), especially of solving problems-in-the-world, and the emergence of the mode (3) form of knowledge producer render problematic the category of academic, but they do not extinguish it.

The key question may appear to be, is it possible to hold on to mode (1) while exhibiting the modes (2) and (3) form of knowledge production? Is it possible to be apart from the world while becoming ever more immersed in it, subject increasingly to the social epistemologies, norms and requirements (of effectiveness, efficiency and economy) of the wider world? The question hints that it just may be that the reading of academic as a past social category is precipitate. It might be possible to hang on to something of the separateness of the academic while serving new 'stakeholders'. The question has the further value in that it implies, rightly, that a challenge of academic life is that of living effectively with multiple discourses and in speaking, at the same time, to audiences having conflicting agendas.

The question has that double worth but it presumes too much. To ask if the internalist category of academic can be retained in the modern world, even if alongside more modern extramural interpretations, is to hang on to a world that is characteristic of a former age. The academics have lost their monopoly over the production of high-status knowledge. The associated category of academic is, therefore, doomed, except as an archaic role, perhaps available to certain 'elite' universities wishing to pretend to offer a site for such epistemological purity. But as a serious social category, this sense of the 'academic' is doomed. Let us not try to hang on to it.

The question is unfortunate in another sense. It pretends that things are simpler than they are. It looks to a simple coupling of the old and the new, of the internal and the external, of the cognitive with the operational, and of the conceptual with the performative. But just to list those tensions indicates that there can be no simple such coupling. The character of the modern academic as an epistemological hybrid has to be reformulated, independently of its inheritance.

The sociological story of the modern academic cannot be understood simply as a loss of the category of the academic. Purity is lost. *That* conception of the academic has to be cast aside. But the world is still in need of knowing competences, even if it denies that academic competences are sufficient in the modern world. The knowledge society has need of knowledge (Stehr, 1994). The academic life is not yet expunged. Sociologically, therefore, the category of the academic should not be written off just yet. The announcement of its demise is premature.

Radical practising epistemologists

Philosophically, too, it is a little early to read the last rites of the category of academic. It may seem odd to speak of a philosophical sense of the category of academic, but we can legitimately do so. Academics claim to know the world, if only in a particular way. Knowing the world has always been problematic and, to that extent, academics have always been practising epistemologists. But, in an age that threatens to become postmodern, knowing the world is especially problematic for academics. For the academic role was built on the project of modernism. The academic role took for granted that there was a world to know: the academic task was to produce methodologies for coming to know the world in secure ways. Knowing the world was possible; progress in knowledge, whether gradual or revolutionary, was assured.

Such assuredness has collapsed. The spectre of postmodernism, with its insistence on there being all kinds of legitimate but incommensurable readings of our situations, is not the only cause of this anomie. Much more to the point is the shift in our social epistemologies, in which knowledge as contemplation, celebrated by academicism, gives way to knowledge-as-action and even knowledge-as-(mere)-performance. As Gibbons and his associates (1994) insist, this is not the applied knowledge with which academics are more or less familiar and which, it should be noted, would maintain the academics' epistemological hegemony. Rather, it is a form of knowledge created in action. It is working knowledge; knowledge that works for its users. It has no other locus.

Academics, then, are finding that their epistemological standing is undermined. What counts as knowledge is more open, being more subject to definition by others. Picking up a term from our last chapter, academics have to become practising epistemologists, but in a radical sense. They have to go on continually legitimating themselves. They have to demonstrate that their definitions of knowledge matter. They cannot demonstrate that their definitions of knowledge are the only true way; there are too many other claimants now. Accordingly, the academics' claim to epistemological supremacy lies, if at all, in their competence to handle knowledge as such. They demonstrate their competence in metaknowledge, that they really know about knowledge. They practise epistemology through and through. They not only live this perspective rather than that, but also are able to give a plausible story about its worthwhileness. The academics give us plausible stories about the stories.

The academic lives, then, but in a somewhat different form. Sociologically, the academic is inserted into society as society itself claims knowledge as a defining category of its self-constitution. The academic, far from being an extinct species, is now a necessary social species. Philosophically, the academic has to know about knowledge in a radical way. In a world in which everyone is an epistemologist, the academics are radical practising epistemologists. They secure their legitimacy by demonstrating that they understand the rules for generating and for choosing between knowledges. And they still possess the capacity for producing new knowledge.

But this academic is not the academic of academicism. This is an academic both in-the-world and of-the-world. This academic secures her living through being able to demonstrate a societal value. This academic has to live in society, like it or not. Even disciplines are now taken over by society, as forms of production. Disciplines are sites not only of academic power but also of societal and economic power, sustained only because of their perceived extramural value. So this academic has the world in her bones. Her discourse only gains a hearing in so far as it has value alongside the multitudinous others. She has to carry the world with her, epistemologically speaking. There is an in-the-world incorporation, and there is an of-the-world identity. This is a streetwise academic. She knows that she makes it academically because she makes it in the world.

The academic is dead; long live the academic. This new academic, this worldly academic, eschews academicism. She knows that, in the knowledge society, everyone is an epistemologist. There is no virtue in knowing as such any more. To claim epistemological superiority just because one knows something is to exhibit hubris of the most embarrassing kind. The emperor is without clothes. On the other hand, the new academic understands the real world. The new academic sees that she has to sell her epistemological wares to the world. And that means engaging with the world. The new academic is an epistemological entrepreneur, finding customers for her wares. This is an academic fully immersed in the world, not one separate from it.

The academic, therefore, is displaced into the world and, in the process, is changed. Of course, we need a new term for this hybrid role; since this is not a role solely within the academy, it is not purely academic. Nor does 'intellectual' appear to be appropriate for this role, for this epistemological wheeling and dealing (often, quite literally, as patents are taken out, as book rights are determined, and as possibilities for technological transfer are worked out). As the new worldy academic is born, the category of *practising epistemologist* beckons.

The new endorsers

Three roles are opening up for the new academic in the world. First, as problem solver in the grand style. Society has problems, whether in transport, the economy, business organization, food technology or foreign policy. The academic, therefore, should be able to offer solutions. Second, as endorser of state policies, especially in welfare fields such as health and education. The problems and solutions effectively have already been determined. The academic's role is to legitimate them by filling in the detail, by offering sophisticated performance indicators, modes of organization and human resource management so as to enable the policies to work. Third, as cultural voyeur. For postmodernism, especially in the arts, all the world offers delight. Disneyworld rivals Versailles. In this milieu, the academic lives it up, pointing out to us what we have been missing all this time and helping us to see how we have become aesthetic dupes, saturated with unexamined traditions and canons of apparent right taste but which were discourses loaded with power.

All these roles could be said to be critical, but the critical element is limited in each case. The problem solvers not only take identified problems but even refashion them so that we see the problems in new ways. The problem of communicating computerized information is suddenly seen in pictorial terms, and so the PC screen is transformed into icons and windows. This is a critique of conventional frames of doing things, but it springs from an intent on achievement, on getting things done and on profitability. This critique is fine, but it is limited in taking ends largely for granted, focusing instead on producing imaginative new means of attaining them.

The endorsers also have their critical moments. In the health service and in education, new structures are put in place, new kinds of manager are called for, and new roles and relationships are developed in fulfilment of the new and growing performance indicators. This systems approach contains implicit critiques of producer-led cultures, of a lack of explicitness and of professional collegiality. The planning, the structures and the new managerialism are inherently critical of traditional practices, which are seen as inadequate to the challenges of the modern age. But these endorsers of state policies exhibit a limited form of critical thinking, since their systems frameworks, their allegiance to surveillance techniques and their concerns for bottom-line outcomes are givens. This is a decisionism that brooks no critique of itself.

Lastly, the postmodernists look to be thoroughly critical, illuminating the pretentiousness underlying frameworks for knowing and experiencing the world. Now, everyone in their own locale can and should have a hearing. There are no grand narratives to order claims on the world in any hierarchy of worth or truth or emancipatory potential. This debunking is certainly critical. Indeed, it is a thoroughgoing critique, undermining all claims on universal knowledges and values; and, thereby, on frameworks for knowing, valuing and communicating about the world. But this cognitive egalitarianism underplays and, indeed, denies the strength of the dominant ideologies (so much so that ideology itself becomes a worn-out category). This is a naive form of critique. It will be no match for the real world's messiness and power structures despite its insistence – especially by Foucault – on the link between knowledge and power.

So the academics, now being enjoined to come into the world, embrace critical stances. But there are limits in each case to this critical spirit. The modern academics conduct their critical sorties respectively within given horizons of means not ends, of techniques not real communication, and of cognitive egalitarianism not social realism.

The first two roles are not entirely separable and are to be observed in the role of academic-as-consultant. Here, we see a defining instance of the hybrid nature of the modern academic. The jibes aimed at consultants are familiar enough: that they tell us what we know already or that they are paid to articulate what the managers have been saying for years without impact. The jibes only have point because consultants operate within limits. It may be that one of the tasks of the consultant is to educate the client and to reformulate the problem. Nevertheless, there will be limits not only to what can be said but also to the voice in which it is said.

'Executive summaries' are a nice commentary not only on consultancy but also on the spirit of our times. Clear recommendations leading to precise action-based decisions are called for. A careful weighing of the values or purposes of the initiative or organization being evaluated is usually off-limits. Nor is this form of evaluation normally encouraged explicitly to critique those in power who, after all, are characteristically the commissioners of the report. The academic in *this* world of bullet points is necessarily an endorser, or will find his life as consultant short-lived.

Reclaiming the intellectual

The argument can be simply stated. In the Victorian age, a role of intellectual was available to university teachers in which many attempted to educate the public directly. But with the birth of the modern academic, knowledge was captured by the academic class becoming a class in and for itself, sequestering knowledge production and dissemination. The external role of the intellectual was displaced by the internal role of the academic. Today, that inner-directedness is being challenged and the academic is having to become an actor-in-the-world again. However, the social spaces opening up are limited. This critical reason has its locus within instrumental reasoning, intent on bringing about effects in a world of given ends and values. The issue therefore is whether, in playing this hybrid role, it is possible for the academic also to be an intellectual; or is the category of intellectual a historical relic to be laid to rest?

The logic of the analysis just offered is that there is a social space available to the modern academic also to be an intellectual, and that there is a responsibility on the academic to take on that role. The social space has opened up as the academic world has been drawn into the wider society. But precisely because the academic world has been drawn into the wider society, because the impetus comes from that wider world, forces are at work that would constrain the realization of that larger construal of what it is to be an academic. The shift in our social epistemologies to more operational forms of knowing the world, the call for demonstrable outcomes of interactions, the drive for more efficient means to preconceived ends, and the opening of the academic as consultant supplying knowledge services to clients wherever they might be found: these strategic imperatives would limit the functioning of the academic in the wider world.

But there are larger issues at stake. Postmodernism believes that we have reached the end of ideology. The real situation is entirely the other way around. We are so saturated with ideology that the postmodernists can't see it. Postmodernism is an indication not that we have reached the end of ideology but that we are seeing the triumph of ideology. The growth of state apparatuses, of state insistence on outcomes and competences as definitions of education, of universities as organizations, of state surveillance through state agencies, of the construal of education as a means of economic production, of science and technology as unrivalled forms of knowing, of numerical performance indicators, and of performance-based modes of knowing: all of these spring from ideologies of economic production and of control of the social environment.

There is, then, an urgent need for the academic role to be recast so that, just as it is inserted into the world, it contends with the dominant ideologies. Unless the academic role is so reconceived, the academics will end up by being dupes of those ideologies.

'Endorsers' is too polite a term for these modern academics. Endorsers, at least, might be expected to have a sense of the product with which they are identifying. Academics now have their livings in the world and simply fall in with the dominant frameworks. The analysts of the economy, of the health 'service' and of the transport 'system' offer solutions to the problems as defined by the state and its dominant powers. Yet the possibility opens up for the academics to reclaim the role of intellectual by situating their analyses in more critical frames of reference which include purposes and values.

Being an intellectual in the modern age is not easy. Three challenges open up: of framing, of voice and of strategy. Alternative frames of construing problems and situations call for alternative intellectual resources. But from where are such alternative sources of intellectual capital to be found? Secondly, when they are found and when new frames of understanding a problem have been formulated (which, by definition, challenge the conventional frames and sites of power), how are these frames of understanding to be expressed in such a way that they are likely to be listened to? Is it possible to find a voice such that it both resonates to some degree with those occupying sites of power and yet does justice to the new insights being offered? (Dare a report on education include words such as 'epistemology' and 'emancipation'?) Lastly, what strategies are to be employed so that one is given a sympathetic hearing? What forms of communication are available such that this intellectual product – which could be literally revolutionary, presenting not just new understandings but new values – might have positive effects?

All these questions are before those who would wish to be serious intellectuals in the modern age. It is easy enough to be a dilettante intellectual, offering ideas but in an effete manner, in such a sophisticated inner-directed voice and with such inept strategies that no-one in sites of power would ever accord one a hearing. In other words, serious critique in the modern world has to engage with the world and to do so with some adroitness. It may not be possible fully to combine the critical spirit with a significant impact. However much different discourses are intertwined in the one text, such that quite different readings are possible and different communities can see something of their own interests, still punches may have to be pulled. Being an intellectual, a critical intellectual, in the modern world is the art of the possible. Agendas may be incompatible. But the responsibility remains to proffer new ways of reading the world. That the role of the intellectual is not easily constructed today is no reason for not attempting the task. On the contrary, the opening up of discursive space in society is a task that lies before the new academic as intellectual. Unless academics are willing to be accomplices in the closing of the discursive space in society, the task of being a critical intellectual cannot be shirked.

But the critical intellectual occupies an intellectual role that is not just intellectual. The role is both task and achievement: it has to be worked at in the world. It is necessarily political, active and communicative. Dominant ideologies and interests have to be not just understood cerebrally but also contended with in a positive and constructive spirit. This calls for personal qualities of persistence, of courage and of resilience. In other words, the critical intellectual in the modern world has to embrace the three domains of critique identified in this book, of thought, action and self. Indeed, critique in the world calls for self-development as the relevant institutions and sites of power are constructively engaged, but with an unflinching eye on the alternative frames that one is offering. In this combination of critical thought, critical action and critical self, the critical intellectual necessarily is his or her own person. He and she become critical persons.

Conclusion

The academics are being brought back into the world and not before time. Many will resist it but the forces at work are unstoppable. Separate roles of technologist, of systems designer and of apologist open up. These new worldly academics still hold on to a rhetoric of critical thinking in their self-descriptions. And they are right. Each of these roles contains critical elements in which conventional frames are critiqued. But the critiques, for the most part, are mounted from within frames of instrumental reason. Critiques to bring about new forms of communication, of self-understanding and of personal and collective emancipation are not envisaged in this critical order.

Academicism is dead; long live academicism – unless we are careful. The new academics will win their spurs through underwriting existing frames of thought and action. In doing so, they will unwittingly assist in bringing about a closing of the cognitive and cultural space. Only by maintaining their distance and by reclaiming the role of intellectual can a narrow reading of the hybrid academic be resisted. The role of intellectual has to be reconstructed. Mannheimian or Gramscian notions of the intellectual are no longer realizable: there is no independent position available, nor is there a public waiting for intellectual leadership. Rather, a new role of critical but engaged intellectual awaits, in and for the world, in which the intellectual engages with the dominant ideologies but does so constructively and collaboratively.

This task calls for discursive powers of a high order, since different discourses will have to be engaged simultaneously. But it also calls for a willingness to engage in critical action and to develop one's self-understanding. The modern critical intellectual is necessarily a critical person in the fullest sense.

12

Critical Thinking for a
Learning Society

Introduction

A learning society is necessarily a critical society. It is a society that has
developed capacities for reflexivity at the societal level. This is not to say
that society is a single entity, or that a single set of critical reflections should
be felt to be desirable. It is to say that a learning society contains open
communicative systems and an openness to conventional practices, such
that radical alternative institutions, policies and arrangements are not just
possible but are *likely*. As is sometimes observed, a genuinely learning society is a democratic society (Ranson, 1994): it is a society in which all voices
can be heard in equal measure and in which there is no fear about expressing a point of view. It is understood that power and learning are mutually
antagonistic entities. Neither can exist in the presence of the other.

These reflections set a number of hares running. In what sense can
a society learn about itself? How can the idea of criticism bite at the level
of society? What, in any case, is meant by 'a learning society'? I shall say
something about each of these matters but they are not our central concern. That remains higher education and the senses in which it can be said
to be critical. Higher education is or can be critical in the developmental
processes prompted by its courses; or it can be critical in the intellectual
interests of its lecturers and even of its students as they take a critical
interest in their cognitive pursuits; or it can be critical in the alignment of
an intellectual field, in the way its dominant stance – as in women's studies
– might be especially evaluative of the world. However, none of those senses
of higher education as a critical enterprise will occupy us here. Instead, the
question before us is this: in what senses can higher education play a part
in bringing about a more critical society? I shall draw upon the notion of
a learning society as a vehicle to make my argument, not because it is
necessary but because, in the interpretation for which I wish to argue, it is
a helpful vehicle for our present purposes.

A society that learns

The idea of a learning society holds out the hope that it is possible for society to develop, but it is not just any kind of development that counts. Learning suggests development of worthwhile kinds. It implies that progress is possible. Secondly, it also suggests that, through the learning that has taken place, the body or entity in question is able to respond to its environment in new ways. Thirdly, it further suggests that that learning must be accompanied by understanding; simply doing things in new ways doesn't qualify as learning. For that, there has to be some insight into the new ways of thought and of action. The new thinking and the new forms of action have to be informed and to be under some degree of control.

Placing the notion of learning in a relationship with the notion of society produces, therefore, an ambitious set of aspirations. It suggests more than that we might be in the presence of a changing society, implying that the changes are *to some degree* considered, under control, worthwhile and imbued with societal understanding. Of course, contemporary society is so complex that such hopes are in some senses unrealizable. They are hopes, not descriptions of reality. But they hold out possibilities. They suggest that enlightened action is still possible.

The idea of a learning society points also to other dimensions of learning. It says that learning can take place at the level of society. This is a profound and complex idea: that learning need not only be an attribute of individuals or even just of organizations, but can also be said to characterize society itself. The suggestion is that society can learn about itself. This idea of learning works not at the level of individuals and is not a matter for psychological investigation, but works at the level of society itself. The notion of learning, as a description of society – as distinct from the individuals in society – is a sociological category. This sense of the learning society points to certain social conditions that have to be met if there is to be any prospect of the learning society coming into being.

First, society has to have available to it a range of perspectives such that its dominant perspectives or ideologies can be placed and kept under critical surveillance. A number of things follow from that bland statement. Society has to be reasonably democratic in the sense that there can be no domination of ideas within it by any group or discourse. There will never be an equality of discourses in society but, for societal learning to take place, there has to be a range of discourses available.

However, it is not sufficient for different discourses to be present; they have to engage with each other. It was the point of the last chapter that academics have to engage seriously with the discourses of the wider society but without becoming their mere endorsers. Admittedly, there are philosophical issues as to whether disparate discourses could ever engage with each other. If they can engage, there are points of contact and they cannot be so different from each other (unless one is dominating the other). If they are incommensurable, there can be no serious contact. In that case, there can be no learning; no societal learning.

That there can be no societal learning is an implication of the postmodern perspective. On the one hand, the available discourses are purely local – so we are assured – and there can be no general narratives or concepts that offer unifying bridges. On the other hand, progress is ruled out. First, progress is a grand narrative in its own right (and the soundness of grand narratives is now denied). Secondly, progress is ruled out as a logical consequence of this endorsement of the local as against the universal. If all we have are our own immediate holds on life, if they cannot be interrogated in any way, at best learning is confined internally to a single discourse. Critical thinking can only be a matter of living by the standards of that discourse, a matter of ensuring that the internal standards are being maintained. But this is low-level critical thought. Fundamental critique is not so much outlawed as never coming into the reckoning. For *that* gets its purchase precisely from external frameworks of thought and action being turned onto the framework in question, and such a move is ruled offside by postmodernism.

A learning society is, therefore, necessarily a critical society. It is a society in which alternative frames of knowing and acting are made available and in which those discourses come – often uncomfortably – into collision with one another. It is a society that asserts that communication, real communication, is possible. Those living in one cognitive house can learn from those living in another. But, to repeat, the category of the learning society achieves its fullest readings as a sociological and as a philosophical concept. Sociologically, it suggests conditions for the discursive structure of society and for its maintenance. The discourses of society have to come into a close relationship with each other: there are, therefore, implications of a structural openness in this idea, but there are the beginnings of the workings of the communicative structures here as well. For societal learning to take place, there have to be in place steering mechanisms, such that there is feedback between ideas and policies on the one hand and their societal evaluation and critique on the other. The critique implied by the notion of the learning society, in other words, cannot be simply a matter of adversarial conversations but must call up hard-nosed structures that make possible this interchange between societal developments and their evaluation. Informed critique, in turn, calls for a high general level of education, a full flow of information and democratic structures.

But there are also what we can legitimately term philosophical components of the learning society. The learning society is not yet realized, nor will it ever be. It stands for a set of ideas, a prospect of what might be. It offers us a set of concepts around society – learning, openness, communication and progress – which together supply a normative standard against which societies can be evaluated. We learn about ourselves in significant ways by holding up against ourselves the full notion of the learning society. We reconstruct ourselves through our imaginary understandings of what might be. We reassemble the basic constituents through which we understand ourselves. We do not learn new facts about ourselves but come to understand ourselves differently.

The matter with critique

The learning society, therefore, stands for critique in three senses: substantively, procedurally and normatively. More than that, it asserts the importance of critique in these three senses. Critique earns its spurs when it illuminates a discourse, when it shows the discourse for what it is, when it reveals its partiality, its hidden interests and its pretentiousness. Substantively, therefore, it comes into play when it shows that that way of looking at a situation is limited and that, instead, we might take on another perspective altogether. It is not just a matter of exchanging one discourse for another, one way of construing things for another. Critique is evaluative as well as liberating. It says that this framework is not just an alternative to that but that it is *better*. For Marx, better was a function of serving a wider and less partial set of class interests. Now, amidst late modernity, we have a sense of there being significant categories of interests other than those founded on class. But a sense of there being better alternative – and not just different – frameworks is built into the notion of critique. We can improve on this partiality; the option is not just that of adopting yet another form of partiality.

Procedurally, too, critique comes into play in the notion of the learning society. The learning society can only learn about itself if it has relatively democratic structures. The different voices have to have a hearing. This is a severe injunction. Power expresses itself surreptitiously. Ideologies gain their purchase through their hiddenness (the 'end of ideology' thesis betrays a complete misunderstanding of the skulduggery of ideology). Voices are not necessarily silenced, but the dominant powers so make their agendas clear that contesting voices are muted simply to gain a hearing. Those contesting voices can only express themselves fully if they feel that no sanction will result. Sanctions need not be overt; simply disapproval from within the laager of the dominant powers will usually be enough to effect a half-silence. Power will convince itself that it is democratic, that everyone has a hearing. And, indeed, voices – half-voices, at least – are heard. Power will not know of the discursive constraint that it effects. Critique needs relatively democratic structures to work; but life being what it is, critique has to accept the presence of unequal discourses.

Three human qualities are required, therefore, from critique itself. First, it has to be brave; it has to be prepared to take on the dominant discourses. Secondly, it has to be persistent. The dominant powers will not lightly accord a hearing to contending voices. Thirdly, it has to be nuanced. Critique is the art of the possible. If critique is not to be dilettante, is not to be self-indulgence, sophisticated discursive strategies have to be adopted. Critique in modern society calls for discursive crafts of the highest order.

Critique matters in modern society. It matters especially because while modern society is characterized by multitudinous discourses, it harbours tendencies that would close off frames of understanding and action. Globalization, in its narrowing of time and distance and in its capacity to transfer dominant modes of thought and action across the globe, is just one element in this closing of the cognitive universe. The more important consideration concerns the inner substance of globalization, the message not the medium. For there we find the adoption of performative epistemologies, the 'can do' *weltanschauung*, the underwriting of technological reason as a dominant mode not just of reason and action but also of interaction, of the way in which we come to evaluate each other. Now, it is the outcomes that the individual effects, not the understanding that he or she possesses, that count. Similarly, it is the impact that our universities have in the world that matters rather than their constitutive values and processes.

Critique matters, therefore, as a means of effecting an awareness of the limitations of the dominant ideologies *and* of feasible alternatives. It matters, too, as a vehicle for ushering in something approximating to the learning society.

But it has to be admitted that, seen against the context just outlined, there is something the matter with critique itself. Critique has the potential, if only it would find a suitable voice, to expand our discursive space in modern society. It holds out the idea of progress. And it can put up alternative frames of knowing and of action. However, by itself, critique is largely bankrupt. This is probably a surprising statement, given the analysis just provided. But the larger thesis of this book has been that, to be effective, critique has to be accompanied by critical self-reflection and critical action. Necessary as it is for a learning society, critique, by itself, will just bounce off its targets. It has to be accompanied by those two other elements of the critical life. The general thesis of this book has been that, through the interlocking of critical reason, critical self-reflection and critical action, we can see develop critical persons. The challenge to higher education is that of bringing off this triple conjunction of the critical life in developing its students. But here, that triple conjunction is also necessary for bringing off the learning society; or, to put it in other terms, the critical society.

The highest learning

If higher education is to be in any kind of business, it has to be in the business of the highest forms of human development. If education is an intentional set of processes aimed at producing worthwhile forms of human development, higher education has to be in the business of producing the most advanced forms of human development. A higher education designed to bring about critical persons capable of working towards a learning society can be no other.

Allowing the academics to monopolize that business over the past one hundred years and then facing those academics with a mass higher education system has produced inadequate notions of the process and point of higher education. In their hands, higher education has come to be seen, at its best, as teaching students in an ethos of research such that they are brought to the frontiers of human knowledge. Elsewhere, I have pointed to the tendentiousness of that phrase, 'the frontiers of human knowledge'; in reality, there are no sharp boundaries of the kind implied by frontiers, only messiness even over where the boundaries lie. It pretends to an authority that academics do not possess, but such tacit imagery plays havoc with their resulting ideas of curriculum and pedagogy. Teaching in higher education is seen as an advanced form of teaching, the particular onus on those teaching in higher education being that they should be intellectually at the frontiers of knowledge and preferably be intent on pushing back those frontiers themselves.

However, if we are serious about bringing about a widespread practice and conception of higher education as the highest form of human development, we have to jettison the notion of teaching. It is true that 'teaching' can be construed very broadly to embrace the activities of establishing an environment in which the desired forms of human development can be nurtured (Oakeshott, 1989), but the notion of teaching has been so curtailed that the term 'teaching' is best abandoned altogether. Even notions of learning, knowing and competence have become so truncated that they, too, are close to losing their developmental potential and should be on any short list of candidates for the linguistic graveyard.

Western higher education has prided itself on placing critical thinking at its educational centre. Some traditions, notably those of England and the USA, have placed that idea in wider contexts of personal development and civic responsibility. The problem before us, and with which we have wrestled in this book, is what is to count as critical thinking in the modern age. In carving up higher education into distinct knowledge territories, critical thinking has lost its larger connotations of enlightenment and emancipation (personal and social) and has been relegated to the mastery of mysterious skills known to the initiated within the distinct knowledge tribes. Far from being a means of expanding the student's understanding and her hold on the wider world, critical thinking has become a means of maintaining the territoriality towards knowledge that the different epistemic communities exhibit.

If higher education is properly to live up to its rhetoric of valuing the critical life, the idea of the critical life has to be given its fullest expression. This means a three-pronged approach, through critical reason, critical self-reflection and critical action. There are tendencies that would play up one at the expense of the others: the academics favour the first, the reflective practitioners favour the second and the operationalists favour the third. Severed from the other two, however, none of the three approaches will be a coherent aim in itself. All three elements of the critical life have to be pursued together. Through integrating thought, reflection and action, we may hope to develop critical persons. And in that conception and practice, higher education may play its part in bringing about a learning society.

Teaching, in so far as it contains *any* hint of transmission of knowledge, of institutional authority or of assimilation on the part of the student, has to be expunged not just from our vocabulary but from our practices in higher education. A higher education that not just anticipates but also embodies the critical life itself can have no truck with such conceptions of teaching. Critical persons embodying the highest form of human development in critical reason, reflection and action will not be taught. This is not an empirical statement but a restatement of what it means to be critical. The critical life is not negative but purposive, imaginary and hopeful. It is also resilient, brave and the embodiment of integrity. Teaching, narrowly conceived, can have no part in the development of such dispositions. The development of human being cannot be taught, but it can flourish amidst an appropriate set of human experiences (Sotto, 1994). The task of the teacher – if we are to retain the term – is that of constructing a range of situations where the critical life in all its demands, its forms of action and its discursive competence can be sustained.

Higher education in the modern age, then, has to be understood as a striving for the highest forms of human development. Unless we do so understand and practise higher education, it will be resiling from its responsibilities not just to its students but also to the wider society and – amidst globalization – to the world. The idea of the learning society will remain another piece of rhetoric, to be captured by those who will use it for the instrumental ends of the regeneration of human capital, rather than a genuinely open society, keeping its cognitive options open and its possibilities for action infinite. Instead, we would see a permanent closure of the cognitive and ethical universe within which we live. This would be a nice irony, since late modernity requires – even to fulfil its instrumental agendas – complete openness of frameworks, of forms of communication and of forms of action. The very reflexivity that late modernity requires, at both personal and social levels, would have been denied. Late modernity would have undermined itself, cutting off the branch on which it rests.

Higher education as the highest learning, as the embodiment of the critical life, would be at the centre of society as a key vehicle by which postmodern society maintains itself. The reflexivity that a critical higher education offers is part of the social maintenance of modern society. But that reformulation of higher education also retains the emancipatory promise of the idea of higher education. If it does not do that, higher education would not be fulfilling the critical life, but would have surrendered to the instrumental agendas of the academics, the operationalists and the so-called reflective practitioners. A higher education for a genuinely critical life would assist in ushering in a learning society *despite* the efforts of precisely those who would claim that that is just what they themselves are doing.

We're all in it together?

We're all in it together, or so we are told. The learning society leaves no-one out. We are all learners, with each of us responsible for our own self-development and our own continuing self-improvement. That that injunction itself contains an instrumental component, I put to one side: we are all responsible for maintaining our value as human capital in the global economy. But even, or especially, in the wider and more normative conception of the learning society that I have just sketched out, human development as a universal aspiration is a necessary ingredient. A learning society, as a utopian ideology, cannot exclude anyone *a priori*. Potentially, all have something to learn and are all capable of learning through life; and, potentially, we all have much to learn from each other. Society is an inclusive category: the learning society is one in which all are continuously in dialogue with one another to some degree. All voices are given room to be heard; no-one is excluded from this discursive space.

But, it may be said, isn't the view of higher education set out in this book one of exclusivity and in three senses? First, it is set at such a stratospheric level that it calls for intellectual and social capital that only a minority in society could possess. Active engaged critique of the kind envisaged here requires intellectual, personal and social resources that are available to only a few. For all its rhetoric of inclusivity, this is an exclusive view of higher education. For all its talk of a learning society, this is a form of learning and human development to which only a minority can realistically aspire.

Secondly, it contains a sense of students owning their own thinking. Critique is a matter of good faith for, unless it is honest and sincere, it loses its edge, a point to which the Tiananmen Square student halting the tanks was testimony. But writing up a view of higher education *as* critique and, not being content with that, specifying the general character of such critique: this is a form of imposition. Especially in a mass higher education system, students – and institutions and their lecturers – will have their own views about higher education. Any attempt to impose a universal view will undermine itself.

Thirdly, all education – if it is to be worthy of the title – has to encourage the development of critical reason. Any attempt to restrict the notion of critical reason to one level of education – higher education – is tantamount to a knowledge policy that would reinforce boundaries between levels of the educational system at a time when they are rightly dissolving.

We can term these three arguments the arguments of exclusivity, of imposition and of stratification. The exclusivity argument is no argument at all. It says, correctly, that the world is stratified intellectually and socially. It reminds us that higher education has been used to heighten such intellectual and social stratification. Arguably, we have now reached the situation where the most important social indicator about individuals is whether they possess a university degree or not. Its possession, quite apart from the economic potential it signifies, indicates as much if not more than any other indicator whether an individual is likely to be within or excluded from the dominant communicative structures of society, not simply the intellectual and the cultural spheres of society in a narrow sense, but the collective and elaborate texts of society through which it constitutes itself.

The exclusivity argument, therefore, is sociologially correct in its reminder about the social stratification of late modernity, now more dependent on intellectual and reasoning capital than ever before (Reich, 1990; Hutton, 1995). It is also right to imply that the social and the interpersonal engagement characteristic of the critical engagement called for here are the natural capacities of only a minority of society. Such engagement calls for social and personal resources that only a narrow stratum of society characteristically possesses. For such engagement brings risk (witness, again, Tiananmen Square), and only those with substantial social and economic resources can afford to bear such risk. Instead, presumably, safer practices should be entertained in which we can demonstrably all share.

But this is a counsel of despair. It asserts *a priori* that the critical strategies sketched out here can only be entertained by the few. And it excludes educators in higher education from the educational challenges and responsibilities of becoming educators in any real sense. It would endorse the existing social and intellectual stratification in society, for everything would be left as it is. This argument is self-defeating: it underwrites precisely the exclusivity that it claims to want to end.

The arguments of imposition and of stratification can now be despatched swiftly. The argument of this book contains the implicit hope and urging that academics in higher education recognize their educational responsibilities towards their students in developing their fullest intellectual and human capacities. No lower expectation can be entertained if higher education is to fulfil its potential for and within late modernity. The argument of imposition is, in effect, an argument that the market should decide on the character of higher education. That, in itself, would let the academics off their educational hook. But, in higher education, we are in the presence of a managed market, not a proper market *per se*. So the argument of imposition again would surrender higher education to the dominant ideological forces at work, the outcomes of contest between the three ideologies of academicism, of operationalism and of the self-referential practices of the wider professional society. An implicit call in this book has been for academics to understand themselves as educators, not in any facile way but within the context of the possibilities of and constraints on human being in modern society.

The argument of stratification, that the argument here pretends to a distinctiveness that higher education does not and should not possess, can be addressed simply enough. Unless we conceive of and practise higher education as the highest form of human development – in short, that of critical engagement – we will be selling short its students certainly. But we will also be failing to offer modern society, in its 'manufactured risk', the possibility of securing any rational control over itself. It misses the point to argue that all education should be of this ilk. Higher education is an education of adults and so has the task of being the fullest form of human development of which adults are capable. It builds upon human and intellectual capacities formed in other parts of education and should not be confused with it.

The problem facing higher education is not that it is separate from the rest of education but that there are moves afoot to bring it into the managed state educational system in its entirety. Universities are on the way to becoming high schools, which talk of a national curriculum for higher education only serves to reinforce. The autonomy of the Western universities offers a discursive space and an independence from the dominant ideologies of the wider society which other parts of the educational system seldom enjoy. Politically, sociologically and educationally, therefore, the argument of stratification fails. The educational system *is* stratified and that stratification offers a degree of cognitive and societal independence which higher education should deploy with vigour. Unhappily, there are forces both outwith and within the universities that would surrender that discursive openness and that would oblige higher education to accept completely its looming position within the educational apparatus of the state.

Higher education for a learning society

A higher education of the kind sketched out in this book, built upon the critical life, is a vehicle for maintaining the discursive space of late modernity. In keeping open the frames of knowing, reflection and action, higher education can be a key institution for bringing about something like a learning society in its fullest sense. In experiencing a higher education of this kind, students are exposed to alternative frameworks for gaining knowledge of the world and for acting in it. But this is more than a postmodern set of experiences, providing the student with a set of cognitive and interpersonal differences with no way of justifiably deciding between them. This higher education shrinks from opening up a decisionistic universe, in which the only criterion is what works. On the contrary, the students are challenged through the interpersonal character of their experiences to justify themselves and to come up with creative formulations, in both their thinking and their actions. In the process, ethical qualities of bravery, persistence, communicative engagement, risk-taking and sincerity will be developed. In the process, too, the potential for self-transformation and for collective transformation is released. The student comes into herself and becomes a critical person through living out the demands of critical being in the three domains of knowledge, self and world.

Such a higher education for a genuinely learning society – a higher education for the critical life – imposes three conditions.

First, students have to be exposed to multiple discourses. This is no mere multidisciplinarity or even interdisciplinarity. It is to understand that slice of the world in which the student is interested from different points of view, and to understand that they may be incommensurable. A student may be interested in mathematics as pure mathematics. Nonetheless, in a higher education for the critical life, she will be encouraged to understand mathematics from other perspectives. Her view about its purity will be endorsed by exposure to the works of those who have articulated just such a view. But it will also be challenged by those who have argued contrary views; for example, Bloor (1976) has insisted that mathematics should not be accorded any such sense of purity but, on the contrary, is replete with social imagery in fulfilment of different social functions that mathematics has been called upon to serve. It might further be observed that the objectivity of mathematics has also been placed in question by constructivism as a commentary on its epistemological status (Glassersfeld, 1995). This will be an uncomfortable exposure for the student who comes to understand that her world is contestable and is contested, and that there is no stable resting point easily available.

The discourses to which the student will be exposed will not be simply intellectual but will be practical and experiential. In the first place, the student will be required to articulate her own views in the critical company of other students. 'The force of the better argument' will be the watchword, and for that knowledge is depersonalized to some extent. That this person or that puts forward this idea is largely immaterial. What counts is that the pedagogical situation is structured such that students feel able individually to expose their own views and so, collectively, see themselves as advancing their interpersonal understandings of the topic in question.

Secondly, and more controversially, the student will be exposed to wider understandings, questionings and potential impact of her intellectual field. Its communication to non-intellectual audiences would be one way of gaining such insight, for example through study service (Goodlad, 1995). If the student is assured of its purity, as with pure mathematics, then let the student be exposed to other views in the wider society which would deny that any intellectual field can retain such purity. The student's view about the purity of her intellectual field should be articulated and justified. Exposure to wider critiques, to instrumental discourses, need not lead the student simply to serving operational agendas uncritically. But it has to lead to engagement with wider perspectives. Only in such exposure and in such engagement, in such cognitive and personal reaching out, can we hope to see developed a higher education for a learning society. In the process, too, the student's own limited self-understandings are likely to be widened. Critical reason, critical self-reflection and critical action can be brought together in an infinite variety of ways, but all three forms of criticality have to be present if a higher education for a learning society is to come about.

If the first condition of a higher education for the critical life is that of exposure to multiple discourses (both practical and intellectual), the second is that of purposive and positive engagement. Half-hearted or resistant engagement is not enough. That will not bring about a learning society in which we move on progressively in our thought and action. This is another large injunction. Curricula, therefore, have to be constructed so as to encourage the formation of critical but positive dispositions. Since there are multiple and conflicting perspectives with which the student has to contend – for example, quite different views as to the responsibilities of the profession to which she is aspiring – she will have to frame not just her own accounts of the world but *herself*. Realizing that no frames of understanding and action are absolute, the student has no alternative but to frame her own, and that means constructing herself. This point alone is sufficient to displace talk of students as products. Nothing could be further from a sense of a higher education for a critical life.

The third and last condition of a higher education for a critical life is a further extension of the previous two conditions. It is not enough to provide the student with multiple and conflicting perspectives, nor even enough also to encourage the student to engage to some purpose with those perspectives. What is further required is a committed orientation on the part of the student to this form of life. The willingness to see one's own world from other perspectives, the willingness to engage with them, the willingness to work things through in a positive spirit, the willingness to risk critique not just from within but also beyond one's own intellectual and professional world, the willingness to go on giving relentlessly of oneself, and the willingness to go on undercutting one's own social and professional identity as one takes on the conflicting perspectives of one's own frameworks: all this calls for heroic dispositions on the part of students. They call for large personal and psychological resources. Yet, unless students begin to take on such dispositions of generosity, of openness and of serious engagement, we shall not have a higher education for a learning society.

Conclusion

A higher education for the critical life will not be comfortable, for students, for their lecturers (now become educators) or for the wider society. Their educators will be discomforted because they will understand that their own hold on the world is not absolute and may be challenged in a genuinely critical education. It will be uncomfortable, too, both for the critiqued and for the critic. Being uncomfortable, the dominant forces in the wider society will be unsure about its presence in higher education, even if late modernity requires openness and a continual re-evaluation of assumptions and frameworks. Being uncomfortable as an educational strategy, it will foster resistance among both students and their lecturers. But unless we see and practise higher education in this way, as a way of ushering in the critical life, we shall neither provide the reflexiveness that the complexity of modern society requires, nor have any prospect of bringing about the discursive openness and continuing critical evaluation needed for a genuinely open society.

As higher education becomes a business securing its position in the marketplace, it is crucial that it takes its rhetoric about criticality seriously; it has to be in the business of critical being without critical being becoming a business. As the forms of knowing and being in late modernity become more pliable, so reflexivity on both the personal and social levels becomes crucial if both individuals and society are to maintain some semblance of self-propulsion. And as instrumentality and performativity tighten their grip, so a higher education for critical being becomes a necessary counter and a means of injecting a creative and transformatory element into society. For the moment, the social space is just available to realize a higher education for critical being. But moments do not last for ever.

Coda: A Critical Space

Critical energy

We have no general account of the purposes of higher education in the modern world. For the most part, we muddle along. And yet, in the dominant concept within the university, that of critical thinking, lies the embryo of just such an idea around which all parties can unite. That idea, which I have offered in this book, is that of critical being.

This is not a matter of old wine in new bottles. The idea of critical thinking as the defining concept of higher education has to give way to a much larger idea of critical being, in which critical reason is but one of three forms of critical being together with critical self-reflection and critical action. But simply widening criticality to include the domains of knowledge, the self and the world is not enough to sustain a higher education for the new millennium. Criticality can be exhibited on different levels, ranging from low-level skills operating within given frameworks to critique, in which transforming frameworks of knowledge, self-understanding or action are brought to bear.

This book, therefore, has been critical of critical thinking as a construal of criticality in the domain of knowledge. The view that critical thinking is a matter of acquiring the tacit rules of a discipline, or is a matter of grasping common rules of critical reasoning, is completely inadequate to meet the challenges facing the university. These are the tired internal agendas of the academic world, intent on carving out a role for itself. One agenda looks to maintain the hegemony of the disciplines as the foundations of students' critical abilities; the other looks to provide a living to the educationalists who can identify the cross-disciplinary rules, standing over and above the practices of the separate fields of thought. That these agendas are internal and are self-serving is clear enough. But they are also tired agendas in that they have run out of steam. They lack the capacity to impart the energy – the critical energy – that graduates are going to need to survive with positive effect in and on the world.

The student standing in front of that line of tanks was invested with critical energy in all three forms of his critical being: in thought, self-reflection and action. The challenge facing higher education in the modern world is to find ways of enabling students to develop that criticality in all three forms and at the highest levels of critical being.

Critical energy cannot be imparted; it cannot be handed on as if it were a commodity. That is one reason why it is wrong to construe higher education as a form of consumption or to see students as products. The two metaphors work in different ways but both speak to a commodification of educational transactions; in both, there is a sense of the inertness of what is passed on or acquired. But being critical – whether in thought, self-reflection or action – requires that the student invest something of herself.

Even to speak of the student imbuing her truth claims and her actions with her own meanings does not quite get at what is at issue here; or even to speak of the student being autonomous; or even of the student being self-motivated. Being critical requires all those conditions, but they are not sufficient. What is further required is that the student injects some energy of her own. The student's own will has to come into play: the student has to will her truth claims or her actions or even her own self-reflections. Being critical – in any of the three domains – is a personal intervention in the world and calls for nothing less than a self-propelling individual. Authentic interventions cannot be made without critical energy. The possession of such personal energy is a condition of being critical: higher education has to be in the business – the critical business – of enabling critical persons to develop and to flourish.

Critical energy has to have a head of steam behind it, and such energy can lead to a derailment. Students can get carried away by their own enthusiasm to take on other voices (whether in the texts that they encounter or in the contending views of the other students). They may be so intent on evaluating what they confront that they forget about the standards of critical reason. Egg-on-the-face is not an unknown syndrome. The student may miscalculate the likely response. The students in Tiananmen Square may have miscalculated the likely response of the authorities, or perhaps not. Normally, at least, one can live to fight another day: critical energy has to be tempered by wisdom, by discretion and by the practice of the art of the possible.

The key point is about critical energy: to what extent do universities really work to generate critical energy in their students? For all their talk – old and new – about critical thinking, we hear precious little talk about energy, excitement and commitment. Indeed, we hear little about the emotional aspects of learning. This is hardly surprising if learning is construed either as the assimilation of cognitions or as the taking on of pre-specified competences. But without a wish to see students come into themselves such that they invest their own utterances and actions with energy, we can *never* see develop critical persons.

Critical space

The reluctance of even the academic community to speak of higher education with a vocabulary of energy, commitment and even excitement is understandable. For such terms point to the student having a space in which her critical dispositions can flourish. From the argument of this book, that critical space has to contain three orientations such that the student has space for critical reason, critical self-reflection and critical action. Epistemological space, personal space and practical space have to be made available to every student.

The space in each domain has to be an active space. A permissive space is insufficient: the critical dispositions will only be developed if they are actively encouraged to develop. Finding one's own voice and expressing it – in thought and in action – requires the moral virtues of courage, independence and persistence. Students will not take on these burdens lightly: why should they? Unless a definite and major feature looms on their horizon (such as a line of tanks), they are not easily going to be persuaded to take on critical dispositions. Mature students often have such an emotional investment in their learning, and often, too, it is the result of a major disjunction in their lives (such as the death of a parent, separation from a partner or loss of a job). For the most part, the personal commitment to and involvement in one's own learning has to be carefully nurtured because, otherwise, the critical energy as the basis of criticality will not be forthcoming.

The critical spirit embodies, as we have seen, qualities of integrity, bravery, resilience and purposive listening. Such qualities are only to be developed intersubjectively. Students take on the critical spirit, with all its demands (in thought, reflection and action), by testing their ideas, but also by testing themselves, in the critical but supportive environment offered by the students acting collectively. The learning situation becomes a critical community.

But all this calls for demanding human and pedagogical capacities on the part of the lecturer. Lecturers have to become educators: their responsibility lies in providing an educational environment in which their students are likely to work together in acquiring the critical capacities in all three domains of knowledge, of self and of the world. These are not to be taught in any straightforward sense, but are to be won by the students themselves. Epistemological, personal and practical space: these are the necessary conditions of the pedagogical environment which have to be made available to the students. Since many lecturers have difficulty in providing even epistemological space in which students can *risk* developing and proffering their own thinking, the challenge being suggested here is likely to prove considerable. Our higher education pedagogies have an inner text of closure and not of the openness that the development of critical persons requires.

Where will it end?

Critical perspectives need critical frameworks. One can only be critical of an argument, or of oneself, or of a practice in the wider world from within a framework. The framework is typically a mixture of presuppositions of correctness, of what is valuable, and of validity. The framework is not purely cognitive; it is not even mainly cognitive. It is invested with values, emotion, commitment, and professional and social identity. All of this, for the most part, the academic world likes to deny. The academic world likes to believe that its frameworks are devoid of values, emotions and commitment, and organizes its pedagogical practices so as to eschew them. How much more comfortable and risk-free is the resulting 'education'.

A vicious circle operates here. Wanting to keep values and emotions out of things, the academic world concentrates its fire-power on cognitions, on propositions and on techniques. The world is allowed in – for example, in professional and practical activities – but values are kept at bay. Strategies for bringing off greater efficiency and effectiveness are held in focus. Certainly, we see increasing attention being given to ethics in business or in the medical world. But these tend to be handled as interesting sub-plots in the taken-for-granted wider narratives of advanced capitalism or a technologically driven health service in which the dominant power lies with the professionals. Value issues are not allowed to get out of hand, so as not to generate critical questions that would interrogate seriously the value and general structure of the enterprise.

The key point is one of frameworks. Critical questioning – whether of ideas, of oneself or of the world – takes place from within a horizon of assumptions (of value, of truth, of being, of right arrangements in the world). Critical questioning may appear to be opening our universe of understanding. But it may, *at the same time*, spring from taken-for-granted frameworks which, in remaining tacit, foreclose understanding. This is implicit in Foucault's (1980) insights about the coupling of knowledge and power. Through the unquestioned and unquestionable frameworks within which knowledge structures are situated, knowledge comes to be a form of power and domination over the world rather than a means of attaining genuine enlightenment. And that point takes on even more force when we seek to embrace action higher education. Whether it is knowledge-for-action (accountancy) or knowledge-in-action (medicine), we are in danger of utilizing unquestionable frameworks. Rather than being vehicles for developing genuinely critical capacities, our higher education programmes are liable to become ideological carriers secreting not just unquestioned but unquestionable views and values about the world.

Our frameworks, therefore, have to be susceptible to challenge. Our frameworks of value, understanding, self-identity and action all have to be continually in the dock. Not that they are necessarily guilty or faulty or invalid, but they may be. A higher education, therefore, will promote uncertainty: it will render questionable every aspect of a student's being. The student will come to recognize that in each of the three domains – of knowledge, self and world – her hold on life is fragile. Putting this differently, a higher education will enable students to live as postmoderns. The postmodern world, in its refusal of absolute principles and categories, does not lie out there to be experienced but is a matter of the student's developing experience.

Again, this is not just a cognitive affair. The student comes to feel the fragility of all her categories and her own self-identity. The uncertain world without becomes the uncertain world within.

Some academics will say that that is what they have always done, that that is the business – the critical business – that they are in. But it is the argument of this book that they have construed that business as generating in the student, at best, only an epistemological uncertainty, an uncertainty in relation to our propositions about the world. That the academics have not lived up to even this limited rhetoric is not the key point. The degree and level of criticality that they have encouraged in their students has been limited even in relation to formal propositional reasoning. The academics have set themselves a limited set of tasks in developing students' critical capacities, and haven't even delivered on those. But the main argument of this book has been that a higher education for the modern age has to do more than generate epistemological uncertainty. It has also to generate personal or ontological uncertainty, and it has to produce practical uncertainty.

Where will it end? Once higher education understands the logic of taking critical thinking seriously and sees its extension into the domains of self and action-in-the-world, once students come to understand that their frameworks for knowing, for their self-identity and for action are all susceptible to continuing interrogation, what will be the result? Rather than being prepared to live effectively in the world, will they not be paralysed into inaction? That is a logical position to reach. Postmodernism likes to talk of the manifold possibilities of thought and action that await us, but the emphasis it gives to the playful and ludic character of postmodernity underlines that it isn't serious. There is no stable hold on the world. In a world, in an epistemological, ontological and practical world in which there are no enduring categories of being and knowing, one can no longer act with assuredness. The critical dialogue, whether internal or intersubjective, can go on for ever. The basis for an assured sense of oneself, of one's ideas or of one's action can never be reached. Or so it might seem.

It's tradition

There is a fundamental issue left open in this book. We started with the image of the lone student resisting a line of tanks that was intent on crushing the critical voice of the students. That was a graphic case of *critical being* in which critical reasoning, critical self-reflection and critical action were fully integrated, so forming a critical person. In all three domains of knowledge, self and the world, we witnessed in that scene utter assuredness: the student was prepared to die for his beliefs, for the world he wished to see and for his self within that world. But modern philosophy and social theory deny the grounds for assuredness. Whether on a Popperian account, or a postmodern story, or the Critical Theory of the more recent Habermas which offers principles for the foundations of a continuing critical dialogue, or the concepts of modern social theory of discourse, reflexivity, detraditional-ization and manufactured risk (of Giddens, 1994 and Beck, 1992), there is no assured basis for being in any of the three domains of knowing or of the formation of one's self or of action. Continuing interrogation of our frame-works on the one hand, and action without foundations on the other: these are the messages of contemporary reflections.

Certainty and uncertainty, these may seem to be the contradictory themes of this book. Can they be reconciled? Goodlad (1976) talks optimistically of 'authoritative uncertainty' but that, of course, begs the question: on what basis can we derive authority for our utterances (in all their forms, includ-ing action-in-the-world)? MacIntyre (1990) points us back to traditions: our identities, our practices (such as universities) and our ways of knowing are founded on traditions. Even Giddens (1994), although playing up the notion of detraditionalization, has begun to wonder about reclaiming traditions of some kind. And in this book, too, the references to 'the Western university' have called up a generalized notion of the University, built on the Enlight-enment project of disinterested reason providing the possibility of progress, if only in our understanding.

There is a facile traditionalism that beckons and there is a more subtle version. Facile traditionalism has sophistications: it is not straightforwardly facile! Facile traditionalism allows that traditions are organic, that they may and should go on being reinterpreted, and even that traditions can go on reconstructing themselves. There is a contradiction here. Either this tradi-tionalism calls up traditions which, as it admits, are susceptible of critical questioning (and, therefore, how can we invest any security in them?), or it tells us that traditions can be reconstructed (in which case, how can we be sure that anything will endure over time and that there is anything that really amounts to a tradition?).

Traditions cannot be worthwhile in themselves: durability is no criterion of worth. And durability of idea has to be distinguished from durability of practice. The university as a critical enterprise has itself to be critiqued both as an idea and as a practice. The practice has never been that durable and, even if it had, it would not be adequate to meet the epistemological, onto-logical and practical demands on higher education in the modern age. So traditions do not wear their value on their sleeve. If traditionalism is to offer us anything – if, say, the idea of the university is to offer us anything in a context of increasing social change and in an era of mass higher edu-cation in which higher education has lost its autonomies and is now called upon to serve a multitude of functions – a more subtle version of tradition-alism is required.

To repeat, a tradition is only valuable if it is valuable. (The tautology has point.) We go on working at traditions, resuscitating them and remaking them if we consider them to be valuable on other grounds. And the grounds themselves may change. Just that has been part of our story here. If the Enlightenment project is itself being questioned (as it is), we can no longer rest our notion of the university as a critical enterprise on the foundation of its providing an assured framework of knowledge and understanding to carry us forward in the world. The tradition has to be reinvented, and its legitimacy has also to be rebuilt at the same time. Both the superstructure and the foundations need major reconstruction.

In the world but not of it

We live with uncertainty in the world. That is our condition. There is no position of 'authoritative uncertainty' available to us. The challenge on higher education is both to problematize our world – its knowledge frameworks, its external features and our own selves – and to enable us to live with good effect within it. Higher education would be falling short of its responsibilities if the critical capacities of students were not grounded in action. Academics would be falling short of what it is to be a modern academic if they were not able to sustain their critical practices in the world.

Technical practices can be sustained easily enough in the modern world. That has been part of our story: critical capacities *are* now wanted but only so long as they are restrained within narrow parameters of finding more efficient means to ends, or producing a pliable self without values, or generating solutions to given problems. Higher-level critical practices are sustained much less easily in the world. Higher education can pat itself on the back by producing critical competences when all the time it is sustaining – in teaching, in research or in consultancy activities – low-level forms of critical being. Everyone speaks the language of critical competence, *and* they end up practising it. Real critical being is nowhere to be seen.

Real critical being runs against the grain; it has to. But if it is to have a positive effect on the world, it has to be in the world. It has to effect its critical purposes on the world in such a way that its messages are taken on board to some extent. Critical being is in the world even if it is not of the world. It has to maintain its distance from the world but be an effective actor in the world. That is one of the challenges of a proper higher education today.

This agenda may seem impossible: living purposively with uncertainty; intervening with positive effect while retaining one's critical stance; having some sense of self amidst a fragmented and contested social and personal identity; and being able to leap the ontological gap that appears to divide action from understanding. Yet all of this is required in the modern age if higher education is to do justice to its own rhetoric of being a critical enterprise.

The project is demanding but it is entirely feasible. It is entirely feasible in the sense that, in the modern world paradoxically, it is called for and higher education enjoys space to go on working at the cluster of tasks that fall under the heading of 'critical enterprise'. As we have seen, the call for it is, admittedly, half-hearted. Critical capacities both for assisting an organization's economic position (including the university's) and for self-reconstitution are now required. More broadly, however, society is now faced with such exogenous forces for change that it has to generate endogenous capacities for change. At the same time, the sheer profusion of information and knowledge, aided by the Internet, and flatter post-Fordist work practices are producing a wider distribution of the resources for reflection and self-reflection. Reflexivity has become the condition of late modern society.

So the call for critical capacities is present. It is a new call and it looks to critical capacities in the domains of both the self and the world, which have been deficient in the interpretation given to critical competence by the university. But it is there. At the same time, despite the calls for a national curriculum, the Western university retains significant pools of autonomy. Institutional space is still on offer.

There is all to play for. The agenda is daunting but it remains feasible in the sense that the university has the space seriously to work at it. Higher education is now a critical business. The only question is whether higher education will also generate its own interpretations of that calling and parley for the education of critical persons.

Glossary

Critical action: that form of *criticality* which finds expression in direct engagement with the world.

Critical being: that state of human being in which is integrated the three forms of *criticality*.

Criticality: a human disposition of engagement where it is recognized that the object of attention could be other than it is. There are three forms of criticality in relation to its three *domains* of expression: *critical reason, critical self-reflection* and *critical action*.

Critical interdisciplinarity: that form of interdisciplinarity in which different epistemological perspectives illuminate not just a common object but themselves, so showing the limitations of specific disciplines.

Critical persons: individuals who have taken on the three forms of *criticality* and so acquired the state of *critical being*.

Critical reason: that form of *criticality* which is oriented towards formal knowledge.

Critical self-reflection: that form of *criticality* which finds expression in being directed towards the self.

Critical thinking: merely a level of critical reason and one of the lower levels of critical reason at that.

Critical thought: one of the higher levels of *critical reason*.

Critique-in-action: the highest form of *critical action*.

Discursive creation: the insertion into the wider polity (for example, by professionals or by academics) of ways of understanding and engaging with the world. Such discursive creation could be, for instance, instrumental or emancipatory in character.

Domains: the different spheres in which *criticality* finds expression. There are three such domains: knowledge, self and the world.

Metacritical capacities: capacities at either the personal or the organizational level for injecting counter and higher-order critical perspectives.

Practising epistemologists: groups such as professionals and academics who live in the world by deploying their knowledge and by demonstrating a critical stance to it.

Professing-in-action: that form of professional life in which professionals live up to their professional calling by engaging critically with the world.

Bibliography

Adorno, T.W., Albert, H., Dahrendorf, R., Habermas, J., Pilot, H. and Popper, K.R. (1977) *The Positivist Dispute in German Sociology*. London: Heinemann.

Agger, B. (1990) *The Decline of Discourse: Reading, Writing and Resistance in Postmodern Capitalism*. London: Falmer Press.

Agger, B. (1991) *A Critical Theory of Public Life: Knowledge, Discourse and Politics in an Age of Decline*. London: Falmer Press.

Argyris, C. and Schön, D. (1974) *Theory in Practice: Increasing Professional Effectiveness*. San Francisco, CA: Jossey-Bass.

Aronowitz, S. and Giroux, H.A. (1986) *Education under Siege: The Conservative, Liberal and Radical Debate over Schooling*. London: Routledge.

Aronowitz, S. and Giroux, H.A. (1991) *Postmodern Education: Politics, Culture and Social Criticism*. London: University of Minnesota Press.

Assister, A. (ed.) (1995) *Transferable Skills in Higher Education*. London: Kogan Page.

Ball, S.J. (ed.) (1990) *Foucault and Education: Disciplines and Knowledge*. London: Routledge.

Bauman, Z. (1991) *Modernity and the Holocaust*. Cambridge: Polity.

Bauman, Z. (1992) *Intimations of Postmodernity*. London: Routledge.

Becher, T. (1989) *Academic Tribes and Territories*. Buckingham: SRHE/Open University Press.

Becher, T. and Kogan, M. (1992) *Process and Structure in Higher Education*. London: Routledge.

Beck, U. (1992) *Risk Society*. London: Sage.

Beck, U. and Beck-Gernsheim, E. (1995) *The Normal Chaos of Love*. Cambridge: Polity.

Beck, U., Giddens, A. and Lasch, S. (1994) *Reflexive Modernization*. Cambridge: Polity.

Bernstein, B. (1996) *Pedagogy, Symbolic Control and Identity: Theory, Research, Critique*. London: Taylor and Francis.

Bernstein, R.J. (1991) *The New Constellation: The Ethical–Political Horizons of Modernity/ Postmodernity*. Cambridge: Polity.

Bjorkland, S. (1995) 'A university constitution for disputation'. *Studies of Higher Education and Research 4*. Stockholm: Council for Studies of Higher Education.

Blake, N. (1997) 'Truth, identity and community in the university', in R.A. Barnett and A. Griffin (eds), *The End of Knowledge in Higher Education*. London: Cassell.

Bloom, A. (1987) *The Closing of the American Mind*. London: Penguin.

Bloor, D. (1976) *Knowledge and Social Imagery*. London: Routledge.

Boud, D. and Feletti, G. (eds) (1991) *The Challenge of Problem Based Learning*. London: Kogan Page.

Bourdieu, P. (1988) *Homo Academicus*. Cambridge: Polity.

Bourdieu, P. (1990) *In Other Words: Essays Towards a Reflexive Sociology*. Cambridge: Polity.

Bourdieu, P., Passeron, J.-C. and de Saint Martin, M. (1994) *Academic Discourse*. Cambridge: Polity.

Brecher, B., Fleischmann, O. and Halliday, J. (eds) (1996) *The University in a Liberal State*. Aldershot: Avebury.

Brookfield, S.D. (1987) *Developing Critical Thinkers*. Milton Keynes: Open University Press.

Brookfield, S.D. (1993) 'On impostorship, cultural suicide, and other dangers: How nurses learn critical thinking', *Journal of Continuing Education in Nursing*, 24(5): 197–205.

Brosnan, G. (1971) 'A polytechnic philosophy', in G. Brosnan, C. Carter, R. Layard, P. Venables and G. Williams, *Patterns and Policies in Higher Education*. London: Penguin.

Burgen, A. (ed.) (1996) *Goals and Purposes of Higher Education in the 21st Century*. London: Jessica Kingsley.

Carr, W. and Kemmis, S. (1986) *Becoming Critical: Education, Knowledge and Action Research*. Lewes: Falmer Press.

Cole, J.R., Barber, E.G. and Graubard, S.R. (eds) (1994) *The Research University in a Time of Discontent*. Baltimore, MD: University of Nebraska Press.

Derrida, J. (1992) 'Mochlos; or, The conflict of the faculties', in R. Rand (ed.), *Logomachia: The Conflict of the Faculties*. Lincoln, NB: University of Nebraska Press.

Downie, R.S. (1990) 'Professions and professionalism'. *Journal of Philosophy of Education*, 24(2): 147–60.

Dunne, J. (1993) *Back to the Rough Ground: 'Phronesis' and 'Techne' in Modern Philosophy and in Aristotle*. Notre Dame: University of Notre Dame.

Eraut, M. (1994) *Developing Professional Knowledge and Competence*. London: Falmer Press.

Fairclough, N. (1993) *Discourse and Social Change*. Cambridge: Polity.

Feyerabend, P. (1978) *Against Method*. London: Verso.

Foucault, M. (1974) *The Archaeology of Knowledge*. London: Tavistock.

Foucault, M. (1980) *Power/Knowledge*. Hemel Hempstead: Harvester Wheatsheaf.

Friedson, E. (1994) *Professionalism Reborn: Theory, Prophecy and Policy*. Cambridge: Polity.

Fromm, E. (1960) *Fear of Freedom*. London: Routledge.

Fuller, S. (1993) *Philosophy of Science and its Discontents*. New York: Guilford.

Gellner, E. (1988) *Plough, Sword and Book*. London: Paladin.

Gellner, E. (1992) *Reason and Culture*. Oxford: Blackwell.

Geuss, R. (1981) *The Idea of a Critical Theory*. Cambridge: Cambridge University Press.

Gibbons, M., Limoges, C., Nowotny, H., Schwartzman, S., Scott, P. and Trow, M. (1994) *The New Production of Knowledge: The Dynamics of Science and Research in Contemporary Societies*. London: Sage.

Gibson, R. (1986) *Critical Theory and Education*. Sevenoaks: Hodder and Stoughton.

Giddens, A. (1990) *The Consequences of Modernity*. Cambridge: Polity.

Giddens, A. (1991) *Modernity and Self-Identity: Self and Society in the Late Modern Age.* Cambridge: Polity.

Giddens, A. (1994) *Beyond Left and Right: The Future of Radical Politics.* Cambridge: Polity.

Glassersfeld, E. von (1995) *Radical Constructivism: A Way of Learning.* London: Routledge.

Goodlad, S. (1976) *Conflict and Consensus in Higher Education.* London: Hodder and Stoughton.

Goodlad, S. (1995) *The Quest for Quality: Sixteen Forms of Heresy in Higher Education.* Buckingham: SRHE/Open University Press.

Gordon, P. and White, J. (1979) *Philosophers as Educational Reformers.* London: Routledge.

Gorz, A. (1989) *Critique of Economic Reason.* London: Verso.

Gouldner, A. (1979) *The Future of Intellectuals and the Rise of the New Class.* Basingstoke: Macmillan.

Gramsci, A. (1980) *The Modern Prince and Other Writings.* New York: International Publishers.

Grundy, S. (1987) *Curriculum: Product or Praxis?* Lewes: Falmer Press.

Haber, H.F. (1994) *Beyond Postmodern Politics.* London: Routledge.

Habermas, J. (1978) *Knowledge and Human Interests.* London: Heinemann.

Habermas, J. (1989) *The Theory of Communicative Action,* Vol. 2. Cambridge: Polity.

Habermas, J.(1991) *The Theory of Communicative Action,* Vol. 1. Cambridge: Polity.

Habermas, J. (1995) *Postmetaphysical Thinking.* Cambridge: Polity.

Halsey, A.H. (1992) *Decline of Donnish Dominion.* Oxford: Clarendon Press.

Handy, C. (1995) *The Age of Unreason.* London: Arrow.

Heyck, T.W. (1982) *The Transformation of Intellectual Life in Victorian England.* Beckenham: Croom Helm.

Hirst, P.H. (1973) 'Education, Knowledge and Practices', in R. Barrow and P. White (eds) *Beyond Liberal Education: Essays in Honour of Paul H. Hirst.* London: Routledge.

Horkheimer, M. (1937) 'Traditional and Critical Theory', in P. Connerton (ed.) (1978) *Critical Sociology.* London: Penguin.

Hoy, D.C. and McCarthy, T. (1994) *Critical Theory.* Oxford: Blackwell.

Hutton, W. (1995) *The State We're In.* London: Jonathan Cape.

Jarvis, P. (1983) *Professional Education.* Beckenham: Croom Helm.

Jarvis, P. (1992) *Paradoxes of Learning: On Becoming an Individual in Society.* San Francisco, CA: Jossey-Bass.

Jaspers, K. (1960) *The Idea of the University.* London: Peter Owen.

Jenkins, S. (1995) *Accountable to None: The Tory Nationalization of Britain.* London: Hamish Hamilton.

Kant, I. (1992) *The Conflict of the Faculties.* London: University of Nebraska Press.

Kress, G. (1995) *Writing the Future.* Sheffield: NATE.

Kuhn, T. (1970) *The Structure of Scientific Revolutions.* London: University of Chicago Press.

Lakatos, I. and Musgrave, A. (eds) (1977) *Criticism and the Growth of Knowledge.* Cambridge: Cambridge University Press.

Leavis, F.R. (1943) *Education and the University.* London: Chatto and Windus.

Leavis, F.R. (1969) *English Literature in our Time and the University.* London: Chatto and Windus.

Lyotard, J.-F. (1984) *The Postmodern Condition: A Report on Knowledge.* Manchester: University of Manchester Press.

MacIntyre, A. (1990) *Three Rival Versions of Moral Inquiry.* London: Duckworth.

Mannheim, K. (1960) *Ideology and Utopia.* London: Routledge.

Marcuse, H. (1968) *One-Dimensional Man.* London: Sphere Books.

Maxwell, N. (1987) *From Knowledge to Wisdom.* Oxford: Blackwell.

McLaren, P. (1995) *Critical Pedagogy and Predatory Culture: Oppositional Politics in a Postmodern Era.* London: Routledge.

McPeck, J.E. (1981) *Critical Thinking and Education.* Oxford: Martin Robertson.

McPeck, J.E. (1990) *Teaching Critical Thinking.* London: Routledge.

Middlehurst, R. (1993) *Leading Academics.* Buckingham: SRHE/Open University Press.

Midgley, M. (1989) *Wisdom, Information and Wonder: What is Knowledge For?* London: Routledge.

Myerson, G. (1994) *Rhetoric, Reason and Society: Rationality as Dialogue.* London: Sage.

Myerson, G. (1997) 'A new university space: A dialogue on argument, democracy and the university', in R.A. Barnett and A. Griffin (eds), *The End of Knowledge in Higher Education.* London: Cassell.

Nash, A.S. (1945) *The University and the Modern World.* London: SCM Press.

Neave, G. (1990) 'On preparing for markets: Trends in higher education in Western Europe 1988–1990'. *European Journal of Education,* 25(2): 105–23.

Newman, J.H. (1976) *The Idea of a University.* Oxford: Oxford University Press.

Nisbet, R. (1971) *The Degradation of the Academic Dogma.* London: Heinemann.

Norris, P. (1992) *Postmodernism, Intellectuals and the Gulf War.* London: Lawrence and Wishart.

Oakeshott, M. (1989) *The Voice of Liberal Learning.* London: Yale University Press.

Pascale, R. (1990) *Managing on the Edge: How Successful Companies Use Conflict to Stay Ahead.* London: Penguin.

Passmore, J. (1980) 'Teaching to be critical', in *The Philosophy of Teaching.* London: Duckworth.

Perry, W.C. (1970) *Forms of Intellectual and Ethical Development in the College Years.* New York: Holt, Rinehart and Winston.

Peters, M. (ed.) (1995) *Education and the Postmodern Condition.* Westport: Bergin and Garvey.

Peters, R.S. (1967) 'Authority', in A. Quinton (ed.), *Political Philosophy.* Oxford: Oxford University Press.

Peters, T. and Waterman, R.H. (1982) *In Search of Excellence.* London: Harper Collins.

Popper, Sir K. (1972) *Objective Knowledge.* Oxford: Oxford University Press.

Popper, Sir K. (1977) 'Normal science and its dangers', in I. Lakatos and A. Musgrave (eds), *Criticism and the Growth of Knowledge.* Cambridge: Cambridge University Press.

Rand, R. (ed.) (1992) *Logomachia: The Conflict of the Faculties.* Lincoln, NB: University of Nebraska Press.

Ranson, S. (1994) *Towards the Learning Society.* London: Cassell.

Reeves, M. (1988) *The Crisis in Higher Education.* Milton Keynes: SRHE/Open University Press.

Reich, R.B. (1990) *The Work of Nations: A Blueprint for the Future.* London: Simon and Schuster.

Ritzer, G. (1996) 'McUniversity in the postmodern consumer society'. Plenary address at a conference on *Dilemmas of Mass Higher Education,* University of Staffordshire, Staffordshire.

Rorty, R. (1989) *Contingency, Irony and Solidarity.* Cambridge: Cambridge University Press.

Rorty, R. (1991) *Essays on Heidegger and Others.* Cambridge: Cambridge University Press.

Russell, C. (1993) *Academic Freedom.* London: Routledge.
Salter, B. and Tapper, T. (1994) *The State and Higher Education.* Ilford: Woburn Press.
Senge, P.M. (1990) *The Fifth Discipline: The Art and Practice of the Learning Organization.* London: Century Business.
Schön, D. (1971) *Beyond the Stable State.* London: Temple Smith.
Schön, D. (1983) *The Reflective Practitioner.* New York: Basic Books.
Schön, D. (1987) *Educating the Reflective Practitioner.* London: Jossey-Bass.
Scott, P. (1984) *The Crisis of the University.* Beckenham: Croom Helm.
Scott, P. (1994) *The Postmodern Challenge.* London: Trentham Books.
Scott, P. (1995) *The Meanings of Mass Higher Education.* Buckingham: SRHE/Open University Press.
Searle, J.R. (1995) *The Construction of Social Reality.* London: Allen Lane.
Shattock, M. (1994) *The UGC and the Management of British Universities.* Buckingham: SRHE/Open University Press.
Siegel, H. (1988) *Educating Reason.* London: Routledge.
Simons, H.W. and Billig, M. (1994) *After Postmodernism: Reconstructing Ideology Critique.* London: Sage.
Smith, A. and Webster, F. (eds) (1997) *The Idea of the University in the Information Age.* Buckingham: Open University Press.
Smyth, J. (ed.) (1995) *Academic Work.* Buckingham: SRHE/Open University Press.
Sotto, E. (1994) *When Teaching Becomes Learning.* London: Cassell.
Squires, G. (1990) *First Degree: The Undergraduate Curriculum.* Buckingham: SRHE/Open University Press.
Stehr, N. (1994) *Knowledge Societies.* London: Sage.
Steiner, G. (1984) 'To civilise our gentlemen', in *A Reader.* London: Penguin.
Stryker, L. (1996) 'The Holocaust and liberal education', in B. Brecher, O. Fleischmann and J. Halliday (eds), *The University in a Liberal State.* Aldershot: Avebury.
Taylor, C. (1991) *The Ethics of Authenticity.* London: Harvard University Press.
Taylor, C. (1992) *Sources of the Self: The Making of the Modern Identity.* Cambridge: Cambridge University Press.
Touraine, A. (1995) *Critique of Modernity.* Oxford: Blackwell.
Trow, M. (1974) 'Problems in the transition from elite to mass higher education', in OECD (ed.), *Policies for Higher Education: General Report.* Paris: OECD.
Usher, R. and Edwards, R. (1994) *Postmodernism and Education.* London: Routledge.
Winter, R. (1995) 'The University of Life plc: The industrialization of higher education?', in J. Smyth (ed.), *Academic Work.* Buckingham: SRHE/Open University Press.
Winter, R. and Maisch, M. (1996) *Professional Competence and Higher Education: The ASSET Programme.* London: Falmer Press.
Wyatt, J. (1990) *Commitment to Higher Education.* Buckingham: SRHE/Open University Press.
Young, R. (1989) *A Critical Theory of Education: Habermas and our Children's Future.* Hemel Hempstead: Harvester Wheatsheaf.
Young, R. (1992) *Critical Theory and Classroom Talk.* Clevedon: Multilingual Matters.
Zweig, F. (1963) *The Student in the Age of Anxiety.* London: Heinemann.

Selected Reports

Association of Graduate Recruiters (1995) *Skills for Graduates in the 21st Century.* Cambridge: AGR.

Atkins, M.J., Beattie, J. and Dockrell, W.B. (1993) *Assessment Issues in Higher Education.* Sheffield: Department of Employment.

Committee of Vice-Chancellors and Principals (1995) *Learning for Change: Building a University System for a New Century.* London: CVCP.

Confederation of British Industry (1994) *Thinking Ahead: Ensuring the Expansion of Higher Education into the Twenty-first Century.* London: CBI.

Council for Industry and Higher Education (1995) *A Wider Spectrum of Opportunities.* London: CIHE.

Employment Department Group (1994) *Higher Education Developments: The Skills Link 2.* Sheffield: Department of Employment.

Hodgkinson, L. (1996) *Changing the Higher Education Curriculum: Towards a Systematic Approach to Skills Development.* Milton Keynes: Open University.

NIACE (1993) *An Adult Higher Education: A Vision.* Leicester: NIACE.

Index

This book offers a presentation, development and interweaving of certain concepts such as critical thinking, critical thought and critique (see the Glossary for a full such listing). This index, accordingly, lists only the key instances of these terms. The same applies to the terms 'higher education' and 'university'.

Page numbers in bold indicate key references.

The Society for Research into Higher Education

The Society for Research into Higher Education exists to stimulate and coordinate research into all aspects of higher education. It aims to improve the quality of higher education through the encouragement of debate and publication on issues of policy, on the organization and management of higher education institutions, and on the curriculum and teaching methods.

The Society's income is derived from subscriptions, sales of its books and journals, conference fees and grants. It receives no subsidies, and is wholly independent. Its individual members include teachers, researchers, managers and students. Its corporate members are institutions of higher education, research institutes, professional, industrial and governmental bodies. Members are not only from the UK, but from elsewhere in Europe, from America, Canada and Australasia, and it regards its international work as among its most important activities.

Under the imprint *SRHE & Open University Press*, the Society is a specialist publisher of research, having some 60 titles in print. The Editorial Board of the Society's Imprint seeks authoritative research or study in the above fields. It offers competitive royalties, a highly recognizable format in both hardback and paperback and the worldwide reputation of the Open University Press.

The Society also publishes *Studies in Higher Education* (three times a year), which is mainly concerned with academic issues, *Higher Education Quarterly* (formerly *Universities Quarterly*), mainly concerned with policy issues, *Research into Higher Education Abstracts* (three times a year), and *SRHE News* (four times a year).

The Society holds a major annual conference in December, jointly with an institution of higher education. In 1994 the topic was 'The Student Experience' at the University of York. In 1995 it was 'The Changing University' at Heriot-Watt University in Edinburgh and in 1996, 'Working in Higher Education' at Cardiff Institute of Higher Education. Conferences in 1997 include 'Beyond the First Degree' at the University of Warwick.

The Society's committees, study groups and branches are run by the members. The groups at present include:

Teacher Education Study Group
Continuing Education Group
Staff Development Group
Excellence in Teaching and Learning

Benefits to members

Individual

Individual members receive:

- *SRHE News*, the Society's publications list, conference details and other material included in mailings.
- Greatly reduced rates for *Studies in Higher Education* and *Higher Education Quarterly*.
- A 35 per cent discount on all SRHE & Open University Press publications.
- Free copies of the Proceedings – commissioned papers on the theme of the Annual Conference.
- Free copies of *Research into Higher Education Abstracts*.
- Reduced rates for conferences.
- Extensive contacts and scope for facilitating initiatives.
- Reduced reciprocal memberships.
- Free copies of the *Register of Members' Research Interests*.

Corporate

Corporate members receive:

- All benefits of individual members, plus.
- Free copies of *Studies in Higher Education*.
- Unlimited copies of the Society's publications at reduced rates.
- Special rates for its members e.g. to the Annual Conference.
- The right to submit application for the Society's research grants.

Membership details: SRHE, 3 Devonshire Street, London W1N 2BA, UK. Tel: 0171 637 2766. Fax: 0171 637 2781. email: srhe@clus1.ulcc.ac.uk
Catalogue: SRHE & Open University Press, Celtic Court, 22 Ballmoor, Buckingham MK18 1XW. Tel: 01280 823388. Fax: 01280 823233. email: enquiries@openup.co.uk

THE LIMITS OF COMPETENCE
KNOWLEDGE, HIGHER EDUCATION AND SOCIETY

Ronald Barnett

Competence is a term which is making its entrance in the university. How might it be understood at this level? *The Limits of Competence* takes an uncompromising line, providing a sustained critique of the notion of competence as wholly inadequate for higher education.

Currently, we are seeing the displacement of one limited version of competence by another even more limited interpretation. In the older definition – one of academic competence – notions of disciplines, objectivity and truth have been central. In the new version, competence is given an operational twist and is marked out by know-how, competence and skills. In this operationalism, the key question is not 'What do students understand?' but 'What can students do?'

The book develops an alternative view, suggesting that, for our universities, a third and heretical conception of human being is worth considering. Our curricula might, instead, offer an education for life.

Contents

222pp   0 335 19341 2 (Paperback)   0 335 19070 7 (Hardback)

THE MEANINGS OF MASS HIGHER EDUCATION

Peter Scott

This book is the first systematic attempt to analyse the growth of mass higher education in a specifically British context, while seeking to develop more theoretical perspectives on this transformation of elite university systems into open post-secondary education systems. It is divided into three main sections. The first examines the evolution of British higher education and the development of universities and other institutions. The second explores the political, social and economic context within which mass systems are developing. What are the links between post-industrial society, a post-Fordist economy and the mass university? The third section discusses the links between massification and wider currents in intellectual and scientific culture.

Contents
Preface – Introduction – Structure and institutions – State and society – Science and culture – Understanding mass higher education – Notes – Index.

208pp   0 335 19442 7 (Paperback)   0 335 19443 5 (Hardback)